G000123291

Oxford
Mini
School
Spelling
Dictionary

Robert Allen

Education Consultant Michele Chapman

OXFORD
UNIVERSITY PRESS

OXFORD
UNIVERSITY PRESS

Great Clarendon Street, Oxford OX2 6DP

Oxford University Press is a department of the University of Oxford.
It furthers the University's objective of excellence in research,
scholarship, and education by publishing worldwide in

Oxford New York

Auckland Bangkok Buenos Aires Cape Town Chennai
Dar es Salaam Delhi Hong Kong Istanbul Karachi Kolkata
Kuala Lumpur Madrid Melbourne Mexico City Mumbai Nairobi
São Paulo Taipei Tokyo Toronto

Oxford is a registered trade mark of Oxford University Press
in the UK and in certain other countries

British Library cataloguing in Publication Data available

ISBN 0-19-910959-1

10 9 8 7 6 5 4 3 2 1

Printed in Italy by Legoprint

Introduction

The *Oxford Mini School Spelling Dictionary* is a special dictionary designed to help students with their spelling. Generally speaking there are three main areas of spelling difficulty for users of English whatever their age.

- Some words are difficult because they have unusual or unpredictable features. **Eighth**, **guard**, and **niece** are often spelt wrongly because they have awkward letter sequences. **Disappear** and **embarrass** are confusing because some letters are doubled while others are not. Words such as **desperate** and **separate** seeminconsistent because one has an **e** in the middle where the other has an **a** for no apparent reason.

- Then there are words that are easily confused. **Vain**, **vein**, and **vane** sound the same but have very different meanings. Some words change their spelling according to how they are used. For example, **dependant** as a *noun* is spelt with an **a**, but as an *adjective*, it is spelt with an **e**.

- The third type of difficulty arises when suffixes and endings are added to words. It is not easy to remember to keep an **e** in **changeable**, to replace **y** with **i** in **happily**, and not to double the **p** in **galloping**.

With increased interest in spelling, reading, and writing in schools today we hope that the *Oxford Mini School Spelling Dictionary* will provide a valuable tool offering useful strategies for dealing with spelling difficulties. We also hope that it will support teachers and parents whose task is to enable young writers to become confident, accurate spellers and to express themselves with a voice of their own.

How to use this book

Entries

Words are listed alphabetically in **bold** and the part of speech or word class (e.g. *noun*, *verb*, *adjective*) follows in italic. If the word has endings (called inflections), these are also listed in black below the headword.

Decide on the first sound of the word you are looking for. Some first sounds can be confusing. If you cannot find the word you are looking for, use the **Try also** tips which will guide you to other possible spellings.

Footnotes

Some words have footnotes attached to them. These identify words that you need to check that you have the right meaning. For example, at **bite** you will find a footnote to tell you that there is another word that sounds like it but is spelt a different way, **!byte**. Words that sound the same but are spelt differently are called homophones. Some footnotes also give extra information on usage and grammar.

Panels

There are about 250 panels which highlight particular problems. For example, you may want to know which words are spelt **-able** like **bendable**, and which ones are spelt **-ible** like **accessible**. Or you may want to know how you form plurals of nouns ending in **-f** such as **calf** or **roof**. Use these information panels to build your knowledge of spelling rules and practices.

It may be useful to keep a spelling jotter for new words. When using a new word, say it aloud several times before you write it down. When you go on to use it in your writing, try not to copy it but to write the word from memory.

Thumb index

Try also

CO   For words beginning with a k- sound, try also ch-

a
b
c
d
e
f
g
h
i
j
k
l
m
n
o
p
q
r
s
t
u
v
w
x
y
z

Entry word

Alphabet

correspondent *noun*
  correspondents
corridor *noun*
  corridors
corrode *verb*
  corrodes
  corroding
  corroded
corrosion
corrosive
corrugated
corrupt
corruption
corset *noun*
  corsets
cosmetics *plural noun*
cosmic
cosmonaut *noun*
  cosmonauts
cost *verb*
  costs
  costing
  cost
cost *noun*
  costs
costly *adjective*
  costlier
  costliest
costume *noun*
  costumes
cosy *adjective*
  cosier
  cosiest
cosy *noun*
  cosies
cot *noun*
  cots

cottage *noun*
  cottages
cotton
couch *noun*
  couches
cough *verb*
  coughs
  coughing
  coughed
cough *noun*
  coughs
could see can
couldn't
council★ *noun*
  councils
councillor☆ *noun*
  councillors
counsel○ *noun*
  counsels
counsel *verb*
  counsels
  counselling
  counselled
counsellor✦ *noun*
  counsellors
count *verb*
  counts
  counting
  counted
count *noun*
  counts
countdown *noun*
  countdowns
countenance *noun*
  countenances

Panel

counter-
counter- makes words
meaning 'opposite',
e.g. a counter-claim
is a claim someone
makes in response to
a claim from someone
else. You often need a
hyphen, but some
words are spelt joined
up, e.g. counteract,
counterbalance.

counter *noun*
  counters
counterfeit
countess *noun*
  countesses
countless
country *noun*
  countries
countryman *noun*
  countrymen
countryside
countrywoman *noun*
  countrywomen
county *noun*
  counties
couple *noun*
  couples
couple *verb*
  couples
  coupling
  coupled
coupling *noun*
  couplings
coupon *noun*
  coupons

Word class (part of speech)

Inflections

Footnote

Do not confuse with

★ A council is a group of people who run the affairs of a town.
  ! counsel.
☆ A councillor is a member of a council. ! counsellor.
○ Counsel means 'advice'. ! council.
✦ A counsellor is someone who gives advice. ! councillor.

52

Aa

-a
Most nouns ending in
-*a*, e.g. **amoeba**,
gala, have plurals
ending in -*as*, e.g.
amoebas, **galas**. A
few technical words
have plurals ending in
-*ae*, e.g. **antennae**.

aback

abacus *noun*
abacuses

abandon *verb*
abandons
abandoning
abandoned

abbey *noun*
abbeys

abbot *noun*
abbots

abbreviate *verb*
abbreviates
abbreviating
abbreviated

abbreviation *noun*
abbreviations

abdomen *noun*
abdomens

abdominal

abduct *verb*
abducts
abducting
abducted

abide *verb*
abides
abiding
abided

ability *noun*
abilities

ablaze

able *adjective*
abler
ablest

-able and **-ible**
You add -*able* to a
verb to make an
adjective that means
'able to be done', e.g.
bendable means
'able to be bent'.
Some adjectives that
have this meaning
end in -*ible*, e.g.
accessible,
convertible, and
incredible. You
cannot use -*ible* to
make new words as
you can with -*able*.

ably

abnormal
abnormally

abnormality *noun*
abnormalities

aboard

abode *noun*
abodes

abolish *verb*
abolishes
abolishing
abolished

abolition

abominable

aboriginal

Aborigines

abort *verb*
aborts
aborting
aborted

abortion *noun*
abortions

abound *verb*
abounds
abounding
abounded

about

above

abrasive

abreast

abroad

abrupt

abscess *noun*
abscesses

abseil *verb*
abseils
abseiling
abseiled

absence *noun*
absences

absent

absentee *noun*
absentees

absent-minded
absent-mindedly

absolute
absolutely

absorb *verb*
absorbs
absorbing
absorbed

absorbent

absorption

abstract *adjective* and
noun
abstracts

abstract *verb*
abstracts
abstracting
abstracted

absurd
absurdly

absurdity *noun*
absurdities

abundance

abundant

a
b
c
d
e
f
g
h
i
j
k
l
m
n
o
p
q
r
s
t
u
v
w
x
y
z

a

abuse verb
abuses
abusing
abused

abuse noun
abuses

abusive
abusively

abysmal

abyss noun
abysses

academic

academy noun
academies

accelerate verb
accelerates
accelerating
accelerated

acceleration

accelerator noun
accelerators

accent noun
accents

accent verb
accents
accenting
accented

accept* verb
accepts
accepting
accepted

acceptable

acceptance

access noun
accesses

access verb
accesses
accessing
accessed

accessibility

accessible

accession noun
accessions

accessory noun
accessories

accident noun
accidents

accidental
accidentally

acclaim verb
acclaims
acclaiming
acclaimed

accommodate verb
accommodates
accommodating
accommodated

accommodation

accompaniment noun
accompaniments

accompanist noun
accompanists

accompany verb
accompanies
accompanying
accompanied

accomplish verb
accomplishes
accomplishing
accomplished

accomplished

accomplishment noun
accomplishments

accord noun
accords

according
accordingly

accordion noun
accordions

account noun
accounts

account verb
accounts
accounting
accounted

accountancy

accountant noun
accountants

accumulate verb
accumulates
accumulating
accumulated

accumulation

accuracy

accurate
accurately

accusation noun
accusations

accuse verb
accuses
accusing
accused

accustomed

ace noun
aces

ache noun
aches

ache verb
aches
aching
ached

achieve verb
achieves
achieving
achieved

achievement
achievements

acid noun
acids

acidic

acidity noun

b
c
d
e
f
g
h
i
j
k
l
m
n
o
p
q
r
s
t
u
v
w
x
y
z

★ To **accept** something is to take it. **! except.**

2

acknowledge *verb*
acknowledges
acknowledging
acknowledged

acknowledgement *noun*
acknowledgements

acne

acorn *noun*
acorns

acoustic

acoustics

acquaint *verb*
acquaints
acquainting
acquainted

acquaintance *noun*
acquaintances

acquire *verb*
acquires
acquiring
acquired

acquisition *noun*
acquisitions

acquit *verb*
acquits
acquitting
acquitted

acquittal *noun*
acquittals

acre *noun*
acres

acrobat *noun*
acrobats

acrobatic *adjective*
acrobatically

acrobatics

acronym *noun*
acronyms

across *adverb* and *preposition*

act *noun*
acts

act *verb*
acts
acting
acted

action *noun*
actions

activate *verb*
activates
activating
activated

active

activity *noun*
activities

actor *noun*
actors

actress *noun*
actresses

actual
actually

acupuncture

acute

Adam's apple *noun*
Adam's apples

adapt *verb*
adapts
adapting
adapted

adaptable

adaptation

adaptor *noun*
adaptors

add *verb*
adds
adding
added

adder *noun*
adders

addict *noun*
addicts

addicted

addiction *noun*
addictions

addictive

addition *noun*
additions

additional

additive *noun*
additives

address *noun*
addresses

address *verb*
addresses
addressing
addressed

adenoids

adequate

adhere *verb*
adheres
adhering
adhered

adhesive *noun*
adhesives

adhesion

adhesive

Adi Granth

adjacent

adjective *noun*
adjectives

adjourn *verb*
adjourns
adjourning
adjourned

adjournment

adjudicate *verb*
adjudicates
adjudicating
adjudicated

adjudication

adjudicator

adjust *verb*
adjusts
adjusting
adjusted

adjustment *noun*
adjustments

a

administer *verb*
administers
administering
administered

administration *noun*
administrations

administrative

administrator

admirable
admirably

admiral *noun*
admirals

admiration

admire *verb*
admires
admiring
admired

admirer *noun*
admirers

admission *noun*
admissions

admit *verb*
admits
admitting
admitted

admittance

admittedly

ado

adolescence

adolescent *noun*
adolescents

adopt *verb*
adopts
adopting
adopted

adoption

adoptive

adorable
adorably

adoration

adore *verb*
adores
adoring
adored

adorn *verb*
adorns
adorning
adorned

adornment

adrenalin

adrift

adult *noun*
adults

adulterer

adultery

advance *noun*
advances

advance *verb*
advances
advancing
advanced

advanced

advantage *noun*
advantages

advantageous

Advent*

adventure *noun*
adventures

adventurous
adjective
adventurously

adverb *noun*
adverbs

adversary *noun*
adversaries

adverse

adversity *noun*
adversities

advertise *verb*
advertises
advertising
advertised

advertisement *noun*
advertisements

advice

advisable

advise *verb*
advises
advising
advised

adviser *noun*
advisers

advisory

advocate *noun*
advocates

advocate *verb*
advocates
advocating
advocated

aerial *adjective* and
noun
aerials

aero-
You use *aero-* to
make words to
do with the air
or aircraft, e.g.
aerobatics.
If the word is a long
one you spell it with
a hyphen, e.g.
aero-engineering.

aerobatic

aerobatics

aerobics

aeronautical

aeronautics

aeroplane *noun*
aeroplanes

aerosol *noun*
aerosols

aesthetic
aesthetically

★ Use a capital A when you mean the period before Christmas.

4

a
b
c
d
e
f
g
h
i
j
k
l
m
n
o
p
q
r
s
t
u
v
w
x
y
z

affair *noun*
affairs

affect★ *verb*
affects
affecting
affected

affection *noun*
affections

affectionate
affectionately

afflict *verb*
afflicts
afflicting
afflicted

affliction *noun*
afflictions

affluence

affluent

afford *verb*
affords
affording
afforded

afforestation

afloat *adjective and adverb*

afraid

afresh

African *adjective and noun*
Africans

aft

after

afternoon *noun*
afternoons

afterwards

again

against

age *noun*
ages

age *verb*
ages
ageing
aged

aged

agency *noun*
agencies

agenda *noun*
agendas

agent *noun*
agents

aggravate *verb*
aggravates
aggravating
aggravated

aggravation

aggression

aggressive
aggressively

aggressor
aggressors

agile

agility

agitate *verb*
agitates
agitating
agitated

agitation

agitator *noun*
agitators

agnostic *noun*
agnostics

ago

agonizing

agony *noun*
agonies

agree *verb*
agrees
agreeing
agreed

agreeable

agreement *noun*
agreements

agriculture

agricultural

aground

ahead

ahoy

aid *noun*
aids

aid *verb*
aids
aiding
aided

Aids☆

ailing

ailment *noun*
ailments

aim *verb*
aims
aiming
aimed

aim *noun*
aims

aimless
aimlessly

air○ *noun*
airs

air *verb*
airs
airing
aired

airborne

air-conditioned

air-conditioning

aircraft *noun*
aircraft

Airedale *noun*
Airedales

....
★ **Affect** means 'to make something change'. **!effect.**
☆ Use a capital A when you mean the disease.
○ You can use a plural in the phrase *to put on airs.*

a

airfield noun
airfields

air force noun
air forces

airgun noun
airguns

airline noun
airlines

airlock noun
airlocks

airmail

airman noun
airmen

airport noun
airports

airship noun
airships

airstream noun
airstreams

airtight

airy adjective
airier
airiest
airily

aisle* noun
aisles

ajar

akela☆ noun
akelas

alarm verb
alarms
alarming
alarmed

alarm noun
alarms

alas

albatross noun
albatrosses

album noun
albums

alcohol

alcoholic adjective
and noun
alcoholics

alcoholism

alcove noun
alcoves

ale○ noun
ales

alert verb
alerts
alerting
alerted

alert adjective and
noun
alerts

algebra

algebraic

alias noun
aliases

alibi noun
alibis

alien adjective and
noun
aliens

alienate verb
alienates
alienating
alienated

alienation

alight

alike

alive

alkali noun
alkalis

alkaline

alkalinity

Allah

allegation noun
allegations

allege verb
alleges
alleging
alleged

allegedly

allegiance noun
allegiances

allegorical

allegory noun
allegories

allergic

allergy noun
allergies

alley noun
alleys

alliance noun
alliances

allied

alligator noun
alligators

allot verb
allots
allotting
allotted

allotment noun
allotments

allow verb
allows
allowing
allowed

allowance noun
allowances

alloy noun
alloys

all right

all-round

all-rounder

ally noun
allies

- -

★ An **aisle** is a passage in a church or cinema. **! isle**.

☆ **Akela** is a Scout leader.

○ You can use a plural when you mean 'different types of ale'.

ally *verb*
allies
allying
allied

almighty

almond *noun*
almonds

almost

aloft

alone

along

alongside

aloud*

alphabet *noun*
alphabets

alphabetical
alphabetically

alpine

already

Alsatian *noun*
Alsatians

also

altar☆ *noun*
altars

alter○ *verb*
alters
altering
altered

alteration

alternate *verb*
alternates
alternating
alternated

alternately

alternation

alternating current

alternative *noun*
alternatives

alternative

alternator *noun*
alternators

although *conjunction*

altitude *noun*
altitudes

altogether

aluminium

always

amalgamate *verb*
amalgamates
amalgamating
amalgamated

amalgamation

amateur *adjective and noun*
amateurs

amateurish

amaze *verb*
amazes
amazing
amazed

amazement

ambassador *noun*
ambassadors

amber

ambiguity
ambiguities

ambiguous
ambiguously

ambition *noun*
ambitions

ambitious
ambitiously

amble *verb*
ambles
ambling
ambled

ambulance *noun*
ambulances

ambush *noun*
ambushes

ambush *verb*
ambushes
ambushing
ambushed

amen

amend *verb*
amends
amending
amended

amendment

amenity *noun*
amenities

American *adjective and noun*
Americans

amiable
amiably

amicable
amicably

amid✢

amidships

ammonia

ammunition

amnesty *noun*
amnesties

amoeba *noun*
amoebas

among*

amount *noun*
amounts

. . . .

★ **Aloud** means 'in a voice that can be heard'. **I allowed.**
☆ An **altar** is a raised surface in religious ceremonies. **! alter.**
○ **Alter** means to change something. **I altar.**
✢ You can also spell this word *amidst.*
● You can also spell this word *amongst.*

a

amount *verb*
amounts
amounting
amounted

amphibian *adjective*
and *noun*
amphibians

amphibious

ample *adjective*
ampler
amplest
amply

amplification

amplfiier *noun*
amplifiers

amplify *verb*
amplifies
amplifying
amplified

amputate *verb*
amputates
amputating
amputated

amputation

amuse *verb*
amuses
amusing
amused

amusement *noun*
amusements

amusing

an★

anaemia

anaemic

anaesthetic *noun*
anaesthetics

anaesthetist

anaesthetize *verb*
anaesthetizes
anaesthetizing
anaesthetized

anagram *noun*
anagrams

analogous

analogue☆

analogy *noun*
analogies

analyse *verb*
analyses
analysing
analysed

analysis *noun*
analyses

analytical

anarchism

anarchist *noun*
anarchists

anarchy

anatomical

anatomy

-ance and -ence
Most nouns ending in
-ance come from
verbs, e.g.
disturbance,
endurance. Some
nouns end in -ence,
e.g. **dependence**,
obedience, and you
need to be careful not
to misspell these.

---

ancestor *noun*
ancestors

ancestral

ancestry *noun*
ancestries

anchor *noun*
anchors

anchorage *noun*
anchorages

ancient

anemone *noun*
anemones

angel *noun*
angels

angelic

anger

angle *noun*
angles

angle *verb*
angles
angling
angled

angler *noun*
anglers

Anglican *adjective*
and *noun*
Anglicans

Anglo-Saxon
adjective **and** *noun*
Anglo-Saxons

angry *adjective*
angrier
angriest
angrily

anguish

angular

animal *noun*
animals

animated

animation

★ You use **an** instead of *a* before a word beginning with a vowel, e.g.
an apple, or before an abbreviation that sounds as though it begins
with a vowel, e.g. *an MP*.
☆ You will sometimes see the spelling *analog*, especially when it is
about computers.

b c d e f g h i j k l m n o p q r s t u v w x y z

animosity *noun*
animosities

aniseed

ankle *noun*
ankles

annex *verb*
annexes
annexing
annexed

annexation

annexe *noun*
annexes

annihilate *verb*
annihilates
annihilating
annihilated

annihilation

anniversary *noun*
anniversaries

announce *verb*
announces
announcing
announced

announcer

announcement *noun*
announcements

annoy *verb*
annoys
annoying
annoyed

annoyance *noun*
annoyances

annual *adjective*
annually

annual *noun*
annuals

anonymity★

anonymous
anonymously

anorak *noun*
anoraks

anorexia

anorexic

another

answer *noun*
answers

answer *verb*
answers
answering
answered

-ant and **-ent**
Many adjectives end
in *-ant*, e.g.
abundant,
important. Some
adjectives end in *-ent*,
e.g. **dependent**
(**dependant** is a
noun), **permanent**,
and you need to be
careful not to misspell
these.

---

antagonism

antagonistic

antagonize *verb*
antagonizes
antagonizing
antagonized

Antarctic *adjective*
and *noun*

anteater *noun*
anteaters

antelope☆ *noun*
antelope *or* antelopes

antenna *noun*
antennae *or* antennas

anthem *noun*
anthems

anthill *noun*
anthills

anthology *noun*
anthologies

anthracite

anthropologist

anthropology

---

anti-
anti- at the beginning
of a word makes a
word meaning
'against something' or
'stopping something',
e.g. **antifreeze** means
'a liquid that stops
water from freezing'. If
the word you are
adding *anti-* to begins
with a vowel, you use
a hyphen, e.g.
anti-aircraft.

---

antibiotic *noun*
antibiotics

anticipate *verb*
anticipates
anticipating
anticipated

anticipation

anticlimax *noun*
anticlimaxes

anticlockwise *adverb*
and *adjective*

anticyclone *noun*
anticyclones

antidote *noun*
antidotes

antifreeze

★ The noun from **anonymous**.
☆ You use **antelope** when you mean a lot of animals and **antelopes**
when you mean several you are thinking about separately.

an - ap

antipodes*

antiquated

antique *adjective and noun*
antiques

antiseptic *noun*
antiseptics

antler *noun*
antlers

anus *noun*
anuses

anvil *noun*
anvils

anxiety *noun*
anxieties

anxious
anxiously

anybody

anyhow

anyone

anything

anyway

anywhere

apart

apartment *noun*
apartments

apathetic

apathy

ape *noun*
apes

aphid *noun*
aphids

apiece

apologetic
apologetically

apologize *verb*
apologizes
apologizing
apologized

apology *noun*
apologies

apostle *noun*
apostles

apostrophe *noun*
apostrophes

appal *verb*
appals
appalling
appalled

appalling

apparatus *noun*
apparatuses

apparent
apparently

appeal *verb*
appeals
appealing
appealed

appeal *noun*
appeals

appear *verb*
appears
appearing
appeared

appearance *noun*
appearances

appease *verb*
appeases
appeasing
appeased

appeasement

appendicitis

appendix☆
appendixes *or*
appendices

appetite *noun*
appetites

appetizing

applaud *verb*
applauds
applauding
applauded

applause

apple *noun*
apples

appliance *noun*
appliances

applicable

applicant *noun*
applicants

application *noun*
applications

applied

apply *verb*
applies
applying
applied

appoint *verb*
appoints
appointing
appointed

appointment *noun*
appointments

appraisal *noun*
appraisals

appraise *verb*
appraises
appraising
appraised

appreciate *verb*
appreciates
appreciating
appreciated

appreciation

appreciative

apprehension *noun*

apprehensive

★ A word Europeans use for Australia and New Zealand.

☆ You use **appendixes** when you mean organs of the body and
appendices when you mean parts of a book.

apprentice noun
apprentices

apprenticeship

approach verb
approaches
approaching
approached

approach noun
approaches

approachable

appropriate

approval

approve verb
approves
approving
approved

approximate
approximately

apricot noun
apricots

April

apron noun
aprons

aptitude noun
aptitudes

aquarium noun
aquariums

aquatic

aqueduct noun
aqueducts

Arab★ noun
Arabs

Arabian★ adjective

Arabic☆

arabic☆

arable

arbitrary

arbitrate verb
arbitrates
arbitrating
arbitrated

arbitration

arbitrator

arc○ noun
arcs

arcade noun
arcades

arch noun
arches

arch verb
arches
arching
arched

archaeology

archaeological

archaeologist

archbishop noun
archbishops

archer noun
archers

archery

architect noun
architects

architecture

-archy
-archy at the end of a
word means 'rule or
government', e.g.
anarchy (= a lack of
rule) and **monarchy**
(= rule by a king or
queen). The plural
form is -archies, e.g.
monarchies.

Arctic

are

area noun
areas

arena noun
arenas

aren't abbreviation

argue verb
argues
arguing
argued

argument noun
arguments

arid

aridity

arise verb
arises
arising
arose
arisen

aristocracy noun
aristocracies

aristocrat noun
aristocrats

aristocratic

arithmetic

arithmetical

ark✦ noun
arks

arm noun
arms

arm verb
arms
arming
armed

armada noun
armadas

a b c d e f g h i j k l m n o p q r s t u v w x y z

- -

★ You use **Arab** when you mean a person or the people, and
Arabian when you mean the place, e.g. *the Arabian desert.*
☆ You use **Arabic** when you mean the language, and **arabic** when
you mean numbers, e.g. *arabic numerals.*
○ **Arc** means a curve. **!ark.**
✦ **Ark** means a boat. **!arc.**

11

a

armadillo noun
armadillos

armaments

armchair noun
armchairs

armful noun
armfuls

armistice noun
armistices

armour

armoured

armpit noun
armpits

army noun
armies

aroma noun
aromas

aromatic

arose see **arise**

around

arouse verb
arouses
arousing
aroused

arrange verb
arranges
arranging
arranged

arrangement

array noun
arrays

arrears

arrest verb
arrests
arresting
arrested

arrest noun
arrests

arrival

arrive verb
arrives
arriving
arrived

arrogance

arrogant

arrow noun
arrows

arsenal noun
arsenals

arsenic

arson

artefact noun
artefacts

artery noun
arteries

artful
artfully

arthritic

arthritis

article noun
articles

articulate adjective

articulate verb
articulates
articulating
articulated

artificial
artificially

artillery noun
artilleries

artist noun
artists

artiste noun
artistes

artistic

artistry

asbestos

ascend verb
ascends
ascending
ascended

ascent noun
ascents

ash* noun
ashes

ashamed

ashen

ashore

ashtray noun
ashtrays

Asian adjective and noun
Asians

aside

ask verb
asks
asking
asked

asleep

aspect noun
aspects

asphalt☆

aspirin noun
aspirins

ass noun
asses

assassin noun
assassins

assassinate verb
assassinates
assassinating
assassinated

assassination noun
assassinations

assault verb
assaults
assaulting
assaulted

. . . .

★ The tree and the burnt powder.
☆ Note that this word is not spelt *ash-*.

assault *noun*
assaults

assemble *verb*
assembles
assembling
assembled

assembly *noun*
assemblies

assent

assert *verb*
asserts
asserting
asserted

assertion

assertive

assess *verb*
assesses
assessing
assessed

assessment

assessor

asset *noun*
assets

assign *verb*
assigns
assigning
assigned

assignment *noun*
assignments

assist *verb*
assists
assisting
assisted

assistance

assistant *noun*
assistants

associate *verb*
associates
associating
associated

associate *noun*
associates

association *noun*
associations

assorted

assortment

assume *verb*
assumes
assuming
assumed

assumption *noun*
assumptions

assurance *noun*
assurances

assure *verb*
assures
assuring
assured

asterisk *noun*
asterisks

asteroid *noun*
asteroids

asthma

asthmatic *adjective*
and *noun*
asthmatics

astonish *verb*
astonishes
astonishing
astonished

astonishment

astound *verb*
astounds
astounding
astounded

astride

astrologer

astrological

astrology

astronaut *noun*
astronauts

astronomer

astronomical

astronomy

> **-asy**
> Not many words end
> in *-asy*. The most
> important are
> **ecstasy, fantasy,**
> **idiosyncrasy.** There
> are a lot of words
> ending in *-acy*,
> however, e.g.
> **accuracy**.

ate★ *see eat*

atheist *noun*
atheists

atheism

athlete *noun*
athletes

athletic

athletics

atlas *noun*
atlases

atmosphere *noun*
atmospheres

atmospheric

atoll *noun*
atolls

atom *noun*
atoms

atomic

atrocious
atrociously

atrocity *noun*
atrocities

attach *verb*
attaches
attaching
attached

attached

attachment *noun*
attachments

b
c
d
e
f
g
h
i
j
k
l
m
n
o
p
q
r
s
t
u
v
w
x
y
z

★ **Ate** is the past tense of eat e.g. *I ate an apple.* ! **eight**.

13

a

attack *verb*
attacks
attacking
attacked

attack *noun*
attacks

attain *verb*
attains
attaining
attained

attainment

attempt *verb*
attempts
attempting
attempted

attempt *noun*
attempts

attend *verb*
attends
attending
attended

attendance *noun*
attendances

attendant *noun*
attendants

attention

attentive

attic *noun*
attics

attitude *noun*
attitudes

attract *verb*
attracts
attracting
attracted

attraction *noun*
attractions

attractive

auburn

auction *noun*
auctions

auctioneer

audibility

audible

audience *noun*
audiences

audio-
audio- makes words
with 'sound' or
'hearing' in their
meaning. Some of
them have hyphens,
e.g. **audio-visual** (=
to do with hearing and
seeing).

audio-visual

audition *noun*
auditions

auditorium *noun*
auditoriums

August

aunt *noun*
aunts

auntie* *noun*
aunties

au pair☆ *noun*
au pairs

aural○

austere

austerity

Australian *adjective*
and *noun*
Australians

authentic
authentically

authenticity

author *noun*
authors

authority *noun*
authorities

authorize *verb*
authorizes
authorizing
authorized

autistic

auto-
auto- at the beginning
of a word means 'self',
e.g. **autobiography**
(= a biography of
yourself), **automatic**
(= done by itself). But
some words
beginning with auto-
are to do with cars,
e.g. **autocross** (= car
racing across
country).

autobiography *noun*
autobiographies

autograph *noun*
autographs

automate *verb*
automates
automating
automated

automatic
automatically

automation

automobile *noun*
automobiles

autumn *noun*
autumns

autumnal

auxiliary *adjective* and
noun
auxiliaries

....

★ You can also spell this word *aunty*.
☆ **Au pair** means a young person from another country who works in
your house.
○ **Aural** means 'to do with hearing'. **!** oral.

14

availability

available

avalanche *noun*
avalanches

avenue *noun*
avenues

average *adjective* and
noun
averages

average *verb*
averages
averaging
averaged

avert *verb*
averts
averting
averted

aviary *noun*
aviaries

aviation

avid

avoid *verb*
avoids
avoiding
avoided

avoidance

await *verb*
awaits
awaiting
awaited

awake *adjective*

awake *verb*
awakes
awaking
awoke
awoken

awaken *verb*
awakens
awakening
awakened

award *noun*
awards

award *verb*
awards
awarding
awarded

aware

awareness

awash

away

awe

awed

awful
awfully

awhile*

awkward

awoke see **awake**

awoken see **awake**

axe *noun*
axes

axe *verb*
axes
axing
axed

axis *noun*
axes

axle *noun*
axles

Aztec *noun*
Aztecs

azure *adjective*

Bb

babble *verb*
babbles
babbling
babbled

baboon *noun*
baboons

baby *noun*
babies

babyish

babysit *verb*
babysits
babysitting
babysat

babysitter *noun*
babysitters

bachelor *noun*
bachelors

back *noun*
backs

back *verb*
backs
backing
backed

backache *noun*
backaches

backbone *noun*
backbones

background *noun*
backgrounds

backing

backlash *noun*
backlashes

backlog *noun*
backlogs

backside *noun*
backsides

backstroke

backward *adjective*
and *adverb*

backwards *adverb*

backwater *noun*
backwaters

backyard *noun*
backyards

bacon

bacteria

bacterial

★ **Awhile** means 'for a short time', e.g. *Wait here awhile*. You spell it
as two words in e.g. *a short while*.

a
b
c
d
e
f
g
h
i
j
k
l
m
n
o
p
q
r
s
t
u
v
w
x
y
z

ba

bad *adjective*
worse
worst
badly

baddy *noun*
baddies

badge *noun*
badges

badger *noun*
badgers

badger *verb*
badgers
badgering
badgered

badminton *noun*

baffle *verb*
baffles
baffling
baffled

bag *noun*
bags

bag *verb*
bags
bagging
bagged

bagel *noun*
bagels

baggage

baggy *adjective*
baggier
baggiest

bagpipes

bail* *noun*
bails

bail☆ *verb*
bails
bailing
bailed

Bairam *noun*
Bairams

Baisakhi

bait *noun*

bait *verb*
baits
baiting
baited

bake *verb*
bakes
baking
baked

baker *noun*
bakers

bakery *noun*
bakeries

baking powder

balance *noun*
balances

balance *verb*
balances
balancing
balanced

balcony *noun*
balconies

bald *adjective*
balder
baldest

bale○ *noun*
bales

bale✛ *verb*
bales
baling
baled

ballad *noun*
ballads

ballerina *noun*
ballerinas

ballet *noun*
ballets

ballistic *adjective*

balloon *noun*
balloons

ballot *noun*
ballots

ballpoint *noun*
ballpoints

ballroom *noun*
ballrooms

balsa

bamboo *noun*
bamboos

ban *verb*
bans
banning
banned

banana *noun*
bananas

band *noun*
bands

band *verb*
bands
banding
banded

bandage *noun*
bandages

bandit *noun*
bandits

bandstand *noun*
bandstands

bandwagon *noun*
bandwagons

bandy *adjective*
bandier
bandiest

- -

★ **Bail** means 'money paid to let a prisoner out of prison' and 'a piece of wood put on the stumps in cricket'. **! bale**.

☆ **Bail** means 'to pay money to let a prisoner out of prison' and 'to scoop water out of a boat'. **! bale**.

○ **Bale** means 'a large bundle'. **! bail**.

✛ **Bale** means 'to jump out of an aircraft'. **! bail**.

bang noun
bangs

bang verb
bangs
banging
banged

banger noun
bangers

banish verb
banishes
banishing
banished

banishment

banisters

banjo noun
banjos

bank noun
banks

bank verb
banks
banking
banked

banknote noun
banknotes

bankrupt

bankruptcy

banner noun
banners

banquet noun
banquets

baptism noun
baptisms

Baptist* noun
Baptists

baptize verb
baptizes
baptizing
baptized

bar noun
bars

bar verb
bars
barring
barred

barb noun
barbs

barbarian noun
barbarians

barbaric

barbarism

barbarity noun
barbarities

barbarous adjective

barbecue noun
barbecues

barber noun
barbers

bar code noun
bar codes

bard noun
bards

bare☆ adjective
barer
barest

bareback

barely

bargain noun
bargains

bargain verb
bargains
bargaining
bargained

barge noun
barges

barge verb
barges
barging
barged

baritone noun
baritones

bark noun
barks

bark verb
barks
barking
barked

barley

barman noun
barmen

bar mitzvah noun
bar mitzvahs

barnacle noun
barnacles

barnyard noun
barnyards

barometer noun
barometers

barometric

baron noun
barons

baroness noun
baronesses

baronial

barrack verb
barracks
barracking
barracked

barracks○ plural noun

barrage noun
barrages

barrel noun
barrels

· ·

★ You use a capital B when you mean a member of the Christian Church.

☆ **Bare** means 'naked' or 'not covered'. **!** bear.

○ **Barracks** is plural but sometimes has a singular verb, e.g. *The barracks is over there.*

barren

barricade *noun*
barricades

barricade *verb*
barricades
barricading
barricaded

barrier *noun*
barriers

barrister *noun*
barristers

barrow *noun*
barrows

barter *verb*
barters
bartering
bartered

base★ *noun*
bases

base *verb*
bases
basing
based

baseball *noun*
baseballs

basement *noun*
basements

bash *verb*
bashes
bashing
bashed

bash *noun*
bashes

bashful *adj*
bashfully

basic *adj*
basically

basin *noun*
basins

basis *noun*
bases

bask *verb*
basks
basking
basked

basket *noun*
baskets

basketball *noun*
basketballs

basketful *noun*
basketfuls

bass☆ *noun*
basses

bassoon *noun*
bassoons

bastard *noun*
bastards

bat *noun*
bats

bat *verb*
bats
batting
batted

batch *noun*
batches

bath *noun*
baths

bath *verb*
baths
bathing
bathed

bathe *verb*
bathes
bathing
bathed

bathroom *noun*
bathrooms

baton○ *noun*
batons

batsman *noun*
batsmen

battalion *noun*
battalions

batten✚ *noun*
battens

batter *verb*
batters
battering
battered

batter *noun*

battery *noun*
batteries

battle *noun*
battles

battlefield *noun*
battlefields

battlements

battleship *noun*
battleships

bawl *verb*
bawls
bawling
bawled

bay *noun*
bays

bayonet *noun*
bayonets

bazaar *noun*
bazaars

beach● *noun*
beaches

beacon *noun*
beacons

bead *noun*
beads

. . . .

★ **Base** means 'a place where things are controlled'. **! bass.**
☆ **Bass** means 'a singer with a low voice'. **! base.**
○ A **baton** is a stick used by a conductor in an orchestra. **! batten.**
✚ A **batten** is a flat strip of wood. **! baton.**
● **Beach** means 'sandy part of the seashore'. **! beech.**

18

beady *adjective*
beadier
beadiest

beagle *noun*
beagles

beak *noun*
beaks

beaker *noun*
beakers

beam *noun*
beams

beam *verb*
beams
beaming
beamed

bean★ *noun*
beans

bear☆ *verb*
bears
bearing
bore
borne

bear☆ *noun*
bears

bearable

beard *noun*
beards

bearded

bearing *noun*
bearings

beast *noun*
beasts

beastly

beat *verb*
beats
beating
beat
beaten

beat *noun*
beats

beautiful
beautifully

beautify *verb*
beautifies
beautifying
beautified

beauty *noun*
beauties

beaver *noun*
beavers

becalmed

became see **become**

because

beckon *verb*
beckons
beckoning
beckoned

become *verb*
becomes
becoming
became
become

bedclothes

bedding

bedlam

bedraggled

bedridden

bedroom *noun*
bedrooms

bedside

bedspread *noun*
bedspreads

bedstead *noun*
bedsteads

bedtime

bee *noun*
bees

beech○ *noun*
beeches

beef

beefburger *noun*
beefburgers

beefeater *noun*
beefeaters

beefy *adjective*
beefier
beefiest

beehive *noun*
beehives

beeline

been✤ see **be**

beer *noun*
beers

beet *noun*
beet or beets

beetle *noun*
beetles

beetroot *noun*
beetroot

before

beforehand

beg *verb*
begs
begging
begged

began see **begin**

beggar *noun*
beggars

begin *verb*
begins
beginning
began
begun

beginner *noun*
beginners

beginning *noun*
beginnings

. . . .

★ A bean is a vegetable. **!** been.
☆ To bear something is to carry it and a bear is an animal. **!** bare.
○ Beech means 'a tree'. **!** beach.
✤ You use been in e.g. *I've been to the zoo.* **!** bean.

be

begrudge verb
begrudges
begrudging
begrudged

begun see begin

behalf

behave verb
behaves
behaving
behaved

behaviour

behead verb
beheads
beheading
beheaded

behind adverb and preposition

behind noun
behinds

beige noun

being noun
beings

belch verb
belches
belching
belched

belch noun
belches

belfry noun
belfries

belief noun
beliefs

believe verb
believes
believing
believed

believable

believer

bellow verb
bellows
bellowing
bellowed

bellows

belly noun
bellies

belong verb
belongs
belonging
belonged

belongings

beloved

below

belt noun
belts

belt verb
belts
belting
belted

bench noun
benches

bend verb
bends
bending
bent

bend noun
bends

beneath

benefaction

benefactor noun
benefactors

benefit noun
benefits

beneficial
beneficially

benevolence

benevolent

bent see bend

bequeath verb
bequeaths
bequeathing
bequeathed

bequest

bereaved★

bereavement

bereft☆

beret noun
berets

berry noun
berries

berserk

berth noun
berths

beside

besides

besiege verb
besieges
besieging
besieged

bestseller noun
bestsellers

bet noun
bets

bet verb
bets
betting
bet
betted

betray verb
betrays
betraying
betrayed

betrayal

better adjective and adverb

....

★ You use **bereaved** when you mean a person with a close relative who has died. **I bereft**.
☆ You use **bereft** when you mean 'deprived of something', e.g. *bereft of hope*. **I bereaved**.

better *verb*
betters
bettering
bettered

between

beware* *verb*

bewilder *verb*
bewilders
bewildering
bewildered

bewilderment

bewitch *verb*
bewitches
bewitching
bewitched

beyond

---

bi-
bi- at the beginning of a word means 'two', e.g. **bicycle** (= a machine with two wheels), **bilateral** (= having two sides).

---

bias *noun*
biases

biased

bib *noun*
bibs

Bible *noun*
Bibles

biblical

bicycle *noun*
bicycles

bid *noun*
bids

bid *verb*
bids
bidding
bid

bide *verb*
bides
biding
bided

big *adjective*
bigger
biggest

bigamist

bigamous

bigamy

bike *noun*
bikes

bikini *noun*
bikinis

bile

bilge *noun*
bilges

bilingual

billiards

billion *noun*
billions

billionth

billow *noun*
billows

billow *verb*
billows
billowing
billowed

billy goat *noun*
billy goats

binary

bind *verb*
binds
binding
bound

bingo

binoculars

---

bio-
bio- at the beginning of a word means 'life', e.g. **biography** (= a story of a person's life), **biology** (= the study of living things).

---

biodegradable

biographer

biographical

biography *noun*
biographies

biological

biologist

biology

bionic

biosphere

birch *noun*
birches

bird *noun*
birds

birdseed

Biro *noun*
Biros

birth *noun*
births

birth control

birthday *noun*
birthdays

birthmark *noun*
birthmarks

birthplace *noun*
birthplaces

biscuit *noun*
biscuits

bisect *verb*
bisects
bisecting
bisected

bishop *noun*
bishops

★ **Beware** has no other forms.

bison noun
bison

bit noun
bits

bit see bite

bitch noun
bitches

bitchy adjective
bitchier
bitchiest

bite verb
bites
biting
bit
bitten

bite* noun
bites

bitter

black adjective
blacker
blackest

black noun
blacks

blackberry noun
blackberries

blackbird noun
blackbirds

blackboard noun
blackboards

blacken verb
blackens
blackening
blackened

blackmail verb
blackmails
blackmailing
blackmailed

blackout noun
blackouts

blacksmith noun
blacksmiths

bladder noun
bladders

blade noun
blades

blame verb
blames
blaming
blamed

blame noun

blancmange noun
blancmanges

blank adjective and noun
blanks

blanket noun
blankets

blare verb
blares
blaring
blared

blaspheme verb
blasphemes
blaspheming
blasphemed

blasphemous

blasphemy

blast noun
blasts

blast verb
blasts
blasting
blasted

blast-off

blaze noun
blazes

blaze verb
blazes
blazing
blazed

blazer noun
blazers

bleach noun
bleaches

bleach verb
bleaches
bleaching
bleached

bleak adjective
bleaker
bleakest

bleary adjective
blearier
bleariest
blearily

bleat noun
bleats

bleat verb
bleats
bleating
bleated

bleed verb
bleeds
bleeding
bled

bleep noun
bleeps

blemish noun
blemishes

blend verb
blends
blending
blended

blend noun
blends

bless verb
blesses
blessing
blessed

blessing noun
blessings

blew☆ see blow

blight noun
blights

★ A **bite** is an act of biting. **!** byte.

☆ You use **blew** in e.g. the wind blew hard. **!** blue.

blind *adjective*
blinder
blindest

blind *verb*
blinds
blinding
blinded

blind *noun*
blinds

blindfold *noun*
blindfolds

blindfold *verb*
blindfolds
blindfolding
blindfolded

blink *verb*
blinks
blinking
blinked

bliss

blissful
blissfully

blister *noun*
blisters

blitz *noun*
blitzes

blizzard *noun*
blizzards

bloated

block *noun*
blocks

block *verb*
blocks
blocking
blocked

blockade *noun*
blockades

blockage *noun*
blockages

blond *adjective*
blonder
blondest

blonde★ *noun*
blondes

blood

bloodhound *noun*
bloodhounds

bloodshed

bloodshot

bloodstream

bloodthirsty *adjective*
bloodthirstier
bloodthirstiest

bloody *adjective*
bloodier
bloodiest

bloom *verb*
blooms
blooming
bloomed

bloom *noun*
blooms

blossom *noun*
blossoms

blossom *verb*
blossoms
blossoming
blossomed

blot *noun*
blots

blot *verb*
blots
blotting
blotted

blotch *noun*
blotches

blotchy *adjective*
blotchier
blotchiest

blouse *noun*
blouses

blow *noun*
blows

blow *verb*
blows
blowing
blew
blown

blowlamp *noun*
blowlamps

blowtorch *noun*
blowtorches

blue *adjective*
bluer
bluest

blue☆ *noun*
blues

bluebell *noun*
bluebells

bluebottle *noun*
bluebottles

blueprint *noun*
blueprints

bluff *verb*
bluffs
bluffing
bluffed

bluff *noun*
bluffs

blunder *verb*
blunders
blundering
blundered

blunder *noun*
blunders

blunt *adjective*
blunter
bluntest

blur *verb*
blurs
blurring
blurred

- -
★ You use **blonde** when you are talking about a girl or woman.
☆ Blue is the colour. **!** blew.

blur *noun*
blurs

blush *verb*
blushes
blushing
blushed

bluster *verb*
blusters
blustering
blustered

blustery

boa constrictor *noun*
boa constrictors

boar* *noun*
boars

board☆ *noun*
boards

board *verb*
boards
boarding
boarded

boarder *noun*
boarders

board game *noun*
board games

boast *verb*
boasts
boasting
boasted

boastful
boastfully

boat *noun*
boats

boating

bob *verb*
bobs
bobbing
bobbed

bobble *noun*
bobbles

bobsled *noun*
bobsleds

bobsleigh *noun*
bobsleighs

bodice *noun*
bodices

bodily

body *noun*
bodies

bodyguard *noun*
bodyguards

boggy *adjective*
boggier
boggiest

bogus

boil *verb*
boils
boiling
boiled

boil *noun*
boils

boiler *noun*
boilers

boisterous
boisterously

bold *adjective*
bolder
boldest

bollard *noun*
bollards

bolster *verb*
bolsters
bolstering
bolstered

bolster *noun*
bolsters

bolt *noun*
boits

bolt *verb*
bolts
bolting
bolted

bomb *noun*
bombs

bomb *verb*
bombs
bombing
bombed

bombard *verb*
bombards
bombarding
bombarded

bombardment

bomber *noun*
bombers

bond *noun*
bonds

bondage

bone *noun*
bones

bonfire *noun*
bonfires

bonnet *noun*
bonnets

bonus *noun*
bonuses

bony *adjective*
bonier
boniest

boo *verb*
boos
booing
booed

booby *noun*
boobies

book *noun*
books

book *verb*
books
booking
booked

bookcase *noun*
bookcases

booklet *noun*
booklets

★ A **boar** is a wild pig. **!** bore.
☆ A **board** is a piece of wood. **!** bored.

bookmaker *noun*
bookmakers

bookmark *noun*
bookmarks

boom *noun*
booms

boom *verb*
booms
booming
boomed

boomerang *noun*
boomerangs

boost *verb*
boosts
boosting
boosted

booster *noun*
boosters

boot *noun*
boots

boot *verb*
boots
booting
booted

booth *noun*
booths

border *noun*
borders

borderline

bore *verb*
bores
boring
bored

bore* *noun*
bores

boredom

boring

born☆

borne○ see **bear**

borough *noun*
boroughs

borrow *verb*
borrows
borrowing
borrowed

bosom *noun*
bosoms

boss *noun*
bosses

boss *verb*
bosses
bossing
bossed

bossy *adjective*
bossier
bossiest

botanical

botanist

botany

both

bother *verb*
bothers
bothering
bothered

bother *noun*

bottle *noun*
bottles

bottle *verb*
bottles
bottling
bottled

bottleneck *noun*
bottlenecks

bottom *noun*
bottoms

bottomless

bough✝ *noun*
boughs

bought

boulder *noun*
boulders

bounce *verb*
bounces
bouncing
bounced

bounce *noun*
bounces

bouncing

bouncy *adjective*
bouncier
bounciest

bound *verb*
bounds
bounding
bounded

bound *adjective* and
noun
bounds

bound see **bind**

boundary *noun*
boundaries

bounds

bouquet *noun*
bouquets

bout *noun*
bouts

boutique *noun*
boutiques

bow✻ *noun*
bows

★ **Bore** means 'something boring'. ! **boar**.

☆ You use **born** in e.g. *He was born in June.* ! **borne**.

○ You use **borne** in e.g. *She has borne three children* and *The cost is borne by the government.* ! **born**.

✝ A **bough** is a part of a tree. ! **bow**.

✻ A **bow** is a knot with loops and rhymes with 'go'. A **bow** is also the front of a ship or a bending of the body and rhymes with 'cow'.

a
b
c
d
e
f
g
h
i
j
k
l
m
n
o
p
q
r
s
t
u
v
w
x
y
z

bow* verb
bows
bowing
bowed

bowels

bowl noun
bowls

bowl verb
bowls
bowling
bowled

bow-legged

bowler noun
bowlers

bowling

bowls

bow tie noun
bow ties

box noun
boxes

box verb
boxes
boxing
boxed

boxer noun
boxers

Boxing Day noun

boy noun
boys

boycott verb
boycotts
boycotting
boycotted

boyfriend noun
boyfriends

boyhood

boyish

bra noun
bras

brace noun
braces

bracelet noun
bracelets

braces

bracken

bracket noun
brackets

bracket verb
brackets
bracketing
bracketed

brag verb
brags
bragging
bragged

braid noun
braids

braille

brain noun
brains

brainy adjective
brainier
brainiest

brake☆ noun
brakes

bramble noun
brambles

branch noun
branches

branch verb
branches
branching
branched

brand noun
brands

brand verb
brands
branding
branded

brandish verb
brandishes
brandishing
brandished

brand new

brandy noun
brandies

brass

brassière noun
brassières

brassy adjective
brassier
brassiest

brave adjective
braver
bravest

brave noun
braves

bravery

brawl noun
brawls

brawn

brawny adjective
brawnier
brawniest

bray verb
brays
braying
brayed

brazen

brazier noun
braziers

breacho noun
breaches

bread

breadth noun
breadths

breadwinner noun
breadwinners

......

★ To **bow** is to bend the body and rhymes with 'cow'.
☆ A **brake** is what makes a car stop. **I break**.
o A **breach** is a gap or a breaking of a rule. **I breech**.

break* *verb*
breaks
breaking
broke
broken

break *noun*
breaks

breakable

breakage *noun*
breakages

breakdown *noun*
breakdowns

breaker *noun*
breakers

breakfast *noun*
breakfasts

breakneck

breakthrough *noun*
breakthroughs

breakwater *noun*
breakwaters

breast *noun*
breasts

breaststroke

breath *noun*
breaths

breathalyse
breathalyses
breathalysing
breathalysed

breathalyser *noun*
breathalysers

breathe *verb*
breathes
breathing
breathed

breather *noun*
breathers

breathless

breathtaking

bred see **breed**

breech☆ *noun*
breeches

breeches *plural noun*

breed *verb*
breeds
breeding
bred

breed *noun*
breeds

breeder *noun*
breeders

breeze *noun*
breezes

breezy *adjective*
breezier
breeziest

brethren

brevity

brew *verb*
brews
brewing
brewed

brewer *noun*
brewers

brewery *noun*
breweries

briar○ *noun*
briars

bribe *noun*
bribes

bribe *verb*
bribes
bribing
bribed

bribery

brick *noun*
bricks

bricklayer *noun*
bricklayers

bride *noun*
brides

bridal✢

bridegroom *noun*
bridegrooms

bridesmaid *noun*
bridesmaids

bridge *noun*
bridges

bridle* *noun*
bridles

brief *adjective*
briefer
briefest

brief *noun*
briefs

brief *verb*
briefs
briefing
briefed

briefcase *noun*
briefcases

brigade *noun*
brigades

brigadier *noun*
brigadiers

brigand *noun*
brigands

bright *adjective*
brighter
brightest

★ To **break** something is to make it go into pieces. **!** brake.

☆ A **breech** is a part of a gun. **!** breach.

○ **Briar** means 'a prickly bush' and 'a pipe'. You will sometimes see it spelt *brier*.

✢ **Bridal** means 'to do with a bride'. **!** bridle.

✱ A **bridle** is part of a horse's harness. **!** bridal.

a
b
c
d
e
f
g
h
i
j
k
l
m
n
o
p
q
r
s
t
u
v
w
x
y
z

br

a
b
c
d
e
f
g
h
i
j
k
l
m
n
o
p
q
r
s
t
u
v
w
x
y
z

brighten *verb*
brightens
brightening
brightened

brilliance

brilliant

brim *noun*
brims

brimming

brine

bring *verb*
brings
bringing
brought

brink

brisk *adjective*
brisker
briskest

bristle *noun*
bristles

bristly
bristlier
bristliest

British

Briton *noun*
Britons

brittle *adjective*
brittler
brittlest

broach* *verb*
broaches
broaching
broached

broad *adjective*
broader
broadest
broadly

broadcast *noun*
broadcasts

broadcast *verb*
broadcasts
broadcasting
broadcast

broadcaster

broaden *verb*
broadens
broadening
broadened

broad-minded

broadside *noun*
broadsides

brochure *noun*
brochures

brogue *noun*
brogues

broke see **break**

broken see **break**

bronchitis

bronze

brooch☆ *noun*
brooches

brood *noun*
broods

brood *verb*
broods
brooding
brooded

broody *adjective*
broodier
broodiest

brook *noun*
brooks

broom *noun*
brooms

broomstick *noun*
broomsticks

broth *noun*
broths

brother *noun*
brothers

brotherly

brother-in-law *noun*
brothers-in-law

brought see **bring**

brow *noun*
brows

brown *adjective*
browner
brownest

brownie○ *noun*
brownies

Brownie✥ *noun*
Brownies

browse *verb*
browses
browsing
browsed

bruise *noun*
bruises

bruise *verb*
bruises
bruising
bruised

brunette *noun*
brunettes

brush *noun*
brushes

brush *verb*
brushes
brushing
brushed

Brussels sprout *noun*
Brussels sprouts

brutal
brutally

brutality *noun*
brutalities

. . . .

★ **Broach** means 'to mention something'. **!broach**.
☆ A **brooch** is an ornament you wear. **!broach**.
○ A **brownie** is a chocolate cake.
✥ A **Brownie** is a junior Guide.

28

brute *noun*
brutes

bubble *noun*
bubbles

bubble *verb*
bubbles
bubbling
bubbled

bubble gum

bubbly *adjective*
bubblier
bubbliest

buccaneer *noun*
buccaneers

buck *noun*
bucks

buck *verb*
bucks
bucking
bucked

bucket *noun*
buckets

bucketful *noun*
bucketfuls

buckle *noun*
buckles

buckle *verb*
buckles
buckling
buckled

bud *noun*
buds

Buddhism

Buddhist

budding

budge *verb*
budges
budging
budged

budgerigar *noun*
budgerigars

budget *noun*
budgets

budget *verb*
budgets
budgeting
budgeted

budgie *noun*
budgies

buff

buffalo *noun*
buffalo *or* buffaloes

buffer *noun*
buffers

buffet *noun*
buffets

bug *noun*
bugs

bug *verb*
bugs
bugging
bugged

bugle *noun*
bugles

bugler *noun*
buglers

build *verb*
builds
building
built

builder *noun*
builders

building *noun*
buildings

built-in

built-up

bulb *noun*
bulbs

bulge *noun*
bulges

bulge *verb*
bulges
bulging
bulged

bulk

bulky *adjective*
bulkier
bulkiest

bull *noun*
bulls

bulldog *noun*
bulldogs

bulldoze *verb*
bulldozes
bulldozing
bulldozed

bulldozer *noun*
bulldozers

bullet *noun*
bullets

bulletin *noun*
bulletins

bulletproof

bullfight *noun*
bullfights

bullfighter

bullion

bullock *noun*
bullocks

bull's-eye *noun*
bull's-eyes

bully *verb*
bullies
bullying
bullied

bully *noun*
bullies

bulrush *noun*
bulrushes

bulwark* *noun*
bulwarks

bulwarks☆ *plural noun*
bulwarks

bum *noun*
bums

....

★ A **bulwark** is a strong wall.
☆ **Bulwarks** are the sides of a ship.

a
b
c
d
e
f
g
h
i
j
k
l
m
n
o
p
q
r
s
t
u
v
w
x
y
z

29

bu

bumblebee noun
bumblebees

bump verb
bumps
bumping
bumped

bump noun
bumps

bumper adjective and noun
bumpers

bumpy adjective
bumpier
bumpiest

bunch noun
bunches

bundle noun
bundles

bundle verb
bundles
bundling
bundled

bung verb
bungs
bunging
bunged

bung noun
bungs

bungalow noun
bungalows

bungle verb
bungles
bungling
bungled

bungler noun
bunglers

bunk noun
bunks

bunk bed noun
bunk beds

bunker noun
bunkers

bunny noun
bunnies

bunsen burner noun
bunsen burners

buoy noun
buoys

buoyancy

buoyant

burden noun
burdens

burdensome

bureau* noun
bureaux

burglar noun
burglars

burglary noun
burglaries

burgle verb
burgles
burgling
burgled

burial noun
burials

burly adjective
burlier
burliest

burn☆ verb
burns
burning
burnt or burned

burn noun
burns

burner noun
burners

burning

burp noun
burps

burp verb
burps
burping
burped

burr noun
burrs

burrow noun
burrows

burrow verb
burrows
burrowing
burrowed

burst verb
bursts
bursting
burst

burst noun
bursts

bury verb
buries
burying
buried

bus noun
buses

bus stop noun
bus stops

bush noun
bushes

bushy adjective
bushier
bushiest

busily

business noun
businesses

businesslike

busker noun
buskers

....

★ **Bureau** is a French word used in English. It means 'a writing desk' or 'an office'.

☆ You use **burned** in e.g. *I burned the cakes*. You use **burnt** in e.g. *I can smell burnt cakes*. You use **burned** or **burnt** in e.g. *I have burned/burnt the cakes*.

a
b
c
d
e
f
g
h
i
j
k
l
m
n
o
p
q
r
s
t
u
v
w
x
y
z

bust verb
busts
busting
bust

bust noun
busts

bust adjective

bustle verb
bustles
bustling
bustled

busy adjective
busier
busiest

busybody noun
busybodies

but*

butcher noun
butchers

butchery

butler noun
butlers

butt☆ noun
butts

butt○ verb
butts
butting
butted

butter

buttercup noun
buttercups

butterfingers noun
butterfingers

butterfly noun
butterflies

butterscotch noun
butterscotches

buttocks

button noun
buttons

button verb
buttons
buttoning
buttoned

buttonhole noun
buttonholes

buttress noun
buttresses

buy verb
buys
buying
bought

buy noun
buys

buyer noun
buyers

buzz noun
buzzes

buzz verb
buzzes
buzzing
buzzed

buzzard noun
buzzards

buzzer noun
buzzers

by✢ preposition

bye✱ noun
byes

bye-bye

by-election noun
by-elections

by-law noun
by-laws

bypass noun
bypasses

by-product noun
by-products

bystander noun
bystanders

byte✱ noun

Cc

CAB abbreviation

cab noun
cabs

cabaret noun
cabarets

cabbage noun
cabbages

cabin noun
cabins

cabinet noun
cabinets

cable noun
cables

cackle verb
cackles
cackling
cackled

cackle noun
cackles

cactus noun
cacti

caddie○ noun
caddies

....

★ You use but in e.g. *I like fish but I'm not hungry*. **!** but.
☆ A **butt** is a barrel or part of a gun. **!** but.
○ **Butt** means 'to hit with your head' **!** but.
✢ You use by in e.g. *a book by J. K. Rowling*. **!** bye.
✱ You use **bye** in e.g *bye for now*. **!** by.
✱ A byte is a unit in computing. **!** bite.
○ A **caddie** is a person who helps a golfer. **!** caddy..

caddy* *noun*
caddies

cadet *noun*
cadets

cadge *verb*
cadges
cadging
cadged

cafe *noun*
cafes

cafeteria *noun*
cafeterias

caffeine

caftan *noun*
caftans use **kaftan**

cage *noun*
cages

cagey *adjective*
cagier
cagiest

cagoule *noun*
cagoules

cake *noun*
cakes

caked

calamine

calamitous

calamity *noun*
calamities

calcium

calculate *verb*
calculates
calculating
calculated

calculation *noun*
calculations

calculator *noun*
calculators

calendar *noun*
calendars

calf☆ *noun*
calves

calico

call *noun*
calls

call *verb*
calls
calling
called

calling *noun*
callings

callipers *plural noun*

callous

calm *adjective*
calmer
calmest
calmly

calmness

calorie *noun*
calories

calves○ see **calf**

calypso *noun*
calypsos

camcorder *noun*
camcorders

came see **come**

camel *noun*
camels

camera *noun*
cameras

cameraman *noun*
cameramen

camouflage

camp *noun*
camps

camp *verb*
camps
camping
camped

campaign *noun*
campaigns

campaign *verb*
campaigns
campaigning
campaigned

camper *noun*
campers

campsite *noun*
campsites

campus *noun*
campuses

can *verb*
could

can✛ *verb*
cans
canning
canned

can *noun*
cans

canal *noun*
canals

canary *noun*
canaries

cancel *verb*
cancels
cancelling
cancelled

cancellation *noun*
cancellations

cancer *noun*
cancers

candidate *noun*
candidates

....

★ A **caddy** is a container for tea. **! caddie**.
☆ **Calf** means 'a young cow' and 'a part of your leg'.
○ **Calves** is the plural of calf. **! carves**.
✛ This verb **can** means 'to put food in a can', and it has normal forms.

a b c d e f g h i j k l m n o p q r s t u v w x y z

32

candle noun
candles

candlelight

candlestick noun
candlesticks

candy noun
candies

candyfloss

cane noun
canes

cane verb
canes
caning
caned

canine

cannabis

canned music

cannibal noun
cannibals

cannibalism

cannon* noun
cannon or cannons

cannonball noun
cannonballs

cannot

canoe noun
canoes

canoe verb
canoes
canoeing
canoed

canoeist

canon☆ noun
canons

canopy noun
canopies

can't verb

canteen noun
canteens

canter verb
canters
cantering
cantered

canton noun
cantons

canvas○ noun
canvases

canvass✢ verb
canvasses
canvassing
canvassed

canyon noun
canyons

cap verb
caps
capping
capped

cap noun
caps

capable
capably

capability

capacity noun
capacities

cape noun
capes

caper verb
capers
capering
capered

caper noun
capers

capital noun
capitals

capitalism

capitalist

capsize verb
capsizes
capsizing
capsized

capsule noun
capsules

captain noun
captains

caption noun
captions

captivating

captive adjective and noun
captives

captivity

captor noun
captors

capture verb
captures
capturing
captured

capture noun
captures

car noun
cars

caramel noun
caramels

carat noun
carats

caravan noun
caravans

carbohydrate noun
carbohydrates

carbon

car boot sale noun
car boot sales

★ A **cannon** is a gun. ! **canon**. You use **cannons** in e.g. *There are ten cannons on the walls* and **cannon** in e.g. *They use all their cannon.*

☆ A **canon** is a member of the clergy. ! **cannon**.

○ **Canvas** means 'a strong cloth'. ! **canvass**.

✢ **Canvass** means 'to ask people for their support'. ! **canvas**.

carburettor *noun*
carburettors

carcass *noun*
carcasses

card *noun*
cards

cardboard

cardigan *noun*
cardigans

cardinal *noun*
cardinals

cardphone *noun*
cardphones

care *noun*
cares

care *verb*
cares
caring
cared

career *noun*
careers

career *verb*
careers
careering
careered

carefree

careful *adjective*
carefully

careless *adjective*
carelessly
carelessness

caress *verb*
caresses
caressing
caressed

caress *noun*
caresses

caretaker *noun*
caretakers

cargo *noun*
cargoes

Caribbean

caricature *noun*
caricatures

carnation *noun*
carnations

carnival *noun*
carnivals

carnivore *noun*
carnivores

carnivorous

carol *noun*
carols

caroller *noun*
carollers

carolling

carp *noun*
carp

carpenter *noun*
carpenters

carpentry

carpet *noun*
carpets

carriage *noun*
carriages

carriageway *noun*
carriageways

carrier *noun*
carriers

carrot *noun*
carrots

carry *verb*
carries
carrying
carried

cart *noun*
carts

cart *verb*
carts
carting
carted

carthorse *noun*
carthorses

cartilage

carton *noun*
cartons

cartoon *noun*
cartoons

cartoonist *noun*
cartoonists

cartridge *noun*
cartridges

cartwheel *noun*
cartwheels

carve* *verb*
carves
carving
carved

cascade *noun*
cascades

case *noun*
cases

cash *verb*
cashes
cashing
cashed

cash *noun*

cashier *noun*
cashiers

cash register *noun*
cash registers

cask *noun*
casks

casket *noun*
caskets

casserole *noun*
casseroles

cassette *noun*
cassettes

cast *verb*
casts
casting
cast

cast *noun*
casts

castanets *plural noun*

★ You use **carves** in e.g. *He carves the meat with a knife.* ! **calves.**

34

castaway *noun*
castaways

castle *noun*
castles

castor *noun*
castors

castor sugar

casual *adjective*
casually

casualty *noun*
casualties

cat *noun*
cats

catalogue *noun*
catalogues

catalyst *noun*
catalysts

catamaran *noun*
catamarans

catapult *noun*
catapults

catastrophe *noun*
catastrophes

catastrophic

catch *verb*
catches
catching
caught

catch *noun*
catches

catching

catchphrase *noun*
catchphrases

catchy *adjective*
catchier
catchiest

category *noun*
categories

cater *verb*
caters
catering
catered

caterer *noun*
caterers

caterpillar *noun*
caterpillars

cathedral *noun*
cathedrals

Catherine wheel
noun
Catherine wheels

cathode *noun*
cathodes

Catholic *adjective* and
noun
Catholics

catkin *noun*
catkins

Cat's-eye *noun*
Cat's-eyes

cattle

caught see **catch**

cauldron *noun*
cauldrons

cauliflower *noun*
cauliflowers

cause *verb*
causes
causing
caused

cause *noun*
causes

caution *noun*
cautions

cautious *adjective*
cautiously

cavalier *noun*
cavaliers

cavalry *noun*
cavalries

cave *noun*
caves

cave *verb*
caves
caving
caved

caveman *noun*
cavemen

cavern *noun*
caverns

cavity *noun*
cavities

CD

CD-ROM *noun*
CD-ROMs

cease *verb*
ceases
ceasing
ceased

ceasefire *noun*
ceasefires

ceaseless *adjective*
ceaselessly

cedar *noun*
cedars

ceiling *noun*
ceilings

celebrate *verb*
celebrates
celebrating
celebrated

celebration *noun*
celebrations

celebrity *noun*
celebrities

celery

cell* *noun*
cells

cellar *noun*
cellars

cello *noun*
cellos

cellular

celluloid

cellulose

a
b
c
d
e
f
g
h
i
j
k
l
m
n
o
p
q
r
s
t
u
v
w
x
y
z

★ A **cell** is a small room or a part of an organism. **I sell**.

35

Celsius

Celt *noun*
Celts

Celtic

cement

cemetery *noun*
cemeteries

censor *verb*
censors
censoring
censored

censor★ *noun*
censors

censorship

censure *verb*
censures
censured
censuring

censure☆ *noun*

census *noun*
censuses

cent° *noun*
cents

centenary *noun*
centenaries

centigrade

centimetre *noun*
centimetres

centipede *noun*
centipedes

central *adjective*
centrally

centre *noun*
centres

centrifugal force

centurion *noun*
centurions

century *noun*
centuries

ceramic *adjective*

ceramics *plural noun*

cereal✢ *noun*
cereals

ceremony *noun*
ceremonies

ceremonial *adjective*
ceremonially

certain

certainly

certainty *noun*
certainties

certificate *noun*
certificates

certify *verb*
certifies
certifying
certified

chaffinch *noun*
chaffinches

chain *noun*
chains

chair *noun*
chairs

chairlift *noun*
chairlifts

chairman *noun*
chairmen

chairperson *noun*
chairpersons

chalet *noun*
chalets

chalk *noun*
chalks

chalky *adjective*
chalkier
chalkiest

challenge *verb*
challenges
challenging
challenged

challenge *noun*
challenges

challenger *noun*
challengers

chamber *noun*
chambers

champagne

champion *noun*
champions

championship *noun*
championships

chance *noun*
chances

chancel *noun*
chancels

chancellor *noun*
chancellors

Chancellor of the Exchequer

chandelier *noun*
chandeliers

change *verb*
changes
changing
changed

change *noun*
changes

changeable

channel *noun*
channels

chant *noun*
chants

. . . .

★ A **censor** is someone who makes sure books and films are suitable for people to see. **!** censure.

☆ **Censure** means 'harsh criticism'. **!** censor.

✪ A **cent** is a coin used in America. **!** scent, sent.

✢ A **cereal** is something you eat. **!** serial.

chant *verb*
chants
chanting
chanted

chaos

chaotic *adjective*
chaotically

chap *noun*
chaps

chapatti *noun*
chapattis

chapel *noun*
chapels

chapped

chapter *noun*
chapters

char *verb*
chars
charring
charred

character *noun*
characters

characteristic *adjective*
characteristically

characteristic *noun*
characteristics

characterize *verb*
characterizes
characterizing
characterized

charades *plural noun*

charcoal

charge *verb*
charges
charging
charged

charge *noun*
charges

chariot *noun*
chariots

charioteer *noun*
charioteers

charitable *adjective*
charitably

charity *noun*
charities

charm *verb*
charms
charming
charmed

charm *noun*
charms

charming

chart *noun*
charts

charter *noun*
charters

charter *verb*
charters
chartering
chartered

charwoman *noun*
charwomen

chase *verb*
chases
chasing
chased

chase *noun*
chases

chasm *noun*
chasms

chassis *noun*
chassis

chat *verb*
chats
chatting
chatted

chat *noun*
chats

chatty *adjective*
chattier
chattiest

chateau* *noun*
chateaux

chatter *verb*
chatters
chattering
chattered

chauffeur *noun*
chauffeurs

chauvinism

chauvinist

cheap☆ *adjective*
cheaper
cheapest

cheat *verb*
cheats
cheating
cheated

cheat *noun*
cheats

check *verb*
checks
checking
checked

check *noun*
checks

checkmate *noun*
checkmates

checkout *noun*
checkouts

check-up *noun*
check-ups

cheek *noun*
cheeks

cheek *verb*
cheeks
cheeking
cheeked

a
b
c
d
e
f
g
h
i
j
k
l
m
n
o
p
q
r
s
t
u
v
w
x
y
z

. . . .

★ **Chateau** is a French word used in English. It means 'a castle or large house'.

☆ **Cheap** means 'not costing much'. **!cheep.**

37

ch

cheeky *adjective*
cheekier
cheekiest
cheekily

cheep* *verb*
cheeps
cheeping
cheeped

cheer *verb*
cheers
cheering
cheered

cheer *noun*
cheers

cheerful *adjective*
cheerfully

cheerio

cheese *noun*
cheeses

cheesy *adjective*
cheesier
cheesiest

cheetah *noun*
cheetahs

chef *noun*
chefs

chemical *adjective*
chemically

chemical *noun*
chemicals

chemist *noun*
chemists

chemistry

cheque *noun*
cheques

chequebook *noun*
chequebooks

chequered

cherish *verb*
cherishes
cherishing
cherished

cherry *noun*
cherries

chess

chest *noun*
chests

chestnut *noun*
chestnuts

chest of drawers
noun
chests of drawers

chew *verb*
chews
chewing
chewed

chewy *adjective*
chewier
chewiest

chic☆

chick *noun*
chicks

chicken *noun*
chickens

chicken *verb*
chickens
chickening
chickened

chickenpox

chief *adjective*
chiefly

chief *noun*
chiefs

chieftain *noun*
chieftains

chilblain *noun*
chilblains

child *noun*
children

childhood *noun*
childhoods

childish

childminder *noun*
childminders

childproof

chill *noun*
chills

chill *verb*
chills
chilling
chilled

chilli○ *noun*
chillies

chilly✦ *adjective*
chillier
chilliest

chime *noun*
chimes

chime *verb*
chimes
chiming
chimed

chimney *noun*
chimneys

chimpanzee *noun*
chimpanzees

chin *noun*
chins

china

. . . .

★ **Cheep** is the noise a bird makes. **!cheap**.

☆ Chic is a French word and means 'smart or elegant'. There is no word *chicly*.

○ A **chilli** is a type of hot pepper, added to meat or vegetable dishes. **!chilly**.

✦ You use **chilly** to describe cold, bleak weather or atmosphere. **!chilli**.

38

chink noun
chinks

chip noun
chips

chip verb
chips
chipping
chipped

chirp verb
chirps
chirping
chirped

chirpy adjective
chirpier
chirpiest

chisel noun
chisels

chisel verb
chisels
chiselling
chiselled

chivalrous adjective
chivalrously

chivalry

chlorine

chlorophyll

choc ice noun
choc ices

chock-a-block

chock-full

chocolate noun
chocolates

choice noun
choices

choir noun
choirs

choirboy noun
choirboys

choirgirl noun
choirgirls

choke verb
chokes
choking
choked

choke noun
chokes

cholera

cholesterol

choose verb
chooses
choosing
chose
chosen

choosy adjective
choosier
choosiest

chop verb
chops
chopping
chopped

chop noun
chops

chopper noun
choppers

choppy adjective
choppier
choppiest

chopsticks

choral

chord* noun
chords

chore noun
chores

chorister noun
choristers

chorus noun
choruses

chose see **choose**

chosen see **choose**

christen verb
christens
christening
christened

christening

Christian adjective
and noun
Christians

Christianity

Christmas noun
Christmases

chrome

chromium

chromosome noun
chromosomes

chronic adjective
chronically

chronicle noun
chronicles

chronological
adjective
chronologically

chronology

chrysalis noun
chrysalises

chrysanthemum
noun
chrysanthemums

chubby adjective
chubbier
chubbiest

chuck verb
chucks
chucking
chucked

chuckle verb
chuckles
chuckling
chuckled

chuckle noun
chuckles

chug verb
chugs
chugging
chugged

chum noun
chums

. . . .

★ A **chord** is a number of musical notes played together. ! **cord**.

chummy *adjective*
chummier
chummiest

chunk *noun*
chunks

chunky *adjective*
chunkier
chunkiest

church *noun*
churches

churchyard *noun*
churchyards

churn *noun*
churns

churn *verb*
churns
churning
churned

chute *noun*
chutes

chutney *noun*
chutneys

cider *noun*
ciders

cigar *noun*
cigars

cigarette *noun*
cigarettes

cinder *noun*
cinders

cine camera *noun*
cine cameras

cinema *noun*
cinemas

cinnamon

circle *noun*
circles

circle *verb*
circles
circling
circled

circuit *noun*
circuits

circular *adjective and
noun*
circulars

circulate *verb*
circulates
circulating
circulated

circulation *noun*
circulations

circumference *noun*
circumferences

circumstance *noun*
circumstances

circus *noun*
circuses

cistern *noun*
cisterns

citizen *noun*
citizens

citizenship

citric acid

citrus

city *noun*
cities

civic

civil

civilian *noun*
civilians

civilization *noun*
civilizations

civilize *verb*
civilizes
civilizing
civilized

clad

claim *verb*
claims
claiming
claimed

claim *noun*
claims

claimant *noun*
claimants

clam *noun*
clams

clamber *verb*
clambers
clambering
clambered

clammy *adjective*
clammier
clammiest

clamp *noun*
clamps

clamp *verb*
clamps
clamping
clamped

clan *noun*
clans

clang *verb*
clangs
clanging
clanged

clanger *noun*
clangers

clank *verb*
clanks
clanking
clanked

clap *verb*
claps
clapping
clapped

clap *noun*
claps

clapper *noun*
clappers

clarification

clarify *verb*
clarifies
clarifying
clarified

★ A **chute** is a funnel for sending things down. I **shoot**.

clarinet *noun*
clarinets

clarinettist

clarity

clash *verb*
clashes
clashing
clashed

clash *noun*
clashes

clasp *verb*
clasps
clasping
clasped

clasp *noun*
clasps

class *noun*
classes

class *verb*
classes
classing
classed

classic *noun*
classics

classic

classical *adjective*
classically

classification

classified

classify *verb*
classifies
classifying
classified

classmate *noun*
classmates

classroom *noun*
classrooms

clatter *noun*

clatter *verb*
clatters
clattering
clattered

clause* *noun*
clauses

claw☆ *noun*
claws

claw○ *verb*
claws
clawing
clawed

clay

clayey

clean *adjective*
cleaner
cleanest
cleanly

clean *verb*
cleans
cleaning
cleaned

cleaner *noun*
cleaners

cleanliness

cleanse *verb*
cleanses
cleansing
cleansed

cleanser

clear *adjective*
clearer
clearest
clearly

clear *verb*
clears
clearing
cleared

clearance *noun*
clearances

clearing *noun*
clearings

clef *noun*
clefs

clench *verb*
clenches
clenching
clenched

clergy

clergyman *noun*
clergymen

clergywoman *noun*
clergywomen

clerical

clerk *noun*
clerks

clever *adjective*
cleverer
cleverest

cliché *noun*
clichés

click *noun*
clicks

client *noun*
clients

cliff *noun*
cliffs

cliffhanger *noun*
cliffhangers

climate *noun*
climates

climatic

climax *noun*
climaxes

climb *verb*
climbs
climbing
climbed

★ A **clause** is a part of a sentence or contract. **!claws**.

☆ **Claws** are the hard sharp nails that some animals have on their feet. **!clause**.

○ To **claw** is to scratch, maul, or pull a person or thing.

climb noun
climbs

climber noun
climbers

cling verb
clings
clinging
clung

clingfilm

clinic noun
clinics

clink verb
clinks
clinking
clinked

clip verb
clips
clipping
clipped

clip noun
clips

clipboard noun
clipboards

clipper noun
clippers

clippers plural noun

clipping noun
clippings

cloak noun
cloaks

cloakroom noun
cloakrooms

clobber verb
clobbers
clobbering
clobbered

clock noun
clocks

clockwise

clockwork

clog verb
clogs
clogging
clogged

clog noun
clogs

cloister noun
cloisters

clone noun
clones

clone verb
clones
cloning
cloned

close verb
closes
closing
closed

close adjective and
noun
closer
closest
closely

close noun
closes

close-up noun
close-ups

closure noun
closures

clot noun
clots

clot verb
clots
clotting
clotted

cloth noun
cloths

clothe verb
clothes
clothing
clothed

clothes

clothing

cloud noun
clouds

cloud verb
clouds
clouding
clouded

cloudless

cloudy adjective
cloudier
cloudiest

clout verb
clouts
clouting
clouted

clove noun
cloves

clover

clown noun
clowns

clown verb
clowns
clowning
clowned

club noun
clubs

club verb
clubs
clubbing
clubbed

cluck verb
clucks
clucking
clucked

clue noun
clues

clueless

clump noun
clumps

clumsiness

clumsy adjective
clumsier
clumsiest
clumsily

clung see **cling**

cluster noun
clusters

clutch verb
clutches
clutching
clutched

clutch noun
  clutches

clutter verb
  clutters
  cluttering
  cluttered

clutter noun

co-
  co- makes words
  meaning 'together',
  e.g. a **co-pilot** is
  another pilot who sits
  together with the chief
  pilot. You often need a
  hyphen, e.g.
  co-author, **co-driver**,
  but some words are
  spelt joined up, e.g.
  cooperate,
  coordinate.

coach verb
  coaches
  coaching
  coached

coach noun
  coaches

coal noun

coarse* adjective
  coarser
  coarsest
  coarsely

coast noun
  coasts

coast verb
  coasts
  coasting
  coasted

coastal

coastguard noun
  coastguards

coastline

coat noun
  coats

coat verb
  coats
  coating
  coated

coating noun
  coatings

coax verb
  coaxes
  coaxing
  coaxed

cobalt

cobbled

cobbler noun
  cobblers

cobbles plural noun

cobblestone noun
  cobblestones

cobra noun
  cobras

cobweb noun
  cobwebs

cock noun
  cocks

cock verb
  cocks
  cocking
  cocked

cockerel noun
  cockerels

cocker spaniel noun
  cocker spaniels

cockle noun
  cockles

cockney noun
  cockneys

cockpit noun
  cockpits

cockroach noun
  cockroaches

cocky adjective
  cockier
  cockiest

cocoa noun
  cocoas

coconut noun
  coconuts

cocoon noun
  cocoons

cod☆ noun
  cod

code noun
  codes

code verb
  codes
  coding
  coded

coeducation

coeducational

coffee noun
  coffees

coffin noun
  coffins

cog noun
  cogs

cohort noun
  cohorts

coil verb
  coils
  coiling
  coiled

coil noun
  coils

coin noun
  coins

coin verb
  coins
  coining
  coined

coinage noun
  coinages

....

★ Coarse means 'rough' or 'crude'. **I course**.

☆ You use **cod** for the plural: *The sea is full of cod.*

coincide *verb*
coincides
coinciding
coincided

coincidence *noun*
coincidences

coincidentally

coke

cola *noun*
colas

colander *noun*
colanders

cold *adjective*
colder
coldest
coldly

cold *noun*
colds

cold-blooded

coldness

coleslaw

collaborate *verb*
collaborates
collaborating
collaborated

collaboration

collaborator

collage *noun*
collages

collapse *verb*
collapses
collapsing
collapsed

collapse *noun*
collapses

collapsible

collar *noun*
collars

collate *verb*
collates
collating
collated

colleague *noun*
colleagues

collect *verb*
collects
collecting
collected

collection *noun*
collections

collective

collector

college *noun*
colleges

collide *verb*
collides
colliding
collided

collie *noun*
collies

collision *noun*
collisions

colloquial *adjective*
colloquially

colon *noun*
colons

colonel★ *noun*
colonels

colonial

colonist *noun*
colonists

colony *noun*
colonies

colossal *adjective*
colossally

colour *noun*
colours

colour *verb*
colours
colouring
coloured

colour-blind

coloured

colourful *adjective*
colourfully

colouring

colourless

colt *noun*
colts

column *noun*
columns

coma *noun*
comas

comb *noun*
combs

comb *verb*
combs
combing
combed

combat *noun*
combats

combat *verb*
combats
combating
combated

combatant *noun*
combatants

combination *noun*
combinations

combine *verb*
combines
combining
combined

combine *noun*
combines

combustion

come *verb*
comes
coming
came

comeback *noun*
comebacks

comedian *noun*
comedians

comedy *noun*
comedies

....

★ A **colonel** is an army officer. ! **kernel**.

comet noun
comets

comfort verb
comforts
comforting
comforted

comfort noun
comforts

comfortable adjective
comfortably

comic adjective and noun
comics

comical adjective
comically

comma noun
commas

command verb
commands
commanding
commanded

command noun
commands

commander noun
commanders

commandment noun
commandments

commando noun
commandos

commemorate verb
commemorates
commemorating
commemorated

commemoration

commence verb
commences
commencing
commenced

commencement

commend verb
commends
commending
commended

commendable

commendation

comment verb
comments
commenting
commented

comment noun
comments

commentary noun
commentaries

commentate

commentator noun
commentators

commerce

commercial adjective
commercially

commercial noun
commercials

commercialized

commit verb
commits
committing
committed

commitment noun
commitments

committee noun
committees

commodity noun
commodities

common adjective
commoner
commonest

common noun
commons

commonplace

commonwealth noun
commonwealths

commotion noun
commotions

communal adjective
communally

commune noun
communes

communicate verb
communicates
communicating
communicated

communication noun
communications

communicative

communion noun
communions

communism

communist noun
communists

community noun
communities

commute

commuter noun
commuters

compact adjective
compactly

compact noun
compacts

compact disc noun
compact discs

companion noun
companions

companionship

company noun
companies

comparable adjective
comparably

comparative adjective
comparatively

comparative noun
comparatives

compare verb
compares
comparing
compared

comparison noun
comparisons

compartment noun
compartments

compass noun
compasses

compassion

compassionate adjective
compassionately

compatible adjective
compatibly

compel verb
compels
compelling
compelled

compensate verb
compensates
compensating
compensated

compensation noun
compensations

compère noun
compères

compete verb
competes
competing
competed

competence noun

competent adjective
competently

competition noun
competitions

competitive adjective
competitively

competitor noun
competitors

compilation noun
compilations

compile verb
compiles
compiling
compiled

compiler noun
compilers

complacent adjective
complacently

complain verb
complains
complaining
complained

complaint noun
complaints

complement* noun
complements

complementary☆

complete adjective
completely

complete verb
completes
completing
completed

completion noun

complex adjective and noun
complexes

complexion noun
complexions

complexity noun
complexities

complicated

complication noun
complications

compliment° noun
compliments

complimentary✢

component noun
components

compiler noun
compilers

compose verb
composes
composing
composed

composer noun
composers

composition noun
compositions

compost

compound noun
compounds

comprehend verb
comprehends
comprehending
comprehended

comprehension noun
comprehensions

comprehensive adjective
comprehensively

comprehensive noun
comprehensives

compress verb
compresses
compressing
compressed

compression noun

comprise verb
comprises
comprising
comprised

compromise noun
compromises

··

★ A **complement** is a thing that completes something. **! compliment**.

☆ Something **complementary** completes something.
! complimentary.

○ A **compliment** is something good you say about someone.
! complement.

✢ Something **complimentary** praises someone. **! complementary**.

compromise *verb*
compromises
compromising
compromised

compulsory

computation

compute *verb*
computes
computing
computed

computer *noun*
computers

comrade *noun*
comrades

comradeship

con *verb*
cons
conning
conned

concave

conceal *verb*
conceals
concealing
concealed

concealment

conceit

conceited

conceive *verb*
conceives
conceiving
conceived

concentrate *verb*
concentrates
concentrating
concentrated

concentrated

concentration *noun*
concentrations

concentric

concept *noun*
concepts

conception *noun*
conceptions

concern *verb*
concerns
concerning
concerned

concern *noun*
concerns

concerning

concert *noun*
concerts

concertina *noun*
concertinas

concerto *noun*
concertos

concession *noun*
concessions

concise *adjective*
concisely

conclude *verb*
concludes
concluding
concluded

conclusion *noun*
conclusions

concrete *adjective and noun*

concussion

condemn *verb*
condemns
condemning
condemned

condemnation

condensation

condense *verb*
condenses
condensing
condensed

condition *noun*
conditions

condom *noun*
condoms

conduct *verb*
conducts
conducting
conducted

conduct *noun*

conduction

conductor *noun*
conductors

cone *noun*
cones

confectioner *noun*
confectioners

confectionery

confer *verb*
confers
conferring
conferred

conference *noun*
conferences

confess *verb*
confesses
confessing
confessed

confession *noun*
confessions

confetti

confide *verb*
confides
confiding
confided

confidence *noun*
confidences

confident *adjective*
confidently

confidential *adjective*
confidentially

confine *verb*
confines
confining
confined

confinement

confirm *verb*
confirms
confirming
confirmed

confirmation

confiscate *verb*
confiscates
confiscating
confiscated

a
b
c
d
e
f
g
h
i
j
k
l
m
n
o
p
q
r
s
t
u
v
w
x
y
z

47

confiscation noun
confiscations

conflict verb
conflicts
conflicting
conflicted

conflict noun
conflicts

conform verb
conforms
conforming
conformed

conformity

confront verb
confronts
confronting
confronted

confrontation noun
confrontations

confuse verb
confuses
confusing
confused

confusion noun
confusions

congested

congestion

congratulate verb
congratulates
congratulating
congratulated

congratulations
plural noun

congregation noun
congregations

congress noun
congresses

congruence

congruent

conical

conifer noun
conifers

coniferous

conjunction noun
conjunctions

conjure verb
conjures
conjuring
conjured

conjuror noun
conjurors

conker★ noun
conkers

connect verb
connects
connecting
connected

connection noun
connections

conning tower noun
conning towers

conquer☆ verb
conquers
conquering
conquered

conqueror noun
conquerors

conquest noun
conquests

conscience

conscientious
adjective
conscientiously

conscious adjective
consciously

consciousness

conscription

consecutive adjective
consecutively

consensus

consent verb
consents
consenting
consented

consent noun

consequence noun
consequences

consequently

conservation

conservationist

conservative

Conservative○ noun
Conservatives

conservatory noun
conservatories

conserve verb
conserves
conserving
conserved

consider verb
considers
considering
considered

considerable
adjective
considerably

considerate adjective
considerately

consideration noun
considerations

consist verb
consists
consisting
consisted

consistency noun
consistencies

consistent adjective
consistently

consolation noun
consolations

. . . .

★ A **conker** is the fruit of a horse chestnut tree. ! **conquer**.
☆ To **conquer** means 'to invade or take over'. ! **conker**.
○ Use a capital C when you mean a member of the political party.

console verb
consoles
consoling
consoled

consonant noun
consonants

conspicuous adjective
conspicuously

conspiracy noun
conspiracies

conspirator noun

conspire verb
conspires
conspiring
conspired

constable noun
constables

constancy noun

constant adjective
constantly

constant noun
constants

constellation noun
constellations

constipated

constipation

constituency noun
constituencies

constituent noun
constituents

constitute verb
constitutes
constituting
constituted

constitution noun
constitutions

constitutional

construct verb
constructs
constructing
constructed

construction noun
constructions

constructive

consul noun
consuls

consult verb
consults
consulting
consulted

consultant noun
consultants

consultation noun
consultations

consume verb
consumes
consuming
consumed

consumer noun
consumers

consumption

contact noun
contacts

contact verb
contacts
contacting
contacted

contagious

contain verb
contains
containing
contained

container noun
containers

contaminate verb
contaminates
contaminating
contaminated

contamination

contemplate verb
contemplates
contemplating
contemplated

contemplation

contemporary adjective and noun
contemporaries

contempt

contemptible adjective
contemptibly

contemptuous adjective
contemptuously

contend verb
contends
contending
contended

contender noun
contenders

content adjective and noun

contented adjective
contentedly

contentment

contents plural noun

contest verb
contests
contesting
contested

contest noun
contests

contestant noun
contestants

context noun
contexts

continent noun
continents

continental

continual adjective
continually

continuation

continue verb
continues
continuing
continued

continuous adjective
continuously

continuity

contour noun
contours

contraception

contraceptive noun
contraceptives

contract verb
contracts
contracting
contracted

contract noun
contracts

contraction noun
contractions

contractor noun
contractors

contradict verb
contradicts
contradicting
contradicted

contradiction noun
contradictions

contradictory

contraflow noun
contraflows

contraption noun
contraptions

contrary adjective and noun

contrast verb
contrasts
contrasting
contrasted

contrast noun
contrasts

contribute verb
contributes
contributing
contributed

contribution noun
contributions

contributor noun
contributors

contrivance noun
contrivances

contrive verb
contrives
contriving
contrived

control verb
controls
controlling
controlled

control noun
controls

controller noun
controllers

controversial adjective
controversially

controversy noun
controversies

conundrum noun
conundrums

convalescence

convalescent

convection

convector noun
convectors

convenience noun
conveniences

convenient adjective
conveniently

convent noun
convents

convention noun
conventions

conventional adjective
conventionally

converge verb
converges
converging
converged

converse verb
converses
conversing
conversed

converse noun

conversion noun
conversions

convert verb
converts
converting
converted

convert noun
converts

convertible

convex

convey verb
conveys
conveying
conveyed

conveyor belt noun
conveyor belts

convict verb
convicts
convicting
convicted

convict noun
convicts

conviction noun
convictions

convince verb
convinces
convincing
convinced

convoy noun
convoys

cook verb
cooks
cooking
cooked

cook noun
cooks

cooker noun
cookers

cookery

cool adjective
cooler
coolest
coolly

cool *verb*
cools
cooling
cooled

cooler

coolness

coop *noun*
coops

cooperate *verb*
cooperates
cooperating
cooperated

cooperation

cooperative

coordinate *verb*
coordinates
coordinating
coordinated

coordinate *noun*
coordinates

coordination

coordinator *noun*
coordinators

coot *noun*
coots

cop *verb*
cops
copping
copped

cop *noun*
cops

cope *verb*
copes
coping
coped

copier *noun*
copiers

copper *noun*
coppers

copper sulphate

copy *verb*
copies
copying
copied

copy *noun*
copies

coral

cord* *noun*
cords

cordial *adjective*
cordially

cordial *noun*
cordials

cordiality

corduroy

core *noun*
cores

corgi *noun*
corgis

cork *noun*
corks

corkscrew *noun*
corkscrews

cormorant *noun*
cormorants

corn *noun*
corns

corned beef

corner *noun*
corners

corner *verb*
corners
cornering
cornered

cornet *noun*
cornets

cornfield *noun*
cornfields

cornflakes

cornflour

cornflower *noun*
cornflowers

Cornish

Cornish pasty *noun*
Cornish pasties

corny *adjective*
cornier
corniest

coronation *noun*
coronations

coroner *noun*
coroners

corporal *noun*
corporals

corporal *adjective*

corporation *noun*
corporations

corps☆ *noun*
corps

corpse○ *noun*
corpses

corpuscle *noun*
corpuscles

corral *noun*
corrals

correct *adjective*
correctly

correct *verb*
corrects
correcting
corrected

correction *noun*
corrections

correctness

correspond *verb*
corresponds
corresponding
corresponded

correspondence

....

★ A **cord** is a piece of thin rope. **! chord.**

☆ A **corps** is a unit of soldiers. **! corpse.**

○ A **corpse** is a dead body. **! corps.**

a
b
c
d
e
f
g
h
i
j
k
l
m
n
o
p
q
r
s
t
u
v
w
x
y
z

correspondent *noun*
correspondents

corridor *noun*
corridors

corrode *verb*
corrodes
corroding
corroded

corrosion

corrosive

corrugated

corrupt

corruption

corset *noun*
corsets

cosmetics *plural noun*

cosmic

cosmonaut *noun*
cosmonauts

cost *verb*
costs
costing
cost

cost *noun*
costs

costly *adjective*
costlier
costliest

costume *noun*
costumes

cosy *adjective*
cosier
cosiest

cosy *noun*
cosies

cot *noun*
cots

cottage *noun*
cottages

cotton

couch *noun*
couches

cough *verb*
coughs
coughing
coughed

cough *noun*
coughs

could see **can**

couldn't

council* *noun*
councils

councillor☆ *noun*
councillors

counsel○ *noun*
counsels

counsel *verb*
counsels
counselling
counselled

counsellor✢ *noun*
counsellors

count *verb*
counts
counting
counted

count *noun*
counts

countdown *noun*
countdowns

countenance *noun*
countenances

---

counter-
counter- makes words
meaning 'opposite',
e.g. a **counter-claim**
is a claim someone
makes in response to
a claim from someone
else. You often need a
hyphen, but some
words are spelt joined
up, e.g. **counteract**,
counterbalance.

---

counter *noun*
counters

counterfeit

countess *noun*
countesses

countless

country *noun*
countries

countryman *noun*
countrymen

countryside

countrywoman *noun*
countrywomen

county *noun*
counties

couple *noun*
couples

couple *verb*
couples
coupling
coupled

coupling *noun*
couplings

coupon *noun*
coupons

. . . .

★ A **council** is a group of people who run the affairs of a town.
  ! counsel.

☆ A **councillor** is a member of a council. **!** counsellor.

○ **Counsel** means 'advice'. **!** council.

✢ A **counsellor** is someone who gives advice. **!** councillor.

52

courage

courageous *adjective*
courageously

courgette *noun*
courgettes

courier *noun*
couriers

course* *noun*
courses

court *noun*
courts

court *verb*
courts
courting
courted

courteous *adjective*
courteously

courtesy *noun*
courtesies

court martial *noun*
courts martial

courtship *noun*

courtyard *noun*
courtyards

cousin *noun*
cousins

cove *noun*
coves

cover *verb*
covers
covering
covered

cover *noun*
covers

coverage

cover-up *noun*
cover-ups

cow *noun*
cows

coward *noun*
cowards

cowardice

cowardly

cowboy *noun*
cowboys

cowslip *noun*
cowslips

cox *noun*
coxes

coxswain *noun*
coxswains

coy *adjective*
coyly

coyness

crab *noun*
crabs

crack *verb*
cracks
cracking
cracked

crack *noun*
cracks

cracker *noun*
crackers

crackle *verb*
crackles
crackling
crackled

crackling

cradle *noun*
cradles

craft *noun*
crafts

craftsman *noun*
craftsmen

craftsmanship

crafty *adjective*
craftier
craftiest
craftily

craftiness

crag *noun*
crags

craggy *adjective*
craggier
craggiest

cram *verb*
crams
cramming
crammed

cramp *verb*
cramps
cramping
cramped

cramp *noun*
cramps

crane *noun*
cranes

crane *verb*
cranes
craning
craned

crane fly *noun*
crane flies

crank *verb*
cranks
cranking
cranked

crank *noun*
cranks

cranky *adjective*
crankier
crankiest

cranny *noun*
crannies

crash *verb*
crashes
crashing
crashed

crash *noun*
crashes

crate *noun*
crates

crater *noun*
craters

a
b
c
d
e
f
g
h
i
j
k
l
m
n
o
p
q
r
s
t
u
v
w
x
y
z

★ You use **course** in e.g. *a French course*. **I coarse**.

53

crave verb
craves
craving
craved

crawl verb
crawls
crawling
crawled

crawl noun
crawls

crayon noun
crayons

craze noun
crazes

craziness

crazy adjective
crazier
craziest
crazily

creak verb
creaks
creaking
creaked

creak noun
creaks

creaky adjective
creakier
creakiest

cream noun
creams

creamy adjective
creamier
creamiest

crease verb
creases
creasing
creased

crease noun
creases

create verb
creates
creating
created

creation noun
creations

creative adjective
creatively

creativity

creator noun
creators

creature noun
creatures

crèche noun
crèches

credibility

credible adjective
credibly

credit verb
credits
crediting
credited

credit noun

creditable adjective
creditably

creditor noun
creditors

creed noun
creeds

creek noun
creeks

creep verb
creeps
creeping
crept

creep noun
creeps

creeper noun
creepers

creepy adjective
creepier
creepiest

cremate verb
cremates
cremating
cremated

cremation noun
cremations

crematorium noun
crematoria

creosote

crêpe noun
crêpes

crept see **creep**

crescendo noun
crescendos

crescent noun
crescents

cress

crest noun
crests

crevice noun
crevices

crew noun
crews

crib verb
cribs
cribbing
cribbed

crib noun
cribs

cricket* noun
crickets

cricketer noun
cricketers

cried see **cry**

crime noun
crimes

criminal adjective and noun
criminals

crimson

crinkle verb
crinkles
crinkling
crinkled

⋆ **Cricket** means 'a game' and 'an insect like a grasshopper'.

54

crinkly adjective
crinklier
crinkliest

cripple verb
cripples
crippling
crippled

cripple noun
cripples

crisis noun
crises

crisp adjective
crisper
crispest

crisp noun
crisps

criss-cross adjective

critic noun
critics

critical adjective
critically

criticism noun
criticisms

criticize verb
criticizes
criticizing
criticized

croak verb
croaks
croaking
croaked

croak noun
croaks

crochet* noun

crock noun
crocks

crockery

crocodile noun
crocodiles

crocus noun
crocuses

croft noun
crofts

crofter

croissant noun
croissants

crook noun
crooks

crook verb
crooks
crooking
crooked

crooked

croon verb
croons
crooning
crooned

crop noun
crops

crop verb
crops
cropping
cropped

---

cross-
cross- makes words
meaning 'across', e.g.
a cross-channel ferry
is one that goes
across the English
Channel. You usually
need a hyphen, but
some words are spelt
joined up, e.g.
crossroads and
crosswind.

---

cross adjective
crossly

cross verb
crosses
crossing
crossed

cross noun
crosses

crossbar noun
crossbars

crossbow noun
crossbows

cross-country

cross-examine verb
cross-examines
cross-examining
cross-examined

cross-examination
noun
cross-examinations

cross-eyed

crossing noun
crossings

cross-legged

crossness

crossroads noun
crossroads

cross-section noun
cross-sections

crosswise

crossword noun
crosswords

crotchet☆ noun
crotchets

crouch verb
crouches
crouching
crouched

crow noun
crows

crow verb
crows
crowing
crowed

crowbar noun
crowbars

crowd noun
crowds

★ **Crochet** is a kind of needlework. **!** crotchet.
☆ A **crotchet** is a note in music. **!** crochet.

a
b
c
d
e
f
g
h
i
j
k
l
m
n
o
p
q
r
s
t
u
v
w
x
y
z

crowd *verb*
crowds
crowding
crowded

crown *noun*
crowns

crown *verb*
crowns
crowning
crowned

crow's-nest *noun*
crow's-nests

crucial *adjective*
crucially

crucifix *noun*
crucifixes

crucifixion* *noun*
crucifixions

crucify *verb*
crucifies
crucifying
crucified

crude *adjective*
cruder
crudest

cruel *adjective*
crueller
cruellest
cruelly

cruelty *noun*
cruelties

cruise *verb*
cruises
cruising
cruised

cruise *noun*
cruises

cruiser *noun*
cruisers

crumb *noun*
crumbs

crumble *verb*
crumbles
crumbling
crumbled

crumbly *adjective*
crumblier
crumbliest

crumpet *noun*
crumpets

crumple *verb*
crumples
crumpling
crumpled

crunch *noun*
crunches

crunch *verb*
crunches
crunching
crunched

crunchy *adjective*
crunchier
crunchiest

crusade *noun*
crusades

crusader *noun*
crusaders

crush *verb*
crushes
crushing
crushed

crush *noun*
crushes

crust *noun*
crusts

crustacean *noun*
crustaceans

crutch *noun*
crutches

cry *verb*
cries
crying
cried

cry *noun*
cries

crypt *noun*
crypts

crystal *noun*
crystals

crystalline

crystallize *verb*
crystallizes
crystallizing
crystallized

cub *noun*
cubs

cubbyhole *noun*
cubbyholes

cube *noun*
cubes

cube *verb*
cubes
cubing
cubed

cubic

cubicle *noun*
cubicles

cuboid *noun*
cuboids

cuckoo *noun*
cuckoos

cucumber *noun*
cucumbers

cud

cuddle *verb*
cuddles
cuddling
cuddled

cuddly

cue☆ *noun*
cues

cuff *verb*
cuffs
cuffing
cuffed

....
★ Use a capital C when you are talking about Christ.
☆ A **cue** is a signal for action or a stick used in snooker. **!queue**.

56

cuff noun
cuffs

cul-de-sac noun
cul-de-sacs or
culs-de-sac

culminate verb
culminates
culminating
culminated

culmination noun

culprit noun
culprits

cult noun
cults

cultivate verb
cultivates
cultivating
cultivated

cultivation noun

cultivated

culture noun
cultures

cultural adjective
culturally

cultured

cunning

cup noun
cups

cup verb
cups
cupping
cupped

cupboard noun
cupboards

cupful noun
cupfuls

curate noun
curates

curator noun
curators

curb* verb
curbs
curbing
curbed

curd noun
curds

curdle verb
curdles
curdling
curdled

cure verb
cures
curing
cured

cure noun
cures

curfew noun
curfews

curiosity noun
curiosities

curious adjective
curiously

curl verb
curls
curling
curled

curl noun
curls

curly adjective
curlier
curliest

currant☆ noun
currants

currency noun
currencies

current○ noun
currents

current adjective
currently

curriculum noun
curriculums or
curricula

curry verb
curries
currying
curried

curry noun
curries

curse verb
curses
cursing
cursed

curse noun
curses

cursor noun
cursors

curtain noun
curtains

curtsy verb
curtsies
curtsying
curtsied

curtsy noun
curtsies

curvature noun
curvatures

curve verb
curves
curving
curved

curve noun
curves

cushion noun
cushions

cushion verb
cushions
cushioning
cushioned

custard

. . . .

★ To **curb** a feeling is to restrain it. **!** kerb.

☆ A **currant** is a small dried grape. **!** current.

○ A **current** is a flow of water, air, or electricity. **!** currant.

For words beginning with a k- sound, try also ch-

custom noun
customs

customary adjective
customarily

customer noun
customers

customize noun
customizes
customizing
customized

cut verb
cuts
cutting
cut

cut noun
cuts

cute adjective
cuter
cutest

cutlass noun
cutlasses

cutlery noun

cutlet noun
cutlets

cut-out noun
cut-outs

cut-price noun

cutter noun
cutters

cutting noun
cuttings

cycle noun
cycles

cycle verb
cycles
cycling
cycled

cyclist noun
cyclists

cyclone noun
cyclones

cyclonic

cygnet* noun
cygnets

cylinder noun
cylinders

cylindrical

cymbal noun
cymbals

cynic noun
cynics

cynical adjective
cynically

cynicism

cypress noun
cypresses

Dd

dab verb
dabs
dabbing
dabbed

dab noun
dabs

dabble verb
dabbles
dabbling
dabbled

dachshund noun
dachshunds

dad noun
dads

daddy noun
daddies

daddy-long-legs noun
daddy-long-legs

daffodil noun
daffodils

daft adjective
dafter
daftest

dagger noun
daggers

dahlia noun
dahlias

daily adjective and adverb

daintiness

dainty adjective
daintier
daintiest
daintily

dairy noun
dairies

daisy noun
daisies

dale noun
dales

Dalmatian noun
Dalmatians

dam noun
dams

dam☆ verb
dams
damming
dammed

damage verb
damages
damaging
damaged

damage noun

damages plural noun

Dame○ noun
Dames

- -
★ A **cygnet** is a young swan. **!** signet.
☆ **Dam** means 'to build a dam across water'. **!** damn.
○ Use a capital D when it is a title, e.g. *Dame Jane Smith*.

dame* *noun*
dames

damn☆ *verb*
damns
damning
damned

damned

damp *adjective and
noun*
damper
dampest

dampen *verb*
dampens
dampening
dampened

damson *noun*
damsons

dance *verb*
dances
dancing
danced

dance *noun*
dances

dancer *noun*
dancers

dandelion *noun*
dandelions

dandruff

danger *noun*
dangers

dangerous *adjective*
dangerously

dangle *verb*
dangles
dangling
dangled

dappled

dare *verb*
dares
daring
dared

dare *noun*
dares

daredevil *noun*
daredevils

daring

dark *adjective and
noun*
darker
darkest

darken *verb*
darkens
darkening
darkened

darkness

darkroom *noun*
darkrooms

darling *noun*
darlings

darn *verb*
darns
darning
darned

dart *noun*
darts

dartboard *noun*
dartboards

dash *verb*
dashes
dashing
dashed

dash *noun*
dashes

dashboard *noun*
dashboards

data° *plural noun*

database *noun*
databases

date *noun*
dates

date *verb*
dates
dating
dated

daughter *noun*
daughters

dawdle *verb*
dawdles
dawdling
dawdled

dawn *noun*
dawns

dawn *verb*
dawns
dawning
dawned

day *noun*
days

daybreak

daydream *verb*
daydreams
daydreaming
daydreamed

daylight

day-to-day

daze *verb*
dazes
dazing
dazed

daze *noun*

dazzle *verb*
dazzles
dazzling
dazzled

★ Use a small d when you mean a pantomime woman played by a
man.

☆ **Damn** means 'to say that something is very bad'. **I dam**.

° **Data** is strictly a plural noun, but is often used as a singular noun:
Here is the data.

de

de-
de- makes verbs with an opposite meaning, e.g. **deactivate** means 'to stop something working'. You need a hyphen when the word begins with an e or i, e.g. **de-escalate**, **de-ice**.

dead

deaden verb
deadens
deadening
deadened

dead end noun
dead ends

deadline noun
deadlines

deadlock

deadly adjective
deadlier
deadliest

deaf adjective
deafer
deafest

deafness

deafen verb
deafens
deafening
deafened

deal verb
deals
dealing
dealt

deal noun
deals

dealer noun
dealers

dean noun
deans

dear★ adjective
dearer
dearest

death noun
deaths

deathly

debatable

debate noun
debates

debate verb
debates
debating
debated

debris

debt noun
debts

debtor noun
debtors

debug verb
debugs
debugging
debugged

début noun
débuts

decade noun
decades

decay verb
decays
decaying
decayed

decay noun

deceased

deceit

deceitful adjective
deceitfully

deceive verb
deceives
deceiving
deceived

December

decency

decent adjective
decently

deception noun
deceptions

deceptive

decibel noun
decibels

decide verb
decides
deciding
decided

deciduous

decimal noun
decimals

decimalization

decimalize verb
decimalizes
decimalizing
decimalized

decipher verb
deciphers
deciphering
deciphered

decision noun
decisions

decisive adjective
decisively

deck noun
decks

deckchair noun
deckchairs

declaration noun
declarations

declare verb
declares
declaring
declared

decline verb
declines
declining
declined

. . . .

★ **Dear** means 'loved' or 'expensive'. **!** deer.

60

decode *verb*
decodes
decoding
decoded

decompose *verb*
decomposes
decomposing
decomposed

decorate *verb*
decorates
decorating
decorated

decoration *noun*
decorations

decorative

decorator *noun*
decorators

decoy *noun*
decoys

decrease *verb*
decreases
decreasing
decreased

decrease *noun*
decreases

decree *noun*
decrees

decree *verb*
decrees
decreeing
decreed

decrepit

dedicate *verb*
dedicates
dedicating
dedicated

dedication

deduce *verb*
deduces
deducing
deduced

deduct *verb*
deducts
deducting
deducted

deductible

deduction *noun*
deductions

deed *noun*
deeds

deep *adjective*
deeper
deepest
deeply

deepen *verb*
deepens
deepening
deepened

deep-freeze *noun*
deep-freezes

deer* *noun*
deer

deface *verb*
defaces
defacing
defaced

default *noun*
defaults

defeat *verb*
defeats
defeating
defeated

defeat *noun*
defeats

defect *noun*
defects

defect *verb*
defects
defecting
defected

defective *adjective*
defectively

defence *noun*
defences

defenceless

defend *verb*
defends
defending
defended

defendant *noun*
defendants

defender *noun*
defenders

defensible

defensive *adjective*
defensively

defer *verb*
defers
deferring
deferred

deferment

defiance

defiant *adjective*
defiantly

deficiency *noun*
deficiencies

deficient

deficit *noun*
deficits

defile *verb*
defiles
defiling
defiled

define *verb*
defines
defining
defined

definite *adjective*
definitely

definition *noun*
definitions

deflate *verb*
deflates
deflating
deflated

★ A **deer** is an animal. **!** **dear**.

de

deflect *verb*
deflects
deflecting
deflected

deflection

deforestation

deformed

deformity *noun*
deformities

defrost *verb*
defrosts
defrosting
defrosted

deft *adjective*
defter
deftest
deftly

defuse *verb*
defuses
defusing
defused

defy *verb*
defies
defying
defied

degenerate *verb*
degenerates
degenerating
degenerated

degeneration

degradation

degrade *verb*
degrades
degrading
degraded

degree *noun*
degrees

dehydrated

dehydration

de-ice *verb*
de-ices
de-icing
de-iced

de-icer

deity *noun*
deities

dejected

dejection

delay *verb*
delays
delaying
delayed

delay *noun*
delays

delegate *noun*
delegates

delegate *verb*
delegates
delegating
delegated

delegation

delete *verb*
deletes
deleting
deleted

deletion

deliberate *adjective*
deliberately

deliberate *verb*
deliberates
deliberating
deliberated

deliberation

delicacy *noun*
delicacies

delicate *adjective*
delicately

delicatessen *noun*
delicatessens

delicious *adjective*
deliciously

delight *verb*
delights
delighting
delighted

delight *noun*
delights

delightful *adjective*
delightfully

delinquency

delinquent *noun*
delinquents

delirious *adjective*
deliriously

delirium *noun*

deliver *verb*
delivers
delivering
delivered

delivery *noun*
deliveries

delta *noun*
deltas

delude *verb*
deludes
deluding
deluded

deluge *noun*
deluges

deluge *verb*
deluges
deluging
deluged

delusion *noun*
delusions

de luxe

demand *verb*
demands
demanding
demanded

demand *noun*
demands

demanding

demerara

demist *verb*
demists
demisting
demisted

demo *noun*
demos

democracy *noun*
democracies

democrat *noun*
democrats

democratic *adjective*
democratically

demolish *verb*
demolishes
demolishing
demolished

demolition

demon *noun*
demons

demonstrate *verb*
demonstrates
demonstrating
demonstrated

demonstration *noun*
demonstrations

demonstrator *noun*
demonstrators

demoralize *verb*
demoralizes
demoralizing
demoralized

demote *verb*
demotes
demoting
demoted

den *noun*
dens

denial *noun*
denials

denim

denominator *noun*
denominators

denote *verb*
denotes
denoting
denoted

denounce *verb*
denounces
denouncing
denounced

denunciation

dense *adjective*
denser
densest
densely

density *noun*
densities

dent *noun*
dents

dental

dentist *noun*
dentists

dentistry

denture *noun*
dentures

deny *verb*
denies
denying
denied

deodorant *noun*
deodorants

depart *verb*
departs
departing
departed

department *noun*
departments

departure *noun*
departures

depend *verb*
depends
depending
depended

dependable

dependant* *noun*
dependants

dependence

dependent☆ *adjective*

depict *verb*
depicts
depicting
depicted

deplorable *adjective*
deplorably

deplore *verb*
deplores
deploring
deplored

deport *verb*
deports
deporting
deported

deposit *verb*
deposits
depositing
deposited

deposit *noun*
deposits

depot *noun*
depots

depress *verb*
depresses
depressing
depressed

depression *noun*
depressions

deprivation

deprive *verb*
deprives
depriving
deprived

depth *noun*
depths

deputize *verb*
deputizes
deputizing
deputized

deputy *noun*
deputies

derail *verb*
derails
derailing
derailed

★ **Dependant** is a noun: *She has three dependants.* **!** dependent.
☆ **Dependent** is an adjective: *She has three dependent children.*
! dependant.

a b c **d** e f g h i j k l m n o p q r s t u v w x y z

de

derby *noun*
derbies

derelict

deride *verb*
derides
deriding
derided

derision

derive *verb*
derives
deriving
derived

derrick *noun*
derricks

derv

descant* *noun*
descants

descend *verb*
descends
descending
descended

descendant *noun*
descendants

descent☆

describe *verb*
describes
describing
described

description *noun*
descriptions

descriptive *adjective*
descriptively

desert° *noun*
deserts

desert *verb*
deserts
deserting
deserted

deserter *noun*
deserters

desertion

deserve *verb*
deserves
deserving
deserved

design *verb*
designs
designing
designed

design *noun*
designs

designate *verb*
designates
designating
designated

designer *noun*
designers

desirable

desire *verb*
desires
desiring
desired

desire *noun*
desires

desk *noun*
desks

desktop

desolate

desolation

despair *verb*
despairs
despairing
despaired

despair *noun*

despatch *verb* use
dispatch

desperate *adjective*
desperately

desperation

despicable *adjective*
despicably

despise *verb*
despises
despising
despised

despite

dessert✢ *noun*
desserts

dessertspoon *noun*
dessertspoons

destination *noun*
destinations

destined

destiny *noun*
destinies

destroy *verb*
destroys
destroying
destroyed

destroyer *noun*
destroyers

destruction

destructive

detach *verb*
detaches
detaching
detached

detachable

detached

detachment *noun*
detachments

detail *noun*
details

detain *verb*
detains
detaining
detained

★ **Descant** is a term in music. **!descent**.
☆ **Descent** is a way down. **!descant**.
○ A **desert** is a very dry area of land. **!dessert**.
✢ A **dessert** is a sweet pudding. **!desert**.

64

detect verb
  detects
  detecting
  detected
detection noun
detector noun
detective noun
  detectives
detention noun
  detentions
deter verb
  deters
  deterring
  deterred
detergent noun
  detergents
deteriorate verb
  deteriorates
  deteriorating
  deteriorated
deterioration noun
determination noun
determine verb
  determines
  determining
  determined
determined adjective
deterrence noun
deterrent noun
  deterrents
detest verb
  detests
  detesting
  detested
detestable adjective
detonate verb
  detonates
  detonating
  detonated
detonation noun

detonator noun
detour noun
  detours
deuce*
devastate verb
  devastates
  devastating
  devastated
devastation noun
develop verb
  develops
  developing
  developed
development noun
  developments
device noun
  devices
devil noun
  devils
devilish adjective
devilment noun
devious adjective
  deviously
devise verb
  devises
  devising
  devised
devolution noun
devote verb
  devotes
  devoting
  devoted
devotee noun
devotion noun
devour verb
  devours
  devouring
  devoured
devout adjective
dew☆

dewy
dhoti⚬ noun
  dhotis
diabetes noun
diabetic
diabolical adjective
  diabolically
diagnose verb
  diagnoses
  diagnosing
  diagnosed
diagnosis noun
  diagnoses
diagonal adjective
  diagonally
diagonal noun
  diagonals
diagram noun
  diagrams
dial noun
  dials
dial verb
  dials
  dialling
  dialled
dialect noun
  dialects
dialogue noun
  dialogues
diameter noun
  diameters
diamond noun
  diamonds
diaphragm noun
  diaphragms
diarrhoea noun
diary noun
  diaries
dice noun
  dice

....

★ **Deuce** is a score in tennis. **!juice**.
☆ **Dew** is moisture on grass and plants. **!due**.
⚬ A **dhoti** is a piece of clothing worn by Hindus.

a
b
c
d
e
f
g
h
i
j
k
l
m
n
o
p
q
r
s
t
u
v
w
x
y
z

di

dictate *verb*
dictates
dictating
dictated

dictation

dictator *noun*
dictators

dictatorial *adjective*
dictatorially

dictionary *noun*
dictionaries

did see do

diddle *verb*
diddles
diddling
diddled

didn't *verb*

die *verb*
dies
dying
died

diesel *noun*
diesels

diet *noun*
diets

diet *verb*
diets
dieting
dieted

differ *verb*
differs
differing
differed

difference *noun*
differences

different *adjective*
differently

difficult

difficulty *noun*
difficulties

dig *verb*
digs
digging
dug

dig *noun*
digs

digest *verb*
digests
digesting
digested

digestible

digestion

digestive

digger *noun*
diggers

digit *noun*
digits

digital *adjective*
digitally

dignified

dignity

dike *noun* use dyke

dilemma *noun*
dilemmas

dilute *verb*
dilutes
diluting
diluted

dilution

dim *adjective*
dimmer
dimmest
dimly

dimension *noun*
dimensions

diminish *verb*
diminishes
diminishing
diminished

dimple *noun*
dimples

din *noun*
dins

dine *verb*
dines
dining
dined

diner* *noun*
diners

dinghy° *noun*
dinghies

dingy○ *adjective*
dingier
dingiest

dinner‡ *noun*
dinners

dinosaur *noun*
dinosaurs

dioxide *noun*
dioxides

dip *verb*
dips
dipping
dipped

dip *noun*
dips

diphtheria

diploma *noun*
diplomas

diplomacy

diplomat

diplomatic *adjective*
diplomatically

dire *adjective*
direr
direst

direct *adjective*
directly

....

★ A **diner** is someone who eats dinner. **! dinner**.
☆ A **dinghy** is a small sailing boat. **! dingy**.
○ **Dingy** means 'dirty-looking, drab, dull-coloured'. **! dinghy**.
‡ **Dinner** is a meal. **! diner**.

66

direct verb
  directs
  directing
  directed

direction noun
  directions

director noun
  directors

directory noun
  directories

dirt

dirtiness

dirty adjective
  dirtier
  dirtiest
  dirtily

---

dis-
dis- makes a word
with an opposite
meaning, e.g.
disobey means 'to
refuse to obey' and
disloyal means 'not
loyal'. These words
are spelt joined up.

---

disability noun
  disabilities

disabled

disadvantage noun
  disadvantages

disagree verb
  disagrees
  disagreeing
  disagreed

disagreeable
adjective
  disagreeably

disagreement noun
  disagreements

disappear verb
  disappears
  disappearing
  disappeared

disappearance noun
  disappearances

disappoint verb
  disappoints
  disappointing
  disappointed

disappointing

disappointment
noun
  disappointments

disapproval

disapprove verb
  disapproves
  disapproving
  disapproved

disarm verb
  disarms
  disarming
  disarmed

disarmament

disaster noun
  disasters

disastrous adjective
  disastrously

disc* noun
  discs

discard verb
  discards
  discarding
  discarded

discharge verb
  discharges
  discharging
  discharged

disciple noun
  disciples

discipline

disc jockey noun
  disc jockeys

disclose verb
  discloses
  disclosing
  disclosed

disclosure

disco noun
  discos

discomfort

disconnect verb
  disconnects
  disconnecting
  disconnected

disconnection

discontent

discontented

discotheque noun
  discotheques

discount noun
  discounts

discourage verb
  discourages
  discouraging
  discouraged

discouragement

discover verb
  discovers
  discovering
  discovered

discovery noun
  discoveries

discreet adjective
  discreetly

discriminate verb
  discriminates
  discriminating
  discriminated

discrimination

discus noun
  discuses

discuss verb
  discusses
  discussing
  discussed

★ A **disc** is a flat round object. **!** disk.

a
b
c
d
e
f
g
h
i
j
k
l
m
n
o
p
q
r
s
t
u
v
w
x
y
z

di

discussion noun
discussions

disease noun
diseases

diseased

disgrace verb
disgraces
disgracing
disgraced

disgrace noun

disgraceful adjective
disgracefully

disguise verb
disguises
disguising
disguised

disguise noun
disguises

disgust verb
disgusts
disgusting
disgusted

disgust noun

disgusting

dish noun
dishes

dish verb
dishes
dishing
dished

dishcloth noun
dishcloths

dishevelled

dishonest adjective
dishonestly

dishonesty

dishwasher noun
dishwashers

disinfect verb
disinfects
disinfecting
disinfected

disinfectant noun
disinfectants

disintegrate verb
disintegrates
disintegrating
disintegrated

disintegration

disinterested

disk* noun
disks

dislike verb
dislikes
disliking
disliked

dislike noun
dislikes

dislocate verb
dislocates
dislocating
dislocated

dislodge verb
dislodges
dislodging
dislodged

disloyal adjective
disloyally

disloyalty

dismal adjective
dismally

dismantle verb
dismantles
dismantling
dismantled

dismay

dismayed

dismiss verb
dismisses
dismissing
dismissed

dismissal

dismount verb
dismounts
dismounting
dismounted

disobedience

disobedient

disobey verb
disobeys
disobeying
disobeyed

disorder noun
disorders

disorderly

dispatch verb
dispatches
dispatching
dispatched

dispense verb
dispenses
dispensing
dispensed

dispenser noun
dispensers

dispersal

disperse verb
disperses
dispersing
dispersed

display verb
displays
displaying
displayed

display noun
displays

displease verb
displeases
displeasing
displeased

disposable

disposal

★ A **disk** is what you put in a computer. ! **disc**.

dispose *verb*
disposes
disposing
disposed

disprove *verb*
disproves
disproving
disproved

dispute *noun*
disputes

disqualification

disqualify *verb*
disqualifies
disqualifying
disqualified

disregard *verb*
disregards
disregarding
disregarded

disrespect

disrespectful
adjective
disrespectfully

disrupt *verb*
disrupts
disrupting
disrupted

disruption

disruptive

dissatisfaction

dissatisfied

dissect *verb*
dissects
dissecting
dissected

dissection

dissolve *verb*
dissolves
dissolving
dissolved

dissuade *verb*
dissuades
dissuading
dissuaded

distance *noun*
distances

distant *adjective*
distantly

distil *verb*
distils
distilling
distilled

distillery *noun*
distilleries

distinct *adjective*
distinctly

distinction *noun*
distinctions

distinctive

distinguish *verb*
distinguishes
distinguishing
distinguished

distinguished

distort *verb*
distorts
distorting
distorted

distortion *noun*
distortions

distract *verb*
distracts
distracting
distracted

distraction *noun*
distractions

distress *verb*
distresses
distressing
distressed

distress *noun*

distribute *verb*
distributes
distributing
distributed

distribution

distributor

district *noun*
districts

distrust

distrustful

disturb *verb*
disturbs
disturbing
disturbed

disturbance *noun*
disturbances

disused

ditch *noun*
ditches

dither *verb*
dithers
dithering
dithered

divan *noun*
divans

dive *verb*
dives
diving
dived

diver *noun*
divers

diverse

diversify *verb*
diversifies
diversifying
diversified

diversion *noun*
diversions

diversity

divert *verb*
diverts
diverting
diverted

divide *verb*
divides
dividing
divided

dividend *noun*
dividends

dividers *plural noun*

divine *adjective*
divinely

di - do

divine *verb*
divines
divining
divined

divinity*

divisible

division *noun*
divisions

divorce *verb*
divorces
divorcing
divorced

divorce *noun*
divorces

Diwali*

dizziness

dizzy *adjective*
dizzier
dizziest
dizzily

do *verb*
does
doing
did
done

docile *adjective*
docilely

dock *noun*
docks

dock *verb*
docks
docking
docked

dock *noun*
docks

docker *noun*
dockers

dockyard *noun*
dockyards

doctor *noun*
doctors

doctrine *noun*
doctrines

document *noun*
documents

documentary *noun*
documentaries

doddery

dodge *verb*
dodges
dodging
dodged

dodge *noun*
dodges

dodgem *noun*
dodgems

dodgy *adjective*
dodgier
dodgiest

doe☆ *noun*
does

doesn't *abbreviation*

dog *noun*
dogs

dog-eared

dogged *adjective*
doggedly

doldrums *plural noun*

dole *verb*
doles
doling
doled

dole *noun*

doll *noun*
dolls

dollar *noun*
dollars

dolly *noun*
dollies

dolphin *noun*
dolphins

-dom
-dom makes nouns,
e.g. **kingdom**. Other
noun suffixes are
-hood, **-ment**, **-ness**,
and **-ship**.

domain *noun*
domains

dome *noun*
domes

domestic *adjective*
domestically

domesticated

dominance

dominant *adjective*
dominantly

dominate *verb*
dominates
dominating
dominated

domination

dominion *noun*
dominions

domino *noun*
dominoes

donate *verb*
donates
donating
donated

donation *noun*
donations

done see **do**

donkey *noun*
donkeys

donor *noun*
donors

don't *abbreviation*

....

★ **Diwali** is a Hindu festival.
☆ A **doe** is a female deer. **!** dough.

70

doodle *verb*
doodles
doodling
doodled

doodle *noun*
doodles

doom *verb*
dooms
dooming
doomed

doom *noun*

door *noun*
doors

doorstep *noun*
doorsteps

doorway *noun*
doorways

dope *noun*
dopes

dopey *adjective*
dopier
dopiest

dormitory *noun*
dormitories

dose *noun*
doses

dossier *noun*
dossiers

dot *verb*
dots
dotting
dotted

dot *noun*
dots

dottiness

dotty *adjective*
dottier
dottiest
dottily

double *adjective*
doubly

double *noun*
doubles

double *verb*
doubles
doubling
doubled

double-cross *verb*
double-crosses
double-crossing
double-crossed

double-decker *noun*
double-deckers

doubt *verb*
doubts
doubting
doubted

doubt *noun*
doubts

doubtful *adjective*
doubtfully

doubtless

dough★

doughnut *noun*
doughnuts

doughy *adjective*
doughier
doughiest

dove *noun*
doves

dowel *noun*
dowels

down

downcast

downfall *noun*
downfalls

downhill

downpour *noun*
downpours

downright *adjective*

downs *plural noun*

downstairs

downstream

downward *adjective*
and *adverb*

downwards *adverb*

downy *adjective*
downier
downiest

doze *verb*
dozes
dozing
dozed

dozen *noun*
dozens

dozy *adjective*
dozier
doziest

drab *adjective*
drabber
drabbest

draft *verb*
drafts
drafting
drafted

draft *noun*
drafts

drag *verb*
drags
dragging
dragged

drag *noun*

dragon *noun*
dragons

dragonfly *noun*
dragonflies

drain *verb*
drains
draining
drained

drain *noun*
drains

drainage

drake *noun*
drakes

drama *noun*
dramas

a
b
c
d
e
f
g
h
i
j
k
l
m
n
o
p
q
r
s
t
u
v
w
x
y
z

★ **Dough** is a mixture of flour and water used for baking. **I doe.**

dr

dramatic adjective
dramatically

dramatist noun
dramatists

dramatization

dramatize verb
dramatizes
dramatizing
dramatized

drank see **drink**

drape verb
drapes
draping
draped

drastic adjective
drastically

draught noun
draughts

draughty adjective
draughtier
draughtiest

draughts noun

draughtsman noun
draughtsmen

draw* verb
draws
drawing
drew
drawn

draw noun
draws

drawback noun
drawbacks

drawbridge noun
drawbridges

drawer☆ noun
drawers

drawing noun
drawings

drawl verb
drawls
drawling
drawled

dread verb
dreads
dreading
dreaded

dread noun

dreadful adjective
dreadfully

dreadlocks

dream noun
dreams

dream verb
dreams
dreaming
dreamt or dreamed

dreamy adjective
dreamier
dreamiest

dreariness

dreary adjective
drearier
dreariest
drearily

dredge verb
dredges
dredging
dredged

dredger

drench verb
drenches
drenching
drenched

dress verb
dresses
dressing
dressed

dress noun
dresses

dresser noun
dressers

dressing noun
dressings

dressmaker noun
dressmakers

drew see **draw**

dribble verb
dribbles
dribbling
dribbled

dried see **dry**

drier noun
driers

drift verb
drifts
drifting
drifted

drift noun
drifts

driftwood

drill verb
drills
drilling
drilled

drill noun
drills

drink verb
drinks
drinking
drank
drunk

drink noun
drinks

drinker noun
drinkers

drip noun
drips

....

★ To **draw** is to make a picture with a pencil, pen, or crayon.
I drawer.

☆ A **drawer** is part of a cupboard. **I draw.**

drip verb
drips
dripping
dripped

dripping

drive verb
drives
driving
drove
driven

drive noun
drives

driver noun
drivers

drizzle verb
drizzles
drizzling
drizzled

drizzle noun

drone verb
drones
droning
droned

drone noun
drones

drool verb
drools
drooling
drooled

droop verb
droops
drooping
drooped

drop verb
drops
dropping
dropped

drop noun
drops

droplet noun
droplets

drought noun
droughts

drove see **drive**

drown verb
drowns
drowning
drowned

drowsiness

drowsy adjective
drowsier
drowsiest
drowsily

drug noun
drugs

drug verb
drugs
drugging
drugged

Druid noun
Druids

drum noun
drums

drum verb
drums
drumming
drummed

drummer noun
drummers

drumstick noun
drumsticks

drunk see **drink**

drunk adjective and noun
drunks

drunkard noun
drunkards

dry adjective
drier
driest
drily

dry verb
dries
drying
dried

dryness

dual* adjective
dually

dub verb
dubs
dubbing
dubbed

duchess noun
duchesses

duck noun
ducks

duck verb
ducks
ducking
ducked

duckling noun
ducklings

duct noun
ducts

dud noun
duds

due☆

duel○ noun
duels

duet noun
duets

duff

duffel coat noun
duffel coats

dug see **dig**

dugout noun
dugouts

duke noun
dukes

a b c **d** e f g h i j k l m n o p q r s t u v w x y z

. . . .

★ **Dual** means 'having two parts'. **!** duel.
☆ **Due** means 'expected'. **!** dew.
○ A **duel** is a fight between two people. **!** dual.

73

dull *adjective*
duller
dullest
dully

dullness

duly

dumb *adjective*
dumber
dumbest

dumbfounded

dummy *noun*
dummies

dump *verb*
dumps
dumping
dumped

dump *noun*
dumps

dumpling *noun*
dumplings

dumpy *adjective*
dumpier
dumpiest

dune *noun*
dunes

dung

dungarees

dungeon *noun*
dungeons

duo *noun*
duos

duplicate *noun*
duplicates

duplicate *verb*
duplicates
duplicating
duplicated

duplication

durability

durable

duration

during

dusk

dust

dust *verb*
dusts
dusting
dusted

dustbin *noun*
dustbins

duster *noun*
dusters

dustman *noun*
dustmen

dustpan *noun*
dustpans

dusty *adjective*
dustier
dustiest

dutiful *adjective*
dutifully

duty *noun*
duties

duvet *noun*
duvets

dwarf *noun*
dwarfs *or* dwarves

dwarf *verb*
dwarfs
dwarfing
dwarfed

dwell *verb*
dwells
dwelling
dwelt

dwelling *noun*
dwellings

dwindle *verb*
dwindles
dwindling
dwindled

dye★ *verb*
dyes
dyeing
dyed

dye *noun*
dyes

dying see **die**

dyke *noun*
dykes

dynamic *adjective*
dynamically

dynamite

dynamo *noun*
dynamos

dynasty *noun*
dynasties

dyslexia

dyslexic

dystrophy *noun*

Ee

e-
e- stands for 'electronic' and makes words about computers and the Internet, e.g. **email** (spelt joined up), **e-commerce** and **e-shopping** (spelt with hyphens).

each

eager *adjective*
eagerly

eagerness

eagle *noun*
eagles

ear *noun*
ears

earache

★ **Dye** means 'to change the colour of something'. **! die.**

eardrum noun
eardrums

earl noun
earls

early adjective and adverb
earlier
earliest

earmark verb
earmarks
earmarking
earmarked

earn verb
earns
earning
earned

earnest adjective
earnestly

earnings plural noun

earphones

earring noun
earrings

earth noun
earths

earthenware

earthly

earthquake noun
earthquakes

earthworm noun
earthworms

earthy adjective
earthier
earthiest

earwig noun
earwigs

ease verb
eases
easing
eased

ease noun

easel noun
easels

east adjective and adverb

east* noun

Easter

easterly adjective and noun
easterlies

eastern

eastward adjective and adverb

eastwards adverb

easy adjective and adverb
easier
easiest
easily

eat verb
eats
eating
ate
eaten

eatable

eaves

ebb verb
ebbs
ebbing
ebbed

ebb

ebony

eccentric

eccentricity noun
eccentricities

echo verb
echoes
echoing
echoed

echo noun
echoes

éclair noun
éclairs

eclipse noun
eclipses

ecological

ecology

economic

economical adjective
economically

economics

economist noun
economists

economize verb
economizes
economizing
economized

economy noun
economies

ecstasy noun
ecstasies

ecstatic adjective
ecstatically

eczema

-ed and **-t**
Some verbs ending in *l, m, n,* and *p* have past forms and past participles ending in *-ed* and *-t,* e.g. **burned/burnt,** leaped/leapt. Both forms are correct, and the *-t* form is especially common when it comes before a noun, e.g. *burnt cakes.*

edge noun
edges

edge verb
edges
edging
edged

edgeways

★ You use a capital E in **the East**, meaning China, Japan, etc.

a
b
c
d
e
f
g
h
i
j
k
l
m
n
o
p
q
r
s
t
u
v
w
x
y
z

ed - el

edgy *adjective*
edgier
edgiest

edible *adjective*

edit *verb*
edits
editing
edited

edition *noun*
editions

editor *noun*
editors

editorial *noun*
editorials

educate *verb*
educates
educating
educated

education *noun*

educational *adjective*

educator *noun*

eel *noun*
eels

eerie *adjective*
eerier
eeriest
eerily

eeriness

effect★ *noun*
effects

effective *adjective*
effectively

effectiveness

effeminate

effervescence

effervescent

efficiency

efficient *adjective*
efficiently

effort *noun*
efforts

effortless *adjective*
effortlessly

egg *noun*
eggs

egg *verb*
eggs
egging
egged

-ei- and **-ie-**
The rule 'i before e except after c' is true when it is pronounced -ee-, e.g. **thief**, **ceiling**. There are a few exceptions, of which the most important are **seize** and **protein**.

Eid☆

eiderdown *noun*
eiderdowns

eight○

eighteen

eighteenth

eighth✢ *adjective* and *noun*
eighthly

eightieth

eighty *noun*
eighties

either

eject *verb*
ejects
ejecting
ejected

ejection

elaborate *adjective*
elaborately

elaborate *verb*
elaborates
elaborating
elaborated

elaboration

elastic

elated

elation

elbow *noun*
elbows

elbow *verb*
elbows
elbowing
elbowed

elder *adjective* and *noun*
elders

elderberry *noun*
elderberries

elderly

eldest

elect *verb*
elects
electing
elected

election *noun*
elections

electorate

electric

electrical *adjective*
electrically

electrician *noun*
electricians

electricity

electrification

....

★ An **effect** is something that is caused by something else. ! **affect**.
☆ **Eid** is a Muslim festival.
○ **Eight** is the number. ! **ate**.
✢ Note that there are two h's in **eighth**.

electrify verb
electrifies
electrifying
electrified

electrocute verb
electrocutes
electrocuting
electrocuted

electrocution

electromagnet noun
electromagnets

electron noun
electrons

electronic adjective
electronically

electronics

elegance

elegant adjective
elegantly

element noun
elements

elementary

elephant noun
elephants

elevate verb
elevates
elevating
elevated

elevation noun
elevations

eleven

eleventh

elf noun
elves

eligibility

eligible

eliminate verb
eliminates
eliminating
eliminated

elimination

élite noun
élites

elk noun
elk or elks

ellipse noun
ellipses

elliptical adjective
elliptically

elm noun
elms

elocution

eloquence

eloquent

else

elsewhere

elude verb
eludes
eluding
eluded

elusive adjective
elusively

elves see elf

email★ noun
emails

email verb
emails
emailing
emailed

emancipate verb
emancipates
emancipating
emancipated

emancipation

embankment noun
embankments

embark verb
embarks
embarking
embarked

embarkation

embarrass☆ verb
embarrasses
embarrassing
embarrassed

embarrassment

embassy noun
embassies

embedded

embers plural noun

emblem noun
emblems

embrace verb
embraces
embracing
embraced

embroider verb
embroiders
embroidering
embroidered

embroidery noun
embroideries

embryo noun
embryos

emerald noun
emeralds

emerge verb
emerges
emerging
emerged

emergence

emergency noun
emergencies

emery paper

emigrant noun
emigrants

emigrate verb
emigrates
emigrating
emigrated

★ **Email** is short for **electronic mail**.
☆ Note that there are two rs in **embarrass** and **embarrassment**.

a
b
c
d
e
f
g
h
i
j
k
l
m
n
o
p
q
r
s
t
u
v
w
x
y
z

a

b

c

d

e

f

g

h

i

j

k

l

m

n

o

p

q

r

s

t

u

v

w

x

y

z

emigration noun

eminence

eminent

emission* noun
emissions

emit verb
emits
emitting
emitted

emotion noun
emotions

emotional adjective
emotionally

emperor noun
emperors

emphasis noun
emphases

emphasize verb
emphasizes
emphasizing
emphasized

emphatic adjective
emphatically

empire noun
empires

employ verb
employs
employing
employed

employee noun
employees

employer noun
employers

employment

empress noun
empresses

empties plural noun

emptiness

empty adjective
emptier
emptiest

empty verb
empties
emptying
emptied

emu noun
emus

emulsion noun
emulsions

enable verb
enables
enabling
enabled

enamel noun
enamels

encampment noun
encampments

-ence
See the note at **-ance**.

enchant verb
enchants
enchanting
enchanted

enchantment

encircle verb
encircles
encircling
encircled

enclose verb
encloses
enclosing
enclosed

enclosure

encore noun
encores

encounter verb
encounters
encountering
encountered

encourage verb
encourages
encouraging
encouraged

encouragement

encyclopedia noun
encyclopedias

encyclopedic

end verb
ends
ending
ended

end noun
ends

endanger verb
endangers
endangering
endangered

endeavour verb
endeavours
endeavouring
endeavoured

ending noun
endings

endless adjective
endlessly

endurance

endure verb
endures
enduring
endured

enemy noun
enemies

energetic adjective
energetically

energy noun
energies

enforce verb
enforces
enforcing
enforced

....

★ An **emission** is something that escapes, like fumes. **!** omission.

78

enforceable	enlist *verb*	ensure *verb*
enforcement	enlists	ensures
engage *verb*	enlisting	ensuring
engages	enlisted	ensured
engaging		
engaged	enmity *noun*	**-ent**
	enmities	See the note at **-ant**.
engagement *noun*		
engagements	enormity★ *noun*	entangle *verb*
engine *noun*	enormities	entangles
engines		entangling
	enormous *adjective*	entangled
engineer *noun*	enormously	
engineers		entanglement
	enormousness	
engineering		enter *verb*
	enough	enters
engrave *verb*		entering
engraves	enquire *verb*	entered
engraving	enquires	
engraved	enquiring	enterprise *noun*
	enquired	enterprises
engraver		
	enquiry☆ *noun*	enterprising
engrossed	enquiries	
		entertain *verb*
engulf *verb*	enrage *verb*	entertains
engulfs	enrages	entertaining
engulfing	enraging	entertained
engulfed	enraged	
		entertainer *noun*
enhance *verb*	enrich *verb*	entertainers
enhances	enriches	
enhancing	enriching	entertainment *noun*
enhanced	enriched	entertainments
enhancement	enrichment	enthusiasm *noun*
		enthusiasms
enjoy *verb*	enrol *verb*	
enjoys	enrols	enthusiast *noun*
enjoying	enrolling	enthusiasts
enjoyed	enrolled	
		enthusiastic
enjoyable	enrolment	*adjective*
		enthusiastically
enjoyment	ensemble *noun*	
	ensembles	entire *adjective*
enlarge *verb*		entirely
enlarges	ensue *verb*	
enlarging	ensues	entirety
enlarged	ensuing	
	ensued	entitle *verb*
enlargement *noun*		entitles
enlargements		entitling
		entitled

....

★ An **enormity** is a wicked act. If you mean 'large size', use **enormousness**.

☆ An **enquiry** is a question. **! inquiry**.

a
b
c
d
e
f
g
h
i
j
k
l
m
n
o
p
q
r
s
t
u
v
w
x
y
z

a **entrance** noun
entrances

b **entrance** verb
entrances
entrancing
c entranced

d **entrant** noun
entrants

entreat verb
entreats
f entreating
entreated
g
entreaty noun
h entreaties

entrust verb
i entrusts
entrusting
j entrusted

k **entry** noun
entries
l
envelop verb
m envelops
enveloping
n enveloped

envelope noun
o envelopes

envious adjective
p enviously

environment noun
q environments

environmental

r **environmentalist**
noun
s environmentalists

envy verb
t envies
envying
u envied

envy noun
v envies

w **enzyme** noun
enzymes

x **epic** noun
epics

y **epidemic** noun
z epidemics

epilepsy

epileptic adjective and
noun
epileptics

epilogue noun
epilogues

episode noun
episodes

epistle noun
epistles

epitaph noun
epitaphs

epoch noun
epochs

equal adjective
equally

equal verb
equals
equalling
equalled

equal noun
equals

equality

equalize verb
equalizes
equalizing
equalized

equalizer noun
equalizers

equation noun
equations

equator

equatorial

equestrian

equilateral

equilibrium noun
equilibria

equinox noun
equinoxes

equip verb
equips
equipping
equipped

equipment

equivalence

equivalent

-er and **-est**
-er and -est make
adjectives and
adverbs meaning
'more' or 'most', e.g.
faster, **slowest**. You
can do this when the
word has one syllable,
and when a
consonant comes at
the end of the word
after a single vowel
you double it, e.g.
fatter, **bigger**. You
can use -er and -est
with some
two-syllable
adjectives, e.g.
commoner,
pleasantest, and
words ending in y,
which change to -ier
and -iest, e.g.
angrier, **happiest**.

-er and **-or**
-er makes nouns
meaning 'a person or
thing that does
something', e.g. a
helper is a person
who helps and an
opener is a tool that
opens things. You can
make new words this
way, e.g. **complainer**,
repairer. Some words
end in -or, e.g. **actor**,
visitor, but you can't
use -or to make new
words.

---

era noun
eras

erase *verb*
erases
erasing
erased

eraser

erect *adjective*

erect *verb*
erects
erecting
erected

erection *noun*
erections

ermine *noun*
ermine

erode *verb*
erodes
eroding
eroded

erosion

errand *noun*
errands

erratic *adjective*
erratically

erroneous *adjective*
erroneously

error *noun*
errors

erupt *verb*
erupts
erupting
erupted

eruption *noun*
eruptions

escalate *verb*
escalates
escalating
escalated

escalation

escalator *noun*
escalators

escape *verb*
escapes
escaping
escaped

escape *noun*
escapes

escort *verb*
escorts
escorting
escorted

escort *noun*
escorts

Eskimo *noun*
Eskimos or Eskimo

especially

espionage

esplanade *noun*
esplanades

-ess
-ess makes nouns for
female people and
animals, e.g.
manageress,
lioness.

essay *noun*
essays

essence *noun*
essences

essential *adjective*
essentially

essential *noun*
essentials

establish *verb*
establishes
establishing
established

establishment *noun*
establishments

estate *noun*
estates

esteem *verb*
esteems
esteeming
esteemed

estimate *noun*
estimates

estimate *verb*
estimates
estimating
estimated

estuary *noun*
estuaries

etch *verb*
etches
etching
etched

etching *noun*
etchings

eternal *adjective*
eternally

eternity

ether

ethnic

etymology *noun*
etymologies

eucalyptus *noun*
eucalyptuses

euphemism *noun*
euphemisms

euphemistic
adjective
euphemistically

Eurasian

euro *noun*
euro or euros

European *adjective*
and *noun*
Europeans

euthanasia

evacuate *verb*
evacuates
evacuating
evacuated

evacuation

evacuee

evade *verb*
evades
evading
evaded

evaluate *verb*
evaluates
evaluating
evaluated

evaluation

evangelical

evangelism

evangelist *noun*
evangelists

evaporate *verb*
evaporates
evaporating
evaporated

evaporation

evasion *noun*
evasions

evasive

eve *noun*
eves

even *adjective*
evenly

even *adverb*

even *verb*
evens
evening
evened

evening *noun*
evenings

evenness

event *noun*
events

eventful *adjective*
eventfully

eventual *adjective*
eventually

ever

evergreen *adjective*
and *noun*
evergreens

everlasting

every

everybody

everyday

everyone

everything

everywhere

evict *verb*
evicts
evicting
evicted

eviction

evidence

evident *adjective*
evidently

evil *adjective*
evilly

evil *noun*
evils

evolution

evolutionary

evolve *verb*
evolves
evolving
evolved

ewe★ *noun*
ewes

---

ex-
ex- makes nouns with
the meaning 'former'
or 'who used to be',
e.g. **ex-president**,
ex-wife. You use a
hyphen to make these
words.

---

exact *adjective*
exactly

exactness

exaggerate *verb*
exaggerates
exaggerating
exaggerated

exaggeration

exalt *verb*
exalts
exalting
exalted

exam *noun*
exams

examination *noun*
examinations

examine *verb*
examines
examining
examined

examiner *noun*
examiners

example *noun*
examples

exasperate *verb*
exasperates
exasperating
exasperated

exasperation

excavate *verb*
excavates
excavating
excavated

excavation *noun*
excavations

excavator *noun*
excavators

exceed *verb*
exceeds
exceeding
exceeded

exceedingly

excel *verb*
excels
excelling
excelled

excellence

excellent *adjective*
excellently

★ A **ewe** is a female sheep. **!** yew, you.

except*

exception noun
exceptions

exceptional adjective
exceptionally

excerpt noun
excerpts

excess noun
excesses

excessive adjective
excessively

exchange verb
exchanges
exchanging
exchanged

exchange noun
exchanges

excitable adjective
excitably

excite verb
excites
exciting
excited

excitedly

excitement noun
excitements

exclaim verb
exclaims
exclaiming
exclaimed

exclamation noun
exclamations

exclude verb
excludes
excluding
excluded

exclusion

exclusive adjective
exclusively

excrement

excrete verb
excretes
excreting
excreted

excretion

excursion noun
excursions

excusable

excuse verb
excuses
excusing
excused

excuse noun
excuses

execute verb
executes
executing
executed

execution noun
executions

executioner noun
executioners

executive noun
executives

exempt adjective

exemption noun
exemptions

exercise noun
exercises

exercise☆ verb
exercises
exercising
exercised

exert verb
exerts
exerting
exerted

exertion noun
exertions

exhale verb
exhales
exhaling
exhaled

exhalation

exhaust verb
exhausts
exhausting
exhausted

exhaust noun
exhausts

exhaustion

exhibit verb
exhibits
exhibiting
exhibited

exhibit noun
exhibits

exhibition noun
exhibitions

exhibitor noun
exhibitors

exile verb
exiles
exiling
exiled

exile noun
exiles

exist verb
exists
existing
existed

existence noun
existences

exit verb
exits
exiting
exited

exit noun
exits

exorcism

exorcist

· ·

★ You use **except** in e.g. *everyone except me.* ! **accept.**

☆ To **exercise** is to keep your body fit. ! **exorcise.**

ex

a
b
c
d
e
f
g
h
i
j
k
l
m
n
o
p
q
r
s
t
u
v
w
x
y
z

exorcize* *verb*
exorcizes
exorcizing
exorcized

exotic *adjective*
exotically

expand *verb*
expands
expanding
expanded

expanse *noun*
expanses

expansion *noun*

expect *verb*
expects
expecting
expected

expectant *adjective*
expectantly

expectation *noun*
expectations

expedition *noun*
expeditions

expel *verb*
expels
expelling
expelled

expenditure

expense *noun*
expenses

expensive

experience *verb*
experiences
experiencing
experienced

experience *noun*
experiences

experienced

experiment *verb*
experiments
experimenting
experimented

experiment *noun*
experiments

experimental
adjective
experimentally

experimentation

expert *adjective* and
noun
experts

expertise

expire *verb*
expires
expiring
expired

expiry

explain *verb*
explains
explaining
explained

explanation *noun*
explanations

explanatory

explode *verb*
explodes
exploding
exploded

exploit *noun*
exploits

exploit *verb*
exploits
exploiting
exploited

exploitation

exploration *noun*
explorations

exploratory

explore *verb*
explores
exploring
explored

explorer *noun*
explorers

explosion *noun*
explosions

explosive *adjective*
and *noun*
explosives

export *verb*
exports
exporting
exported

export *noun*
exports

exporter *noun*
exporters

expose *verb*
exposes
exposing
exposed

exposure *noun*
exposures

express *adjective* and
noun
expresses

express *verb*
expresses
expressing
expressed

expression *noun*
expressions

expressive *adjective*
expressively

expulsion *noun*
expulsions

exquisite *adjective*
exquisitely

extend *verb*
extends
extending
extended

extension *noun*
extensions

extensive *adjective*
extensively

extent *noun*
extents

. . . .

★ To **exorcize** is to get rid of evil spirits. **! exercise**.

exterior *noun*
exteriors

exterminate *verb*
exterminates
exterminating
exterminated

extermination

external *adjective*
externally

extinct

extinction

extinguish *verb*
extinguishes
extinguishing
extinguished

extinguisher *noun*
extinguishers

extra *adjective and noun*
extras

extract *verb*
extracts
extracting
extracted

extract *noun*
extracts

extraction *noun*
extractions

extraordinary *adjective*
extraordinarily

extrasensory

extraterrestrial *adjective and noun*
extraterrestrials

extravagance

extravagant *adjective*
extravagantly

extreme *adjective*
extremely

extreme *noun*
extremes

extremity *noun*
extremities

exuberance

exuberant *adjective*
exuberantly

exult *verb*
exults
exulting
exulted

exultant

exultation

eye *noun*
eyes

eye *verb*
eyes
eyeing
eyed

eyeball *noun*
eyeballs

eyebrow *noun*
eyebrows

eyelash *noun*
eyelashes

eyelid *noun*
eyelids

eyepiece *noun*
eyepieces

eyesight

eyesore *noun*
eyesores

eyewitness *noun*
eyewitnesses

Ff

-f
Most nouns ending in -f have plurals ending in -ves, e.g. **shelf - shelves**, but some have plurals ending in -fs, e.g. **chiefs**. Nouns ending in -ff have plurals ending in -ffs, e.g. **cuffs**.

fable *noun*
fables

fabric *noun*
fabrics

fabricate *verb*
fabricates
fabricating
fabricated

fabulous *adjective*
fabulously

face *noun*
faces

face *verb*
faces
facing
faced

facet *noun*
facets

facetious *adjective*
facetiously

facial *adjective*
facially

facilitate *verb*
facilitates
facilitating
facilitated

facility *noun*
facilities

fact *noun*
facts

factor *noun*
factors

factory *noun*
factories

factual *adjective*
factually

fad *noun*
fads

fade *verb*
fades
fading
faded

faeces

fag *noun*
fags

a

b

c

d

e

f

g

h

i

j

k

l

m

n

o

p

q

r

s

t

u

v

w

x

y

z

fagged

faggot noun
faggots

Fahrenheit

fail verb
fails
failing
failed

fail noun
fails

failing noun
failings

failure noun
failures

faint adjective
fainter
faintest
faintly

faint verb
faints
fainting
fainted

faint-hearted

faintness

fair adjective
fairer
fairest

fair* noun
fairs

fairground noun
fairgrounds

fairly

fairness

fairy noun
fairies

fairyland

faith noun
faiths

faithful adjective
faithfully

faithfulness

fake noun
fakes

fake verb
fakes
faking
faked

faker

falcon noun
falcons

falconry

fall verb
falls
falling
fell
fallen

fall noun
falls

fallacious adjective
fallaciously

fallacy noun
fallacies

fallen see **fall**

fallout

fallow

falls plural noun

false adjective
falser
falsest
falsely

falsehood noun
falsehoods

falseness

falter verb
falters
faltering
faltered

fame

famed

familiar adjective
familiarly

familiarity

family noun
families

famine noun
famines

famished

famous adjective
famously

fan verb
fans
fanning
fanned

fan noun
fans

fanatic noun
fanatics

fanatical adjective
fanatically

fanciful adjective
fancifully

fancy adjective
fancier
fanciest

fancy verb
fancies
fancying
fancied

fancy noun
fancies

fanfare noun
fanfares

fang noun
fangs

fantastic adjective
fantastically

fantasy noun
fantasies

far adjective and adverb
farther
farthest

far-away

farce noun
farces

★ A **fair** is a group of outdoor entertainments or an exhibition. **!fare**.

86

farcical adjective
farcically

fare verb
fares
faring
fared

fare* noun
fares

farewell

far-fetched

farm noun
farms

farm verb
farms
farming
farmed

farmer noun
farmers

farmhouse noun
farmhouses

farmyard noun
farmyards

farther☆

farthest○

farthing noun
farthings

fascinate verb
fascinates
fascinating
fascinated

fascination

fascism

fascist noun
fascists

fashion noun
fashions

fashion verb
fashions
fashioning
fashioned

fashionable

fast adjective and
adverb
faster
fastest

fast verb
fasts
fasting
fasted

fasten verb
fastens
fastening
fastened

fastener

fastening

fat adjective
fatter
fattest

fat noun
fats

fatal adjective
fatally

fatality noun
fatalities

fate✛ noun
fates

father noun
fathers

father-in-law noun
fathers-in-law

fathom noun
fathoms

fathom verb
fathoms
fathoming
fathomed

fatigue

fatigued

fatten verb
fattens
fattening
fattened

fattening

fatty adjective
fattier
fattiest

fault noun
faults

fault verb
faults
faulting
faulted

faultless adjective
faultlessly

faulty adjective
faultier
faultiest

fauna

favour noun
favours

favour verb
favours
favouring
favoured

favourable adjective
favourably

favourite adjective
and noun
favourites

favouritism

★ A fare is money you pay, for example on a bus. **!** fair.
☆ You can use farther or further in e.g. farther up the road. See further.
○ You can use farthest or furthest in e.g. the place farthest from here. See furthest.
✛ Fate is a power that is thought to make things happen. **!** fête.

a

fawn noun
fawns

fax noun
faxes

fax verb
faxes
faxing
faxed

-fe
Most nouns ending in
-fe have plurals
ending in -ves, e.g.
life - lives.

fear noun
fears

fear verb
fears
fearing
feared

fearful adjective
fearfully

fearless adjective
fearlessly

fearsome

feasible

feast noun
feasts

feast verb
feasts
feasting
feasted

feat* noun
feats

feather noun
feathers

feathery

feature noun
features

feature verb
features
featuring
featured

February☆ noun
Februaries

fed see **feed**

federal

federation

fee noun
fees

feeble adjective
feebler
feeblest
feebly

feed verb
feeds
feeding
fed

feed noun
feeds

feedback

feel verb
feels
feeling
felt

feel noun
feels

feeler noun
feelers

feeling noun
feelings

feet○ see **foot**

feline

fell see **fall**

fell verb
fells
felling
felled

fell noun
fells

fellow noun
fellows

fellowship noun
fellowships

felt see **feel**

felt noun

felt-tip pen or
felt-tipped pen noun
felt-tip pens or
felt-tipped pens

female adjective and
noun
females

feminine

femininity

feminism

feminist noun
feminists

fen noun
fens

fence noun
fences

fence verb
fences
fencing
fenced

fencer adjective
fencers

fencing

fend verb
fends
fending
fended

fender noun
fenders

ferment verb
ferments
fermenting
fermented

fermentation

- -

★ A **feat** is an achievement. ! **feet**.
☆ Note that **February** has two rs.
○ **Feet** is the plural of foot. ! **feat**.

ferment

fern noun
ferns

ferocious adjective
ferociously

ferocity

ferret noun
ferrets

ferret verb
ferrets
ferreting
ferreted

ferry noun
ferries

ferry verb
ferries
ferrying
ferried

fertile

fertility

fertilization

fertilize verb
fertilizes
fertilizing
fertilized

fertilizer noun
fertilizers

fervent adjective
fervently

fervour

festival noun
festivals

festive

festivity

festoon verb
festoons
festooning
festooned

fetal

fetch verb
fetches
fetching
fetched

fête★ noun
fêtes

fetlock noun
fetlocks

fetters plural noun

fetus☆ noun
fetuses

feud noun
feuds

feudal

feudalism

fever noun
fevers

fevered

feverish adjective
feverishly

few adjective
fewer
fewest

fez noun
fezzes

fiancé○ noun
fiancés

fiancée✛ noun
fiancées

fiasco noun
fiascos

fib noun
fibs

fibber noun
fibbers

fibre noun
fibres

fibreglass

fibrous

fickle

fiction noun
fictions

fictional adjective
fictionally

fictitious adjective
fictitiously

fiddle verb
fiddles
fiddling
fiddled

fiddle noun
fiddles

fiddler noun
fiddlers

fiddling

fiddly

fidelity

fidget verb
fidgets
fidgeting
fidgeted

fidgety

field noun
fields

field verb
fields
fielding
fielded

fielder noun
fielders

field marshal noun
field marshals

fieldwork

fiend noun
fiends

fiendish adjective
fiendishly

....
★ A **fête** is an outdoor entertainment with stalls. **!** fate.
☆ You will also see this word spelt **foetus**.
○ A woman's **fiancé** is the man who is going to marry her.
✛ A man's **fiancée** is the woman who is going to marry him.

a
b
c
d
e
f
g
h
i
j
k
l
m
n
o
p
q
r
s
t
u
v
w
x
y
z

a
b
c
d
e
f
g
h
i
j
k
l
m
n
o
p
q
r
s
t
u
v
w
x
y
z

fierce *adjective*
fiercer
fiercest
fiercely

fierceness

fiery *adjective*
fierier
fieriest

fife *noun*
fifes

fifteen

fifteenth

fifth

fifthly

fiftieth

fifty *noun*
fifties

fig *noun*
figs

fight *verb*
fights
fighting
fought

fight *noun*
fights

fighter *noun*
fighters

figurative *adjective*
figuratively

figure *noun*
figures

figure *verb*
figures
figuring
figured

filament *noun*
filaments

file *verb*
files
filing
filed

file *noun*
files

filings *plural noun*

fill *verb*
fills
filling
filled

fill *noun*
fills

filler *noun*
fillers

fillet *noun*
fillets

filling *noun*
fillings

filly *noun*
fillies

film *noun*
films

film *verb*
films
filming
filmed

filter *noun*
filters

filter *verb*
filters
filtering
filtered

filth

filthy *adjective*
filthier
filthiest

fin *noun*
fins

final *adjective*
finally

final *noun*
finals

finale *noun*
finales

finalist *noun*
finalists

finality

finance

finance *verb*
finances
financing
financed

finances *plural noun*

financial *adjective*
financially

financier *noun*
financiers

finch *noun*
finches

find *verb*
finds
finding
found

finder *noun*
finders

findings *plural noun*

fine *adjective*
finer
finest
finely

fine *noun*
fines

fine *verb*
fines
fining
fined

finger *noun*
fingers

finger *verb*
fingers
fingering
fingered

fingernail *noun*
fingernails

fingerprint *noun*
fingerprints

finicky

finish *verb*
finishes
finishing
finished

finish *noun*
finishes

fir* noun
firs

fire noun
fires

fire verb
fires
firing
fired

firearm noun
firearms

firefighter noun
firefighters

fireman noun
firemen

fireplace noun
fireplaces

fireproof

fireside noun
firesides

firewood

firework noun
fireworks

firm adjective
firmer
firmest
firmly

firm noun
firms

firmness

first adjective and
adverb
firstly

first class

first floor noun
first floors

first-hand adjective

first-rate

fish noun
fish or fishes

fish verb
fishes
fishing
fished

fisherman noun
fishermen

fishmonger noun
fishmongers

fishy adjective
fishier
fishiest

fission

fist noun
fists

fit adjective
fitter
fittest

fit verb
fits
fitting
fitted

fit noun
fits

fitness

fitter noun
fitters

fitting adjective

fitting noun
fittings

five

fiver noun
fivers

fix verb
fixes
fixing
fixed

fix noun
fixes

fixture noun
fixtures

fizz verb
fizzes
fizzing
fizzed

fizzy adjective
fizzier
fizziest

fizzle verb
fizzles
fizzling
fizzled

fjord noun
fjords

flabbergasted

flabby adjective
flabbier
flabbiest

flag noun
flags

flag verb
flagging
flagged

flagpole noun
flagpoles

flagship noun
flagships

flagstaff noun
flagstaffs

flagstone noun
flagstones

flair☆ noun

flake noun
flakes

flake verb
flakes
flaking
flaked

flaky adjective
flakier
flakiest

. . . .

★ A **fir** is a tree. **!** fur.
☆ **Flair** is a special talent. **!** flare.

fl

flame noun
flames

flame verb
flames
flaming
flamed

flamingo noun
flamingos

flan noun
flans

flank noun
flanks

flannel noun
flannels

flap noun
flaps

flap verb
flaps
flapping
flapped

flapjack noun
flapjacks

flare★ noun
flares

flare verb
flares
flaring
flared

flash noun
flashes

flash verb
flashes
flashing
flashed

flashback noun
flashbacks

flashy adjective
flashier
flashiest

flask noun
flasks

flat adjective
flatter
flattest
flatly

flat noun
flats

flatness

flatten verb
flattens
flattening
flattened

flatter verb
flatters
flattering
flattered

flatterer noun
flatterers

flattery

flaunt verb
flaunts
flaunting
flaunted

flavour noun
flavours

flavour verb
flavours
flavouring
flavoured

flavouring

flaw noun
flaws

flawed

flawless adjective
flawlessly

flax

flea☆ noun
fleas

fleck noun
flecks

flee○ verb
flees
fleeing
fled

fleece noun
fleeces

fleece verb
fleeces
fleecing
fleeced

fleecy adjective
fleecier
fleeciest

fleet noun
fleets

fleeting

flesh

fleshy adjective
fleshier
fleshiest

flew✢ see **fly**

flex noun
flexes

flex verb
flexes
flexing
flexed

flexibility

flexible adjective
flexibly

flick verb
flicks
flicking
flicked

flick noun
flicks

....

★ A **flare** is a bright light. **!** flair.
☆ A **flea** is an insect. **!** flee.
○ To **flee** is to run away. **!** flea.
✢ **Flew** is the past of **fly**. **!** flu, flue.

92

flicker verb
flickers
flickering
flickered

flight noun
flights

flimsy adjective
flimsier
flimsiest

flinch verb
flinches
flinching
flinched

fling verb
flings
flinging
flung

flint noun
flints

flinty adjective
flintier
flintiest

flip verb
flips
flipping
flipped

flippancy

flippant adjective
flippantly

flipper noun
flippers

flirt verb
flirts
flirting
flirted

flirtation

flit verb
flits
flitting
flitted

float verb
floats
floating
floated

float noun
floats

flock verb
flocks
flocking
flocked

flock noun
flocks

flog verb
flogs
flogging
flogged

flood verb
floods
flooding
flooded

flood noun
floods

floodlight noun
floodlights

floodlit

floor noun
floors

floor verb
floors
flooring
floored

floorboard noun
floorboards

flop verb
flops
flopping
flopped

flop noun
flops

floppy adjective
floppier
floppiest

floppy disk noun
floppy disks

flora

floral

florist noun
florists

floss

flounder verb
flounders
floundering
floundered

flour*

flourish verb
flourishes
flourishing
flourished

floury adjective
flourier
flouriest

flow verb
flows
flowing
flowed

flow noun
flows

flower☆ noun
flowers

flower verb
flowers
flowering
flowered

flowerpot noun
flowerpots

flowery

flown

flu○

. . . .

★ **Flour** is powder used in making bread. ! **flower**.
☆ A **flower** is a part of a plant. ! **flour**.
○ **Flu** is an illness. ! **flew**, **flue**.

Try also words beginning with ph-

a

fluctuate *verb*
fluctuates
fluctuating
fluctuated

fluctuation

flue* *noun*
flues

fluency

fluent *adjective*
fluently

fluff

fluffy *adjective*
fluffier
fluffiest

fluid *noun*
fluids

fluke *noun*
flukes

flung see **fling**

fluorescent

fluoridation

fluoride

flurry *noun*
flurries

flush *verb*
flushes
flushing
flushed

flush *noun*
flushes

flush *adjective*

flustered

flute *noun*
flutes

flutter *verb*
flutters
fluttering
fluttered

flutter *noun*
flutters

fly *verb*
flies
flying
flew
flown

fly *noun*
flies

flyleaf *noun*
flyleaves

flyover *noun*
flyovers

flywheel *noun*
flywheels

foal *noun*
foals

foam *noun*

foam *verb*
foams
foaming
foamed

foamy *adjective*
foamier
foamiest

focal

focus *verb*
focuses
focusing
focused

focus *noun*
focuses or foci

fodder

foe *noun*
foes

foetus *noun* see **fetus**

fog *noun*
fogs

foggy☆ *adjective*
foggier
foggiest

foghorn *noun*
foghorns

fogy○ *noun*
fogies

foil *verb*
foils
foiling
foiled

foil *noun*
foils

fold *verb*
folds
folding
folded

fold *noun*
folds

folder *noun*
folders

foliage

folk

folklore

follow *verb*
follows
following
followed

follower *noun*
followers

fond *adjective*
fonder
fondest
fondly

fondness

font *noun*
fonts

food *noun*
foods

fool *noun*
fools

★ A **flue** is a pipe for smoke and fumes. **!** flew, flu.
☆ **Foggy** means 'covered in fog'. **!** fogy.
○ A **fogy** is someone with old-fashioned ideas. **!** foggy.

fool *verb*
fools
fooling
fooled

foolhardiness

foolhardy *adjective*
foolhardier
foolhardiest

foolish *adjective*
foolishly

foolishness

foolproof

foot* *noun*
feet

football *noun*
footballs

footballer *noun*
footballers

foothill *noun*
foothills

foothold *noun*
footholds

footing

footlights

footnote *noun*
footnotes

footpath *noun*
footpaths

footprint *noun*
footprints

footstep *noun*
footsteps

for☆ *preposition* and *conjunction*

forbid *verb*
forbids
forbidding
forbade
forbidden

force *verb*
forces
forcing
forced

force *noun*
forces

forceful *adjective*
forcefully

forceps *plural noun*

forcible *adjective*
forcibly

ford *verb*
fords
fording
forded

ford *noun*
fords

fore○ *adjective* and *noun*

forecast *verb*
forecasts
forecasting
forecast
forecasted

forecast *noun*
forecasts

forecourt *noun*
forecourts

forefathers *plural noun*

forefinger *noun*
forefingers

foregone✦ *adjective*

foreground *noun*
foregrounds

forehead *noun*
foreheads

foreign

foreigner *noun*
foreigners

foreman *noun*
foremen

foremost

forename *noun*
forenames

foresee *verb*
foresees
foreseeing
foresaw
foreseen

foreseeable

foresight

forest *noun*
forests

forester *noun*
foresters

forestry

foretell *verb*
foretells
foretelling
foretold

forever* *adverb*

forfeit *verb*
forfeits
forfeiting
forfeited

forfeit *noun*
forfeits

forgave see **forgive**

....

★ The plural is **foot** in e.g. *a six-foot pole.*
☆ You use **for** in phrases like *a present for you.* **! fore**.
○ You use **fore** in phrases like *come to the fore.* **! for**.
✦ You can use **foregone** in *a foregone conclusion.*
● You use **forever** in e.g. *They are forever complaining.* You can also use **for ever** in e.g. *The rain seemed to go on for ever.*

forge verb
forges
forging
forged

forge noun
forges

forgery noun
forgeries

forget verb
forgets
forgetting
forgot
forgotten

forgetful

forgetfulness

forget-me-not noun
forget-me-nots

forgive verb
forgives
forgiving
forgave
forgiven

forgiveness

fork noun
forks

fork verb
forks
forking
forked

fork-lift truck noun
fork-lift trucks

forlorn

form verb
forms
forming
formed

form noun
forms

formal adjective
formally

formality noun
formalities

format noun
formats

formation noun
formations

former adjective
formerly

formidable adjective
formidably

formula noun
formulas or formulae

formulate verb
formulates
formulating
formulated

forsake verb
forsakes
forsaking
forsook
forsaken

fort noun
forts

forth*

fortieth

fortification noun
fortifications

fortify verb
fortifies
fortifying
fortified

fortnight noun
fortnights

fortnightly

fortress noun
fortresses

fortunate adjective
fortunately

fortune noun
fortunes

fortune-teller noun
fortune-tellers

forty noun
forties

forward adjective and adverb

forward noun
forwards

forwards adverb

fossil noun
fossils

fossilized

foster verb
fosters
fostering
fostered

foster child noun
foster children

foster parent noun
foster parents

fought see fight

foulⓞ adjective
fouler
foulest
foully

foulⓞ verb
fouls
fouling
fouled

foul✦ noun
fouls

foulness

- -

★ You use **forth** in e.g. to go forth. **!fourth**.
☆ **Foul** means 'dirty' or 'disgusting'. **!fowl**.
ⓞ To **foul** is to break a rule in a game. **!fowl**.
✦ A **foul** is breaking a rule in a game. **!fowl**.

found *verb*
founds
founding
founded

found see **find**

foundation *noun*
foundations

founder *noun*
founders

founder *verb*
founders
foundering
foundered

foundry *noun*
foundries

fountain *noun*
fountains

four *noun*
fours

fourteen *noun*
fourteens

fourteenth

fourth★

fourthly

fowl☆ *noun*
fowl *or* fowls

fox *noun*
foxes

fox *verb*
foxes
foxing
foxed

foxglove *noun*
foxgloves

foxy *adjective*
foxier
foxiest

foyer *noun*
foyers

fraction *noun*
fractions

fractionally

fracture *verb*
fractures
fracturing
fractured

fracture *noun*
fractures

fragile *adjective*
fragilely

fragility

fragment *noun*
fragments

fragmentary

fragmentation

fragrance *noun*
fragrances

fragrant

frail *adjective*
frailer
frailest

frailty *noun*
frailties

frame *verb*
frames
framing
framed

frame *noun*
frames

framework *noun*
frameworks

franc○ *noun*
francs

franchise *noun*
franchises

frank✢ *adjective*
franker
frankest
frankly

frank✲ *verb*
franks
franking
franked

frankness

frantic *adjective*
frantically

fraud *noun*
frauds

fraudulent *adjective*
fraudulently

fraught

frayed

freak *noun*
freaks

freakish

freckle *noun*
freckles

freckled

free *adjective*
freer
freest
freely

free *verb*
frees
freeing
freed

freedom *noun*
freedoms

freehand *adjective*

freewheel *verb*
freewheels
freewheeling
freewheeled

a
b
c
d
e
f
g
h
i
j
k
l
m
n
o
p
q
r
s
t
u
v
w
x
y
z

★ You use **fourth** in e.g. *for the fourth time.* ❗**forth.**
☆ A **fowl** is a kind of bird. ❗**foul.**
○ A **franc** is a unit of money in Switzerland. ❗**frank.**
✢ **Frank** means 'speaking honestly'. ❗**franc.**
✲ To **frank** is to mark a letter with a postmark. ❗**franc.**

a b c d e **f** g h i j k l m n o p q r s t u v w x y z

freeze* verb
freezes
freezing
froze
frozen

freezer noun
freezers

freight

freighter noun
freighters

frenzied

frenzy noun
frenzies

frequency noun
frequencies

frequent adjective
frequently

frequent verb
frequents
frequenting
frequented

fresh adjective
fresher
freshest
freshly

freshness

freshen verb
freshens
freshening
freshened

freshwater

fret verb
frets
fretting
fretted

fretful adjective
fretfully

fretsaw noun
fretsaws

fretwork

friar noun
friars

friary noun
friaries

friction

Friday noun
Fridays

fridge noun
fridges

friend noun
friends

friendless

friendliness

friendly adjective
friendlier
friendliest

friendship noun
friendships

frieze☆ noun
friezes

frigate noun
frigates

fright noun
frights

frighten verb
frightens
frightening
frightened

frightful adjective
frightfully

frill noun
frills

frilled

frilly adjective
frillier
frilliest

fringe noun
fringes

fringed

frisk verb
frisks
frisking
frisked

friskiness

frisky adjective
friskier
friskiest
friskily

fritter verb
fritters
frittering
frittered

fritter noun
fritters

frivolous adjective
frivolously

frivolity noun
frivolities

frizzy adjective
frizzier
frizziest

fro°

frock noun
frocks

frog noun
frogs

frogman noun
frogmen

frolic noun
frolics

frolicsome

frolic verb
frolics
frolicking
frolicked

front noun
fronts

frontier noun
frontiers

··

★ To **freeze** is to be very cold. **I frieze**.
☆ A **frieze** is a strip of designs along a wall. **I freeze**.
○ You use **fro** in to and fro.

98

frost noun
frosts

frost verb
frosts
frosting
frosted

frostbite noun

frostbitten

frosty adjective
frostier
frostiest

froth noun

froth verb
froths
frothing
frothed

frothy adjective
frothier
frothiest

froth verb
froths
frothing
frothed

frown verb
frowns
frowning
frowned

frown noun
frowns

froze see **freeze**

frozen see **freeze**

frugal adjective
frugally

frugality

fruit noun
fruit or fruits

fruitful adjective
fruitfully

fruitless adjective
fruitlessly

fruity adjective
fruitier
fruitiest

frustrate verb
frustrates
frustrating
frustrated

frustration noun
frustrations

fry verb
fries
frying
fried

fudge

fuel noun
fuels

fuel verb
fuels
fuelling
fuelled

fug noun
fugs

fuggy adjective
fuggier
fuggiest

fugitive noun
fugitives

-ful
-ful makes nouns for
amounts, e.g.
handful, spoonful.
The plural of these
words ends in -fuls,
e.g. **handfuls**. -ful
also makes
adjectives, e.g.
graceful, and when
the adjective ends in
-y following a
consonant, you
change the y to i, e.g.
beauty - beautiful.

---

fulcrum noun
fulcra or fulcrums

fulfil verb
fulfils
fulfilling
fulfilled

fulfilment noun

full adjective
fully

fullness noun

fumble verb
fumbles
fumbling
fumbled

fume verb
fumes
fuming
fumed

fumes plural noun

fun

function verb
functions
functioning
functioned

function noun
functions

functional adjective
functionally

fund noun
funds

fundamental
adjective
fundamentally

funeral noun
funerals

fungus noun
fungi

funk verb
funks
funking
funked

funnel noun
funnels

funny adjective
funnier
funniest
funnily

a
b
c
d
e
f
g
h
i
j
k
l
m
n
o
p
q
r
s
t
u
v
w
x
y
z

fur* *noun*
furs

furious *adjective*
furiously

furl *verb*
furls
furling
furled

furlong *noun*
furlongs

furnace *noun*
furnaces

furnish *verb*
furnishes
furnishing
furnished

furniture

furrow *noun*
furrows

furry *adjective*
furrier
furriest

further☆ *adjective*

further○ *verb*
furthers
furthering
furthered

furthermore

furthest✦

furtive *adjective*
furtively

fury *noun*
furies

fuse *verb*
fuses
fusing
fused

fuse *noun*
fuses

fuselage *noun*
fuselages

fusion *noun*
fusions

fuss *verb*
fusses
fussing
fussed

fuss *noun*
fusses

fussiness

fussy *adjective*
fussier
fussiest
fussily

futile *adjective*
futilely

futility

futon *noun*
futons

future

fuzz

fuzziness *noun*

fuzzy *adjective*
fuzzier
fuzziest
fuzzily

Gg

gabardine *noun*
gabardines

gabble *verb*
gabbles
gabbling
gabbled

gable *noun*
gables

gabled

gadget *noun*
gadgets

Gaelic

gag *verb*
gags
gagging
gagged

gag *noun*
gags

gaiety

gaily

gain *verb*
gains
gaining
gained

gain *noun*
gains

gala *noun*
galas

galactic

galaxy *noun*
galaxies

gale *noun*
gales

gallant *adjective*
gallantly

gallantry

galleon* *noun*
galleons

gallery *noun*
galleries

galley *noun*
galleys

★ **Fur** is the hair of animals. **!fir**.
☆ You use **further** in e.g. *We need further information.* See **farther**.
○ To **further** something is to make it progress.
✦ You use **furthest** in e.g. *Who has read the furthest?* See **farthest**.
▦ A **galleon** is a type of ship. **!gallon**.

gallon* *noun*
gallons

gallop *verb*
gallops
galloping
galloped

gallop *noun*
gallops

gallows

galore

galvanize *verb*
galvanizes
galvanizing
galvanized

gamble *verb*
gambles
gambling
gambled

gamble *noun*
gambles

gambler *noun*
gamblers

game *noun*
games

gamekeeper *noun*
gamekeepers

gammon

gander *noun*
ganders

gang *noun*
gangs

gang *verb*
gangs
ganging
ganged

gangplank *noun*
gangplanks

gangster *noun*
gangsters

gangway *noun*
gangways

gaol *noun* see **jail**

gaoler *noun* see **jailer**

gap *noun*
gaps

gape *verb*
gapes
gaping
gaped

garage *noun*
garages

garbage

garden *noun*
gardens

gardener *noun*
gardeners

gardening

gargle *verb*
gargles
gargling
gargled

gargoyle *noun*
gargoyles

garland *noun*
garlands

garlic

garment *noun*
garments

garnish *verb*
garnishes
garnishing
garnished

garrison *noun*
garrisons

garter *noun*
garters

gas *noun*
gases

gas *verb*
gasses
gassing
gassed

gaseous

gash *noun*
gashes

gasket *noun*
gaskets

gasoline

gasometer *noun*
gasometers

gasp *verb*
gasps
gasping
gasped

gasp *noun*
gasps

gastric

gate *noun*
gates

gateau☆ *noun*
gateaux

gateway *noun*
gateways

gather *verb*
gathers
gathering
gathered

gathering *noun*
gatherings

gaudy *adjective*
gaudier
gaudiest

gauge *verb*
gauges
gauging
gauged

gauge *noun*
gauges

gaunt

gauntlet *noun*
gauntlets

gauze

gave see **give**

. . . .
★ A **gallon** is a measurement of liquid. **!** **galleon**.
☆ **Gateau** is a French word used in English. It means 'a rich cream cake'.

gay *adjective*
gayer
gayest

gaze *verb*
gazes
gazing
gazed

gaze *noun*
gazes

gazetteer *noun*
gazetteers

gear *noun*
gears

geese see **goose**

Geiger counter *noun*
Geiger counters

gel *noun*
gels

gelatine *noun*

gelding *noun*
geldings

gem *noun*
gems

gender *noun*
genders

gene *noun*
genes

genealogy *noun*
genealogies

general *adjective*
generally

general *noun*
generals

generalization *noun*
generalizations

generalize *verb*
generalizes
generalizing
generalized

generate *verb*
generates
generating
generated

generation *noun*
generations

generator *noun*
generators

generosity *noun*

generous *adjective*
generously

genetic *adjective*
genetically

genetics *plural noun*

genial *adjective*
genially

genie *noun*
genies

genitals *plural noun*

genius *noun*
geniuses

gent *noun*
gents

gentle *adjective*
gentler
gentlest
gently

gentleman *noun*
gentlemen

gentlemanly

gentleness

genuine *adjective*
genuinely

genus *noun*
genera

---

geo-
geo- means 'earth',
e.g. **geography** (the
study of the earth).

---

geographer

geographical
adjective
geographically

geography *noun*

geological *adjective*
geologically

geologist *noun*

geology *noun*

geometric *adjective*
geometrically

geometrical *adjective*
geometrically

geometry *noun*

geranium *noun*
geraniums

gerbil *noun*
gerbils

germ *noun*
germs

germinate *verb*
germinates
germinating
germinated

germination *noun*

gesticulate *verb*
gesticulates
gesticulating
gesticulated

gesture *noun*
gestures

get *verb*
gets
getting
got

getaway *noun*
getaways

geyser *noun*
geysers

ghastly *adjective*
ghastlier
ghastliest

ghetto *noun*
ghettos

ghost *noun*
ghosts

ghostly *adjective*
ghostlier
ghostliest

ghoulish *adjective*
ghoulishly

giant *noun*
giants

giddiness

a b c d e f **g** h i j k l m n o p q r s t u v w x y z

giddy *adjective*
giddier
giddiest
giddily

gift *noun*
gifts

gifted

gigantic *adjective*
gigantically

giggle *verb*
giggles
giggling
giggled

giggle *noun*
giggles

gild* *verb*
gilds
gilding
gilded

gills *plural noun*

gimmick *noun*
gimmicks

gin

ginger

gingerbread

gingerly

gingery

gipsy *noun* see **gypsy**

giraffe *noun*
giraffes

girder *noun*
girders

girdle *noun*
girdles

girl *noun*
girls

girlfriend *noun*
girlfriends

girlhood

girlish

giro☆ *noun*
giros

girth *noun*
girths

gist

give *verb*
gives
giving
gave
given

given see **give**

giver *noun*
givers

glacial

glacier *noun*
glaciers

glad *adjective*
gladder
gladdest
gladly

gladden *verb*
gladdens
gladdening
gladdened

gladiator *noun*
gladiators

gladness

glamorize *verb*
glamorizes
glamorizing
glamorized

glamorous *adjective*
glamorously

glamour

glance *verb*
glances
glancing
glanced

glance *noun*
glances

gland *noun*
glands

glandular

glare *verb*
glares
glaring
glared

glare *noun*
glares

glass *noun*
glasses

glassful *noun*
glassfuls

glassy *adjective*
glassier
glassiest

glaze *verb*
glazes
glazing
glazed

glaze *noun*
glazes

glazier *noun*
glaziers

gleam *noun*
gleams

gleam *verb*
gleams
gleaming
gleamed

glee

gleeful *adjective*
gleefully

glen *noun*
glens

glide *verb*
glides
gliding
glided

glider *noun*
gliders

glimmer *verb*
glimmers
glimmering
glimmered

· ·

★ To **gild** something is to cover it with gold. **! guild**.
☆ A **giro** is a system of paying money. **! gyro**.

a **glimmer** noun
glimmers

b **glimpse** verb
glimpses
c glimpsing
glimpsed

d **glimpse** noun
e glimpses

f **glint** verb
glints
glinting
glinted

g

h **glint** noun
glints

i **glisten** verb
glistens
j glistening
glistened

k **glitter** verb
glitters
l glittering
glittered

m **gloat** verb
gloats
gloating
n gloated

o **global** adjective
globally

p **globe** noun
globes

q **gloom** noun
r **gloominess**

gloomy adjective
s gloomier
gloomiest
gloomily

t **glorification**

u **glorify** verb
glorifies
v glorifying
glorified

glorious adjective
gloriously

glory noun
glories

gloss noun
glosses

glossary noun
glossaries

glossy adjective
glossier
glossiest

glove noun
gloves

glow verb
glows
glowing
glowed

glow noun
glows

glower verb
glowers
glowering
glowered

glow-worm noun
glow-worms

glucose

glue noun
glues

glue verb
glues
gluing
glued

gluey adjective
gluier
gluiest

glum adjective
glummer
glummest
glumly

glutton noun
gluttons

gluttonous

gluttony

gnarled

gnash* verb
gnashes
gnashing
gnashed

gnat* noun
gnats

gnaw* verb
gnaws
gnawing
gnawed

gnome* noun
gnomes

go verb
goes
going
went
gone

go noun
goes

goal noun
goals

goalie noun
goalies

goalkeeper noun
goalkeepers

goalpost noun
goalposts

goat noun
goats

gobble verb
gobbles
gobbling
gobbled

gobbledegook

goblet noun
goblets

goblin noun
goblins

God☆

z

....

★ In these words beginning with **gn-** the 'g' is silent.
☆ You use a capital G when you mean the Christian, Jewish, and Muslim creator.

104

god★ noun
gods

godchild noun
godchildren

goddess noun
goddesses

godparent noun
godparents

goggles plural noun

gold

golden

goldfinch noun
goldfinches

goldfish noun
goldfish

golf

golfer noun
golfers

golfing

gondola noun
gondolas

gondolier noun
gondoliers

gone see go

gong noun
gongs

good adjective
better
best

goodbye interjection

Good Friday

good-looking

good-natured

goodness

goods plural noun

goodwill

gooey adjective
gooier
gooiest

goose noun
geese

gooseberry noun
gooseberries

gore verb
gores
goring
gored

gorge noun
gorges

gorgeous adjective
gorgeously

gorilla☆ noun
gorillas

gorse

gory adjective
gorier
goriest

gosling noun
goslings

gospel noun
gospels

gossip verb
gossips
gossiping
gossiped

gossip noun
gossips

got see get

gouge verb
gouges
gouging
gouged

gourd noun
gourds

govern verb
governs
governing
governed

government noun
governments

governor noun
governors

gown noun
gowns

grab verb
grabs
grabbing
grabbed

grace noun
graces

graceful adjective
gracefully

gracefulness

gracious adjective
graciously

grade noun
grades

grade verb
grades
grading
graded

gradient noun
gradients

gradual adjective
gradually

graduate noun
graduates

graduate verb
graduates
graduating
graduated

graduation

graffiti plural noun

grain noun
grains

grainy adjective
grainier
grainiest

gram noun
grams

....

★ You use a small g when you mean any male divine being.
☆ A **gorilla** is a large ape. **! guerrilla**.

a

grammar *noun*
grammars

b

grammatical *adjective*
grammatically

c

d

gramophone *noun*
gramophones

e

grand *adjective*
grander
grandest
grandly

f

g

grandad *noun*
grandads

h

grandchild *noun*
grandchildren

i

grandeur

j

k

grandfather *noun*
grandfathers

grandma *noun*
grandmas

l

m

grandmother *noun*
grandmothers

n

grandpa *noun*
grandpas

o

grandparent *noun*
grandparents

p

grandstand *noun*
grandstands

q

granite

r

granny *noun*
grannies

s

grant *verb*
grants
granting
granted

t

u

grant *noun*
grants

v

granulated

w

grape *noun*
grapes

x

y

z

grapefruit *noun*
grapefruit

grapevine *noun*
grapevines

graph *noun*
graphs

graphic *adjective*
graphically

graphics *plural noun*

graphite

-graphy
-graphy makes words
for subjects of study,
e.g. **geography** (the
study of the earth). A
bibliography is a list
of books on a subject,
and the plural is
bibliographies.

grapple *verb*
grapples
grappling
grappled

grasp *verb*
grasps
grasping
grasped

grasp *noun*
grasps

grass *noun*
grasses

grasshopper *noun*
grasshoppers

grassy *adjective*
grassier
grassiest

grate* *verb*
grates
grating
grated

grate☆ *noun*
grates

grateful *adjective*
gratefully

grating *noun*
gratings

gratitude

grave *noun*
graves

grave *adjective*
graver
gravest
gravely

gravel

gravelled

gravestone *noun*
gravestones

graveyard *noun*
graveyards

gravitation

gravitational

gravity

gravy

graze *verb*
grazes
grazing
grazed

graze *noun*
grazes

grease

greasy *adjective*
greasier
greasiest

great *adjective*
greater
greatest
greatly

greatness

greed

greediness

★ To **grate** something is to shred it. **! great**.
☆ A **grate** is a fireplace. **! great**.

greedy adjective
greedier
greediest
greedily

green adjective and
noun
greener
greenest

greenery

greengage noun
greengages

greengrocer noun
greengrocers

greengrocery noun
greengroceries

greenhouse noun
greenhouses

greens plural noun

greet verb
greets
greeting
greeted

greeting noun
greetings

grenade noun
grenades

grew see **grow**

grey adjective and
noun
greyer
greyest

greyhound noun
greyhounds

grid noun
grids

grief

grievance noun
grievances

grieve verb
grieves
grieving
grieved

grievous★ adjective
grievously

grill verb
grills
grilling
grilled

grill noun
grills

grim adjective
grimmer
grimmest
grimly

grimace noun
grimaces

grime

grimness

grimy adjective
grimier
grimiest

grin noun
grins

grin verb
grins
grinning
grinned

grind verb
grinds
grinding
ground

grinder noun
grinders

grindstone noun
grindstones

grip verb
grips
gripping
gripped

grip noun
grips

grisly☆ adjective
grislier
grisliest

gristle

gristly adjective
gristlier
gristliest

grit verb
grits
gritting
gritted

grit noun

gritty adjective
grittier
grittiest

grizzly❍ adjective

groan verb
groans
groaning
groaned

groan noun
groans

grocer noun
grocers

grocery noun
groceries

groggy adjective
groggier
groggiest

groin noun
groins

groom verb
grooms
grooming
groomed

groom noun
grooms

groove noun
grooves

a
b
c
d
e
f
g
h
i
j
k
l
m
n
o
p
q
r
s
t
u
v
w
x
y
z

. . . .

★ Note that this word does not end *-ious*.
☆ **Grisly** means 'revolting' or 'horrible'. **! grizzly**.
❍ You use **grizzly** in *grizzly bear*. **! grisly**.

a
b
c
d
e
f
g
h
i
j
k
l
m
n
o
p
q
r
s
t
u
v
w
x
y
z

grope *verb*
gropes
groping
groped

gross *adjective*
grosser
grossest
grossly

gross *noun*
gross

grossness

grotesque* *adjective*
grotesquely

grotty *adjective*
grottier
grottiest

ground *noun*
grounds

ground see **grind**

grounded

grounds *plural noun*

groundsheet *noun*
groundsheets

groundsman *noun*
groundsmen

group *noun*
groups

group *verb*
groups
grouping
grouped

grouse *verb*
grouses
grousing
groused

grouse *noun*
grouse

grove *noun*
groves

grovel *verb*
grovels
grovelling
grovelled

grow *verb*
grows
growing
grew
grown

grower *noun*
growers

growl *verb*
growls
growling
growled

growl *noun*
growls

grown-up *noun*
grown-ups

growth *noun*
growths

grub *noun*
grubs

grubby *adjective*
grubbier
grubbiest

grudge *verb*
grudges
grudging
grudged

grudge *noun*
grudges

grudgingly

gruelling

gruesome

gruff *adjective*
gruffer
gruffest
gruffly

grumble *verb*
grumbles
grumbling
grumbled

grumbler *noun*
grumblers

grumpiness

grumpy *adjective*
grumpier
grumpiest
grumpily

grunt *verb*
grunts
grunting
grunted

grunt *noun*
grunts

guarantee *noun*
guarantees

guarantee *verb*
guarantees
guaranteeing
guaranteed

guard *verb*
guards
guarding
guarded

guard *noun*
guards

guardian *noun*
guardians

guardianship

guerrilla☆ *noun*
guerrillas

guess *verb*
guesses
guessing
guessed

guess *noun*
guesses

guesswork

· ·
★ **Grotesque** means 'strange' and 'ugly'. It sounds like 'grotesk'.
☆ A **guerrilla** is a member of a small army. **!** gorilla.

108

guest noun
guests

guidance noun

guide verb
guides
guiding
guided

guide noun
guides

guidelines plural noun

guild* noun
guilds

guillotine noun
guillotines

guilt

guilty adjective
guiltier
guiltiest

guinea noun
guineas

guinea pig noun
guinea pigs

guitar noun
guitars

guitarist

gulf noun
gulfs

gull noun
gulls

gullet noun
gullets

gullible

gully noun
gullies

gulp verb
gulps
gulping
gulped

gulp noun
gulps

gum noun
gums

gum verb
gums
gumming
gummed

gummy adjective
gummier
gummiest

gun noun
guns

gun verb
guns
gunning
gunned

gunboat noun
gunboats

gunfire

gunman noun
gunmen

gunner noun
gunners

gunnery

gunpowder

gunshot noun
gunshots

gurdwara☆ noun
gurdwaras

gurgle verb
gurgles
gurgling
gurgled

guru noun
gurus

Guru Granth Sahib○

gush verb
gushes
gushing
gushed

gust noun
gusts

gusty adjective
gustier
gustiest

gut noun
guts

gut verb
guts
gutting
gutted

gutter noun
gutters

guy noun
guys

guzzle verb
guzzles
guzzling
guzzled

gym noun
gyms

gymkhana noun
gymkhanas

gymnasium noun
gymnasiums

gymnast noun
gymnasts

gymnastics plural noun

gypsy noun
gypsies

gyro✤ noun
gyros

gyroscope noun
gyroscopes

a
b
c
d
e
f
g
h
i
j
k
l
m
n
o
p
q
r
s
t
u
v
w
x
y
z

. . . .

★ A **guild** is an organization of people. **!** **gild**.
☆ A Sikh place of worship.
○ The holy book of Sikhs.
✤ A **gyro** is type of compass. **!** **giro**.

Hh

habit noun
habits

habitat noun
habitats

habitual adjective
habitually

hack verb
hacks
hacking
hacked

hacker noun
hackers

hacksaw noun
hacksaws

had see **has**

haddock noun
haddock

hadn't verb

hag noun
hags

haggard

haggis noun
haggises

haggle verb
haggles
haggling
haggled

haiku★ noun
haiku

hail verb
hails
hailing
hailed

hail

hailstone noun
hailstones

hair☆ noun
hairs

hairbrush noun
hairbrushes

haircut noun
haircuts

hairdresser noun
hairdressers

hairpin noun
hairpins

hair-raising

hairstyle noun
hairstyles

hairy adjective
hairier
hairiest

hake noun
hake

halal

half adjective and noun
halves

half-baked

half-hearted adjective
half-heartedly

half-life noun
half-lives

half-mast

halfpenny◊ noun
halfpennies or
halfpence

half-term noun
half-terms

half-time noun
half-times

halfway

halibut noun
halibut

hall✧ noun
halls

hallo

Halloween●

hallucination noun
hallucinations

halo noun
haloes

halt verb
halts
halting
halted

halt noun
halts

halter noun
halters

halting adjective
haltingly

halve verb
halves
halving
halved

halves see **half**

ham noun
hams

hamburger noun
hamburgers

hammer noun
hammers

hammer verb
hammers
hammering
hammered

hammock noun
hammocks

- -

★ A Japanese poem.

☆ **Hair** is the covering on the head. I **hare**.

◊ You use **halfpennies** when you mean several coins and **halfpence** for a sum of money.

✧ A **hall** is a large space in a building. I **haul**.

● You will also see this word spelt *Hallowe'en*.

a b c d e f g h i j k l m n o p q r s t u v w x y z

hamper *verb*
hampers
hampering
hampered

hamper *noun*
hampers

hamster *noun*
hamsters

hand *noun*
hands

hand *verb*
hands
handing
handed

handbag *noun*
handbags

handbook *noun*
handbooks

handcuffs *plural noun*

handful *noun*
handfuls

handicap *noun*
handicaps

handicapped *adjective*

handicraft *noun*
handicrafts

handiwork *noun*

handkerchief *noun*
handkerchiefs

handle *noun*
handles

handle *verb*
handles
handling
handled

handlebars *plural noun*

handrail *noun*
handrails

handsome *adjective*
handsomer
handsomest
handsomely

hands-on

handstand *noun*
handstands

handwriting *noun*

handwritten

handy *adjective*
handier
handiest

handyman *noun*
handymen

hang *verb*
hangs
hanging
hung

hangar★ *noun*
hangars

hanger☆ *noun*
hangers

hang-glider *noun*
hang-gliders

hang-gliding

hangman *noun*
hangmen

hangover *noun*
hangovers

hank *noun*
hanks

hanker *verb*
hankers
hankering
hankered

hanky *noun*
hankies

Hanukkah○

haphazard *adjective*
haphazardly

happen *verb*
happens
happening
happened

happening *noun*
happenings

happiness

happy *adjective*
happier
happiest
happily

happy-go-lucky

harass✢ *verb*
harasses
harassing
harassed

harassment

harbour *noun*
harbours

harbour *verb*
harbours
harbouring
harboured

hard *adjective*
harder
hardest

hard *adverb*
harder
hardest

hardboard

hard-boiled

hard disk *noun*
hard disks

harden *verb*
hardens
hardening
hardened

hardly

....

★ A **hangar** is a shed for aircraft. **!** hanger.
☆ A **hanger** is a thing for hanging clothes on. **!** hangar.
○ A Jewish festival.
✢ Note that there is only one r in **harass** and **harassment**.

hardness
hardship *noun*
hardships
hardware *noun*
hardwood *noun*
hardwoods
hardy *adjective*
hardier
hardiest
hare* *noun*
hares
hark *verb*
harks
harking
harked
harm *verb*
harms
harming
harmed
harm *noun*
harmful *adjective*
harmfully
harmless *adjective*
harmlessly
harmonic
harmonica *noun*
harmonicas
harmonious *adjective*
harmoniously
harmonization
harmonize *verb*
harmonizes
harmonizing
harmonized
harmony *noun*
harmonies
harness *verb*
harnesses
harnessing
harnessed
harness *noun*
harnesses

harp *noun*
harps
harp *verb*
harps
harping
harped
harpist *noun*
harpists
harpoon *noun*
harpoons
harpsichord *noun*
harpsichords
harrow *noun*
harrows
harsh *adjective*
harsher
harshest
harshly
harshness
harvest *noun*
harvests
harvest *verb*
harvests
harvesting
harvested
hash *noun*
hashes
hasn't *verb*
hassle *noun*
hassles
haste
hasten *verb*
hastens
hastening
hastened
hastiness
hasty *adjective*
hastier
hastiest
hastily

hatch *verb*
hatches
hatching
hatched
hatch *noun*
hatches
hatchback *noun*
hatchbacks
hatchet *noun*
hatchets
hate *verb*
hates
hating
hated
hate *noun*
hates
hateful *adjective*
hatefully
hatred
hat trick *noun*
hat tricks
haughtiness
haughty *adjective*
haughtier
haughtiest
haughtily
haul☆ *verb*
hauls
hauling
hauled
haul *noun*
hauls
haunt *verb*
haunts
haunting
haunted
have *verb*
has
having
had
haven *noun*
havens

★ A **hare** is an animal like a large rabbit. **!hair**.
☆ To **haul** is to pull something heavy. **!hall**.

haven't *verb*

haversack *noun*
haversacks

hawk *noun*
hawks

hawk *verb*
hawks
hawking
hawked

hawker *noun*
hawkers

hawthorn *noun*
hawthorns

hay fever

haymaking

haystack *noun*
haystacks

hazard *noun*
hazards

hazardous

haze *noun*
hazes

hazel *noun*
hazels

haziness

hazy *adjective*
hazier
haziest
hazily

H-bomb *noun*
H-bombs

head *noun*
heads

head *verb*
heads
heading
headed

headache *noun*
headaches

headdress *noun*
headdresses

header *noun*
headers

heading *noun*
headings

headland *noun*
headlands

headlight *noun*
headlights

headline *noun*
headlines

headlong

headmaster *noun*
headmasters

headmistress *noun*
headmistresses

head-on

headphones

headquarters *noun*
headquarters

headteacher *noun*
headteachers

headway

heal *verb*
heals
healing
healed

healer *noun*
healers

health

healthiness

healthy *adjective*
healthier
healthiest
healthily

heap *verb*
heaps
heaping
heaped

heap *noun*
heaps

hear★ *verb*
hears
hearing
heard

hearing *noun*
hearings

hearse *noun*
hearses

heart *noun*
hearts

hearth *noun*
hearths

heartiness

heartless

hearty *adjective*
heartier
heartiest
heartily

heat *verb*
heats
heating
heated

heat *noun*
heats

heater *noun*
heaters

heath *noun*
heaths

heathen *noun*
heathens

heather

heatwave *noun*
heatwaves

heave☆ *verb*
heaves
heaving
heaved
hove

heaven

heavenly

heaviness

....

★ You use **hear** in e.g. *I can't hear you.* **!** *here.*
☆ You use **hove** in e.g. *the ship hove to.*

heavy *adjective*
heavier
heaviest
heavily

heavyweight *noun*
heavyweights

Hebrew

hectare *noun*
hectares

hectic *adjective*
hectically

he'd *verb*

hedge *noun*
hedges

hedge *verb*
hedges
hedging
hedged

hedgehog *noun*
hedgehogs

hedgerow *noun*
hedgerows

heed *verb*
heeds
heeding
heeded

heed *noun*

heedless

heel *noun*
heels

heel *verb*
heels
heeling
heeled

hefty *adjective*
heftier
heftiest

heifer *noun*
heifers

height *noun*
heights

heighten *verb*
heightens
heightening
heightened

heir *noun*
heirs

heiress *noun*
heiresses

held see **hold**

helicopter *noun*
helicopters

helium

helix *noun*
helices

hell

he'll *verb*

hellish *adjective*
hellishly

hello

helm *noun*
helms

helmsman *noun*
helmsmen

helmet *noun*
helmets

helmeted

help *verb*
helps
helping
helped

help *noun*
helps

helper *noun*
helpers

helpful *adjective*
helpfully

helping *noun*
helpings

helpless *adjective*
helplessly

helter-skelter *noun*
helter-skelters

hem *noun*
hems

hem *verb*
hems
hemming
hemmed

hemisphere *noun*
hemispheres

hemp

hence

henceforth

herald *noun*
heralds

herald *verb*
heralds
heralding
heralded

heraldic

heraldry

herb *noun*
herbs

herbal

herbivore *noun*
herbivores

herd *noun*
herds

herd ☆ *verb*
herds
herding
herded

here °

hereditary

heredity

heritage *noun*
heritages

hermit *noun*
hermits

hermitage

....

★ You do not pronounce the 'h' in **heir** (sounds like *air*).

☆ A **herd** is a group of sheep. **!heard.**

○ You use **here** in e.g. *come here*. **!hear.**

hero noun
heroes

heroic adjective
heroically

heroin★ noun

heroine☆ noun
heroines

heroism

heron noun
herons

herring noun
herring
herrings

hers○

herself

he's verb

hesitant adjective
hesitantly

hesitate verb
hesitates
hesitating
hesitated

hesitation

hexagon noun
hexagons

hexagonal

hibernate verb
hibernates
hibernating
hibernated

hibernation

hiccup noun
hiccups

hide verb
hides
hiding
hidden
hid
hidden

hide-and-seek

hideous adjective
hideously

hideout noun
hideouts

hiding noun
hidings

hieroglyphics plural noun

hi-fi noun
hi-fis

higgledy-piggledy

high adjective
higher
highest

highland adjective

highlands plural noun

highlander noun
highlanders

highlight noun
highlights

highlighter noun
highlighters

highly

Highness noun
Highnesses

high-rise

highway noun
highways

highwayman noun
highwaymen

hijack verb
hijacks
hijacking
hijacked

hijacker noun
hijackers

hike verb
hikes
hiking
hiked

hike noun
hikes

hiker noun
hikers

hilarious adjective
hilariously

hilarity

hill noun
hills

hillside noun
hillsides

hilly adjective
hillier
hilliest

hilt noun
hilts

himself

hind adjective

hind noun
hinds

hinder verb
hinders
hindering
hindered

Hindi

hindrance noun
hindrances

Hindu noun
Hindus

hinge noun
hinges

hinge verb
hinges
hinging
hinged

....

★ **Heroin** is a drug. **!heroine**.
☆ A **heroine** is a woman or girl in a story. **!heroin**
○ You use **hers** in e.g. *the book is hers*. Note that there is no
apostrophe in this word.

a
b
c
d
e
f
g
h
i
j
k
l
m
n
o
p
q
r
s
t
u
v
w
x
y
z

hint *noun*
hints

hint *verb*
hints
hinting
hinted

hip *noun*
hips

hippo *noun*
hippos

hippopotamus *noun*
hippopotamuses

hire *verb*
hires
hiring
hired

hiss *verb*
hisses
hissing
hissed

histogram *noun*
histograms

historian *noun*
historians

historic

historical *adjective*
historically

history *noun*
histories

hit *verb*
hits
hitting
hit

hit *noun*
hits

hitch *verb*
hitches
hitching
hitched

hitch *noun*
hitches

hitch-hike *verb*
hitch-hikes
hitch-hiking
hitch-hiked

hitch-hiker *noun*
hitch-hikers

hi-tech

hither

hitherto

hive *noun*
hives

hoard *verb*
hoards
hoarding
hoarded

hoard★ *noun*
hoards

hoarder *noun*
hoarders

hoarding *noun*
hoardings

hoar frost

hoarse☆ *adjective*
hoarser
hoarsest

hoax *verb*
hoaxes
hoaxing
hoaxed

hoax *noun*
hoaxes

hobble *verb*
hobbles
hobbling
hobbled

hobby *noun*
hobbies

hockey

hoe *noun*
hoes

hoe *verb*
hoes
hoeing
hoed

hog *noun*
hogs

hog *verb*
hogs
hogging
hogged

Hogmanay

hoist *verb*
hoists
hoisting
hoisted

hold *verb*
holds
holding
held

hold *noun*
holds

holdall *noun*
holdalls

holder *noun*
holders

hold-up *noun*
hold-ups

hole○ *noun*
holes

holey✦ *adjective*

Holi✹

holiday *noun*
holidays

holiness

hollow *adjective* and *adverb*

....
★ A **hoard** is a secret store. ❗ **horde**.
☆ A **hoarse** voice is rough or croaking. ❗ **horse**.
○ A **hole** is a gap or opening. ❗ **whole**.
✦ **Holey** means 'full of holes'. ❗ **holy**.
✹ A Hindu festival.

hollow verb
hollows
hollowing
hollowed

hollow noun
hollows

holly

holocaust noun
holocausts

hologram noun
holograms

holster noun
holsters

holy* adjective
holier
holiest

home noun
homes

home verb
homes
homing
homed

homeless

homely

home-made

homesick

homesickness

homestead noun
homesteads

homeward adjective

homewards adjective
and adverb

homework

homing

homosexual
adjective and noun
homosexuals

honest adjective
honestly

honesty

honey noun
honeys

honeycomb noun
honeycombs

honeymoon noun
honeymoons

honeysuckle

honk verb
honks
honking
honked

honk noun
honks

honour verb
honours
honouring
honoured

honour noun
honours

honourable adjective
honourably

hood noun
hoods

-hood
-hood makes nouns,
e.g. **childhood**. Other
noun suffixes are
-dom, **-ment**, **-ness**,
and **-ship**.

---

hooded

hoof noun
hoofs

hook noun
hooks

hook verb
hooks
hooking
hooked

hooligan noun
hooligans

hoop noun
hoops

hoopla

hooray

hoot verb
hoots
hooting
hooted

hoot noun
hoots

hooter noun
hooters

hop verb
hops
hopping
hopped

hop noun
hops

hope verb
hopes
hoping
hoped

hope noun
hopes

hopeful adjective
hopefully

hopeless adjective
hopelessly

hopscotch

horde☆ noun
hordes

horizon noun
horizons

horizontal adjective
horizontally

hormone noun
hormones

horn noun
horns

hornet noun
hornets

★ You use **holy** in e.g. *a holy man*. **!holey**.
☆ A **horde** is a large crowd. **!hoard**.

a
b
c
d
e
f
g
h
i
j
k
l
m
n
o
p
q
r
s
t
u
v
w
x
y
z

horoscope noun
horoscopes

horrible adjective
horribly

horrid

horrific adjective
horrifically

horrify verb
horrifies
horrifying
horrified

horror noun
horrors

horse noun
horses

horseback

horseman noun
horsemen

horsemanship

horsepower noun
horsepower

horseshoe noun
horseshoes

horsewoman noun
horsewomen

horticulture

hose noun
hoses

hospitable adjective
hospitably

hospital noun
hospitals

hospitality

host noun
hosts

hostage noun
hostages

hostel noun
hostels

hostess noun
hostesses

hostile

hostility noun
hostilities

hot adjective
hotter
hottest
hotly

hot verb
hots
hotting
hotted

hotel noun
hotels

hothouse noun
hothouses

hotpot noun
hotpots

hound noun
hounds

hound verb
hounds
hounding
hounded

hour* noun
hours

hourglass noun
hourglasses

hourly adjective and
adverb

house noun
houses

house verb
houses
housing
housed

houseboat noun
houseboats

household noun
households

householder noun
householders

housekeeper noun
housekeepers

housekeeping

housewife noun
housewives

housework

housing noun
housings

hove see **heave**

hover verb
hovers
hovering
hovered

hovercraft noun
hovercraft

however

howl verb
howls
howling
howled

howl noun
howls

howler noun
howlers

hub noun
hubs

huddle verb
huddles
huddling
huddled

hue noun
hues

huff

hug verb
hugs
hugging
hugged

hug noun
hugs

huge adjective
huger
hugest
hugely

hugeness

hulk noun
hulks

....

★ An **hour** is a measure of time. **!** our.

a b c d e f h i j k l m n o p q r s t u v w x y z

hulking

hull noun
hulls

hullabaloo noun
hullabaloos

hullo

hum verb
hums
humming
hummed

hum noun
hums

human adjective and noun
humans

humane adjective
humanely

humanitarian

humanity noun
humanities

humble adjective
humbler
humblest
humbly

humid

humidity

humiliate verb
humiliates
humiliating
humiliated

humiliation

humility

hummingbird noun
hummingbirds

humorous adjective
humorously

humour noun

humour verb
humours
humouring
humoured

hump noun
humps

hump verb
humps
humping
humped

humpback

humus

hunch verb
hunches
hunching
hunched

hunch noun
hunches

hunchback noun
hunchbacks

hunchbacked

hundred noun
hundreds

hundredth

hundredweight noun
hundredweights

hung see **hang**

hunger

hungry adjective
hungrier
hungriest
hungrily

hunk noun
hunks

hunt verb
hunts
hunting
hunted

hunt noun
hunts

hunter noun
hunters

hurdle noun
hurdles

hurdler noun
hurdlers

hurdling

hurl verb
hurls
hurling
hurled

hurrah or **hurray**

hurricane noun
hurricanes

hurriedly

hurry verb
hurries
hurrying
hurried

hurry noun
hurries

hurt verb
hurts
hurting
hurt

hurt noun

hurtle verb
hurtles
hurtling
hurtled

husband noun
husbands

hush verb
hushes
hushing
hushed

hush noun

husk noun
husks

huskiness

husky adjective
huskier
huskiest
huskily

husky noun
huskies

hustle verb
hustles
hustling
hustled

hutch noun
hutches

hyacinth noun
hyacinths

hybrid noun
hybrids

a

hydrangea noun
hydrangeas

b

hydrant noun
hydrants

c

hydraulic adjective
hydraulically

d

hydroelectric

e

hydrofoil noun
hydrofoils

f

hydrogen

g

hydrophobia

h

hyena noun
hyenas

i

hygiene

hygienic adjective
hygienically

j

hymn noun
hymns

k

hyperactive

hypermarket noun
hypermarkets

l

m

hyphen noun
hyphens

n

hyphenated

o

hypnosis

hypnotism

p

hypnotist

q

hypnotize verb
hypnotizes
hypnotizing
hypnotized

r

s

hypocrisy

t

hypocrite noun
hypocrites

u

hypocritical adjective
hypocritically

v

hypodermic

w

hypotenuse noun
hypotenuses

x

hypothermia

y

hypothesis noun
hypotheses

hypothetical
adjective
hypothetically

hysteria

hysterical adjective
hysterically

hysterics plural noun

Ii

-i
Most nouns ending in
-i, e.g. **ski**, **taxi**, have
plurals ending in -is,
e.g. **skis**, **taxis**.

-ible
See the note at **-able**.

-ic and **-ically**
Most adjectives
ending in -ic have
adverbs ending in
-ically, e.g. **heroic** -
heroically, **scientific**
- **scientifically**. An
exception is **public**,
which has an adverb -
publicly.

ice noun
ices

ice verb
ices
icing
iced

iceberg noun
icebergs

ice cream noun
ice creams

icicle noun
icicles

icing

icon noun
icons

icy adjective
icier
iciest
icily

I'd verb

idea noun
ideas

ideal adjective
ideally

ideal noun
ideals

identical adjective
identically

identification

identify verb
identifies
identifying
identified

identity noun
identities

idiocy noun
idiocies

idiom noun
idioms

idiomatic

idiot noun
idiots

idiotic adjective
idiotically

idle* adjective
idler
idlest
idly

z

★ **Idle** means 'lazy'. **!** idol.

idle *verb*
idles
idling
idled

idol* *noun*
idols

idolatry

idolize *verb*
idolizes
idolizing
idolized

-ie-
See the note at **-ei-**.

igloo *noun*
igloos

igneous

ignite *verb*
ignites
igniting
ignited

ignition

ignorance

ignorant

ignore *verb*
ignores
ignoring
ignored

I'll *verb*

ill

illegal *adjective*
illegally

illegible *adjective*
illegibly

illegitimate

illiteracy

illiterate

illness *noun*
illnesses

illogical *adjective*
illogically

illuminate *verb*
illuminates
illuminating
illuminated

illumination *noun*
illuminations

illusion *noun*
illusions

illustrate *verb*
illustrates
illustrating
illustrated

illustration *noun*
illustrations

illustrious

I'm *verb*

image *noun*
images

imagery

imaginable

imaginary

imagination *noun*
imaginations

imaginative *adjective*
imaginatively

imagine *verb*
imagines
imagining
imagined

imam☆ *noun*
imams

imbecile *noun*
imbeciles

imitate *verb*
imitates
imitating
imitated

imitation *noun*
imitations

imitator *noun*
imitators

immature

immaturity

immediate *adjective*
immediately

immense *adjective*
immensely

immensity

immerse *verb*
immerses
immersing
immersed

immersion

immigrant *noun*
immigrants

immigrate *verb*
immigrates
immigrating
immigrated

immigration

immobile

immobility

immobilize *verb*
immobilizes
immobilizing
immobilized

immoral *adjective*
immorally

immorality

immortal

immortality

immune

immunity *noun*
immunities

immunization

immunize *verb*
immunizes
immunizing
immunized

imp *noun*
imps

impish

. . . .

★ An **idol** is someone people admire. **!** idle.
☆ A Muslim religious leader.

a
b
c
d
e
f
g
h
i
j
k
l
m
n
o
p
q
r
s
t
u
v
w
x
y
z

impact noun
impacts

impair verb
impairs
impairing
impaired

impale verb
impales
impaling
impaled

impartial adjective
impartially

impartiality

impassable

impatience

impatient adjective
impatiently

impede verb
impedes
impeding
impeded

imperative

imperceptible adjective
imperceptibly

imperfect adjective
imperfectly

imperfection noun
imperfections

imperial

impersonal adjective
impersonally

impersonate verb
impersonates
impersonating
impersonated

impersonation noun
impersonations

impersonator noun
impersonators

impertinence

impertinent adjective
impertinently

implement verb
implements
implementing
implemented

implement noun
implements

implication noun
implications

implore verb
implores
imploring
implored

imply verb
implies
implying
implied

impolite adjective
impolitely

import verb
imports
importing
imported

import noun
imports

importance

important adjective
importantly

importer noun
importers

impose verb
imposes
imposing
imposed

imposition noun
impositions

impossibility

impossible adjective
impossibly

impostor noun
impostors

impracticable

impractical

impress verb
impresses
impressing
impressed

impression noun
impressions

impressive adjective
impressively

imprison verb
imprisons
imprisoning
imprisoned

imprisonment

improbability

improbable adjective
improbably

impromptu

improper adjective
improperly

impropriety noun
improprieties

improve verb
improves
improving
improved

improvement noun
improvements

improvisation noun
improvisations

improvise verb
improvises
improvising
improvised

impudence

impudent adjective
impudently

impulse noun
impulses

impulsive adjective
impulsively

impure
impurity *adjective*
impurities

in-
in- makes words with
the meaning 'not', e.g.
inedible, **infertile**.
There is a fixed
number of these, and
you cannot freely add
in- as you can with
un-. *in-* changes to *il-*
or *im-* before certain
sounds, e.g. **illogical**,
impossible.

inability
inaccessible
inaccuracy *noun*
inaccuracies
inaccurate *adjective*
inaccurately
inaction
inactive
inactivity
inadequacy
inadequate *adjective*
inadequately
inanimate
inappropriate
adjective
inappropriately
inattention
inattentive
inaudible *adjective*
inaudibly
incapable
incapacity
incendiary
incense *noun*
incense *verb*
incenses
incensing
incensed

incentive *noun*
incentives
incessant *adjective*
incessantly
inch *noun*
inches
incident *noun*
incidents
incidental *adjective*
incidentally
incinerator *noun*
incinerators
inclination *noun*
inclinations
incline *verb*
inclines
inclining
inclined
incline *noun*
inclines
include *verb*
includes
including
included
inclusion
inclusive
income *noun*
incomes
incompatible
incompetence
incompetent
adjective
incompetently
incomplete *adjective*
incompletely
incomprehensible
adjective
incomprehensibly
incongruity
incongruous
adjective
incongruously

inconsiderate
adjective
inconsiderately
inconsistency *noun*
inconsistencies
inconsistent
adjective
inconsistently
inconspicuous
adjective
inconspicuously
inconvenience
inconvenient
adjective
inconveniently
incorporate *verb*
incorporates
incorporating
incorporated
incorporation
incorrect *adjective*
incorrectly
increase *verb*
increases
increasing
increased
increase *noun*
increases
increasingly
incredible *adjective*
incredibly
incredulity
incredulous
incubate *verb*
incubates
incubating
incubated
incubation
incubator *noun*
incubators
indebted

in

indecency
indecent *adjective*
indecently
indeed
indefinite *adjective*
indefinitely
indelible *adjective*
indelibly
indent *verb*
indents
indenting
indented
indentation
independence
independent
adjective
independently
index *noun*
indexes
Indian *adjective* and
noun
Indians
indicate *verb*
indicates
indicating
indicated
indication *noun*
indications
indicative
indicator *noun*
indicators
indifference
indifferent *adjective*
indifferently
indigestible
indigestion
indignant *adjective*
indignantly
indignation
indigo
indirect *adjective*
indirectly

indispensable
adjective
indispensably
indistinct *adjective*
indistinctly
indistinguishable
individual *adjective*
individually
individual *noun*
individuals
individuality
indoctrinate *verb*
indoctrinates
indoctrinating
indoctrinated
indoctrination
indoor *adjective*
indoors *adverb*
induce *verb*
induces
inducing
induced
inducement *noun*
inducements
indulge *verb*
indulges
indulging
indulged
indulgence *noun*
indulgences
indulgent *adjective*
industrial
industrialist *noun*
industrialists
industrialization
industrialize *verb*
industrializes
industrializing
industrialized
industrious *adjective*
industriously
industry *noun*
industries

ineffective *adjective*
ineffectively
ineffectual *adjective*
ineffectually
inefficiency *noun*
inefficiencies
inefficient *adjective*
inefficiently
inequality *noun*
inequalities
inert
inertia
inevitability
inevitable *adjective*
inevitably
inexhaustible
inexpensive *adjective*
inexpensively
inexperience
inexperienced
inexplicable *adjective*
inexplicably
infallibility
infallible *adjective*
infallibly
infamous *adjective*
infamously
infamy
infancy
infant *noun*
infants
infantile
infantry
infect *verb*
infects
infecting
infected
infection *noun*
infections
infectious *adjective*
infectiously

infer *verb*
  infers
  inferring
  inferred

inference *noun*
  inferences

inferior *adjective and noun*
  inferiors

inferiority

infernal *adjective*
  infernally

inferno *noun*
  infernos

infested

infiltrate *verb*
  infiltrates
  infiltrating
  infiltrated

infiltration

infinite *adjective*
  infinitely

infinitive *noun*
  infinitives

infinity

infirm

infirmary *noun*
  infirmaries

infirmity

inflame *verb*
  inflames
  inflaming
  inflamed

inflammable

inflammation *noun*
  inflammations

inflammatory

inflatable

inflate *verb*
  inflates
  inflating
  inflated

inflation

inflect *verb*
  inflects
  inflecting
  inflected

inflection *noun*
  inflections

inflexibility

inflexible *adjective*
  inflexibly

inflict *verb*
  inflicts
  inflicting
  inflicted

influence *verb*
  influences
  influencing
  influenced

influence *noun*
  influences

influential *adjective*
  influentially

influenza

inform *verb*
  informs
  informing
  informed

informal *adjective*
  informally

informality

informant *noun*
  informants

information

informative

informed

informer *noun*
  informers

infrequency

infrequent *adjective*
  infrequently

infuriate *verb*
  infuriates
  infuriating
  infuriated

-ing
-ing makes present participles and nouns, e.g. **hunt - hunting**. You normally drop an e at the end, e.g. **change - changing**, **smoke - smoking**. An exception is **ageing**. Words ending in a consonant following a single vowel double the consonant, e.g. **run - running**.

---

ingenious *adjective*
  ingeniously

ingenuity

ingot *noun*
  ingots

ingrained

ingredient *noun*
  ingredients

inhabit *verb*
  inhabits
  inhabiting
  inhabited

inhabitant *noun*
  inhabitants

inhale *verb*
  inhales
  inhaling
  inhaled

inhaler *noun*
  inhalers

inherent *adjective*
  inherently

inherit *verb*
  inherits
  inheriting
  inherited

inheritance

inhibited

in

inhospitable *adjective*
inhospitably

inhuman *adjective*

inhumanity *noun*

initial *adjective*
initially

initial *noun*
initials

initiate *verb*
initiates
initiating
initiated

initiation

initiative *noun*
initiatives

inject *verb*
injects
injecting
injected

injection *noun*
injections

injure *verb*
injures
injuring
injured

injurious *adjective*
injuriously

injury *noun*
injuries

injustice *noun*
injustices

ink *noun*
inks

inkling *noun*
inklings

inky *adjective*
inkier
inkiest

inland

inlet *noun*
inlets

inn *noun*
inns

innkeeper *noun*
innkeepers

inner

innermost

innings *noun*
innings

innocence

innocent *adjective*
innocently

innocuous *adjective*
innocuously

innovation *noun*
innovations

innovative

innovator *noun*
innovators

innumerable

inoculate *verb*
inoculates
inoculating
inoculated

inoculation

input *verb*
inputs
inputting
input

input *noun*
inputs

inquest *noun*
inquests

inquire *verb*
inquires
inquiring
inquired

inquiry★ *noun*
inquiries

inquisitive *adjective*
inquisitively

insane *adjective*
insanely

insanitary

insanity

inscribe *verb*
inscribes
inscribing
inscribed

inscription *noun*
inscriptions

insect *noun*
insects

insecticide *noun*
insecticides

insecure *adjective*
insecurely

insecurity

insensitive *adjective*
insensitively

insensitivity

inseparable *adjective*
inseparably

insert *verb*
inserts
inserting
inserted

insertion *noun*
insertions

inshore *adjective and adverb*

inside *noun*
insides

inside *adverb, adjective, and preposition*

insight *noun*
insights

insignificance

insignificant *adjective*
insignificantly

insincere *adjective*
insincerely

insincerity

....

★ An **inquiry** is an official investigation. **!enquiry**.

insist *verb*
insists
insisting
insisted

insistence

insistent *adjective*
insistently

insolence

insolent *adjective*
insolently

insolubility

insoluble *adjective*
insolubly

insomnia

inspect *verb*
inspects
inspecting
inspected

inspection *noun*
inspections

inspector *noun*
inspectors

inspiration

inspire *verb*
inspires
inspiring
inspired

install *verb*
installs
installing
installed

installation *noun*
installations

instalment *noun*
instalments

instance *noun*
instances

instant *adjective*
instantly

instant *noun*
instants

instantaneous
adjective
instantaneously

instead

instep *noun*
insteps

instinct *noun*
instincts

instinctive *adjective*
instinctively

institute *verb*
institutes
instituting
instituted

institute *noun*
institutes

institution *noun*
institutions

instruct *verb*
instructs
instructing
instructed

instruction *noun*
instructions

instrument *noun*
instruments

instrumental

insufficient *adjective*
insufficiently

insulate *verb*
insulates
insulating
insulated

insulation

insulin

insult *verb*
insults
insulting
insulted

insult *noun*
insults

insurance

insure *verb*
insures
insuring
insured

intact

intake *noun*
intakes

integer *noun*
integers

integral *adjective*
integrally

integrate *verb*
integrates
integrating
integrated

integration

integrity

intellect *noun*
intellects

intellectual *adjective*
intellectually

intellectual *noun*
intellectuals

intelligence

intelligent *adjective*
intelligently

intelligibility

intelligible *adjective*
intelligibly

intend *verb*
intends
intending
intended

intense *adjective*
intensely

intensification

intensify *verb*
intensifies
intensifying
intensified

intensity *noun*
intensities

intensive *adjective*
intensively

intent *adjective*
intently

intent *noun*
intents

intention *noun*
intentions

in

a

intentional *adjective*
intentionally

b

interact *verb*
interacts
interacting
interacted

c

interaction

d

interactive

e

intercept *verb*
intercepts
intercepting
intercepted

f

interception

g

interchange *noun*
interchanges

h

interchangeable
adjective
interchangeably

i

intercom *noun*
intercoms

j

intercourse

k

interest *verb*
interests
interesting
interested

l

interest *noun*
interests

m

interface *noun*
interfaces

n

interfere *verb*
interferes
interfering
interfered

o

interference

p

interior *noun*
interiors

q

interjection *noun*
interjections

r

interlock *verb*
interlocks
interlocking
interlocked

s

interlude *noun*
interludes

t

intermediate

u

v

w

x

y

z

interminable
adjective
interminably

intermission *noun*
intermissions

intermittent *adjective*
intermittently

intern *verb*
interns
interning
interned

internal *adjective*
internally

international
adjective
internationally

internee

internment

internet

interplanetary

interpret *verb*
interprets
interpreting
interpreted

interpretation *noun*
interpretations

interpreter *noun*
interpreters

interrogate *verb*
interrogates
interrogating
interrogated

interrogation *noun*

interrogative

interrogator *noun*
interrogators

interrupt *verb*
interrupts
interrupting
interrupted

interruption *noun*
interruptions

intersect *verb*
intersects
intersecting
intersected

intersection *noun*
intersections

interval *noun*
intervals

intervene *verb*
intervenes
intervening
intervened

intervention *noun*
interventions

interview *noun*
interviews

interview *verb*
interviews
interviewing
interviewed

interviewer *noun*
interviewers

intestinal

intestine

intimacy

intimate *adjective*
intimately

intimate *verb*
intimates
intimating
intimated

intimation *noun*
intimations

intimidate *verb*
intimidates
intimidating
intimidated

intimidation

into *preposition*

intolerable *adjective*
intolerably

intolerance

intolerant *adjective*
intolerantly

intonation *noun*
intonations

intoxicate *verb*
intoxicates
intoxicating
intoxicated

intoxication

intransitive

intrepid *adjective*
intrepidly

intricacy *noun*
intricacies

intricate *adjective*
intricately

intrigue *verb*
intrigues
intriguing
intrigued

introduce *verb*
introduces
introducing
introduced

introduction *noun*
introductions

introductory

intrude *verb*
intrudes
intruding
intruded

intruder *noun*
intruders

intrusion *noun*
intrusions

intrusive *adjective*
intrusively

intuition

intuitive *adjective*
intuitively

Inuit *noun*
Inuit *or* Inuits

inundate *verb*
inundates
inundating
inundated

inundation *noun*
inundations

invade *verb*
invades
invading
invaded

invader *noun*
invaders

invalid *noun*
invalids

invalid *adjective*
invalidly

invaluable

invariable *adjective*
invariably

invasion *noun*
invasions

invent *verb*
invents
inventing
invented

invention *noun*
inventions

inventive *adjective*
inventively

inventor *noun*
inventors

inverse *noun and
adjective*
inversely

inversion *noun*
inversions

invert *verb*
inverts
inverting
inverted

invertebrate *noun*
invertebrates

invest *verb*
invests
investing
invested

investigate *verb*
investigates
investigating
investigated

investigation *noun*
investigations

investigator *noun*
investigators

investiture *noun*
investitures

investment *noun*
investments

investor *noun*
investors

invigilate *verb*
invigilates
invigilating
invigilated

invigilation

invigilator *noun*
invigilators

invigorate *verb*
invigorates
invigorating
invigorated

invincible

invisibility

invisible *adjective*
invisibly

invitation *noun*
invitations

invite *verb*
invites
inviting
invited

invoice *noun*
invoices

involuntary

involve *verb*
involves
involving
involved

involvement

inward adjective
inwardly

inwards adverb

iodine

ion noun
ions

iris noun
irises

iron noun
irons

iron verb
irons
ironing
ironed

ironic adjective
ironically

ironmonger noun
ironmongers

ironmongery noun

irony noun
ironies

irrational adjective
irrationally

irregular adjective
irregularly

irregularity noun
irregularities

irrelevance

irrelevant adjective
irrelevantly

irresistible adjective
irresistibly

irresponsible adjective
irresponsibly

irresponsibility noun

irreverence

irreverent adjective
irreverently

irrigate verb
irrigates
irrigating
irrigated

irrigation

irritability

irritable adjective
irritably

irritant

irritate verb
irritates
irritating
irritated

irritation noun
irritations

-ish

-ish makes words
meaning 'rather' or
'fairly', e.g. soft -
softish. You normally
drop an e at the end,
e.g. blue - bluish.
Words ending in a
consonant following a
single vowel double
the consonant, e.g.
fat - fattish.

Islam

Islamic

island noun
islands

islander noun
islanders

isle★ noun
isles

isn't verb

isobar noun
isobars

isolate verb
isolates
isolating
isolated

isolation

isosceles adjective

isotope noun
isotopes

issue verb
issues
issuing
issued

issue noun
issues

isthmus noun
isthmuses

italics

itch verb
itches
itching
itched

itch noun
itches

itchy adjective
itchier
itchiest

item noun
items

itinerary noun
itineraries

it'll verb

its☆

it's○ verb

itself

I've verb

ivory adjective and
noun
ivories

ivy

- -

★ An **isle** is a small island. **!** aisle.
☆ You use **its** in e.g. *the cat licked its paw.* **!** it's.
○ You use **it's** in *it's* (it is) *raining* and *it's* (it has) *been raining.* **!** its.

-ize and **-ise**
You can use *-ize* or *-ise* at the end of many verbs, e.g. **realize**, **realise**, **privatize** or **privatise**. This book prefers *-ize*, but some words have to be spelt *-ise*, e.g. **advertise**, **exercise**, **supervise**. Check each spelling if you are not sure.

Jj

jab *verb*
jabs
jabbing
jabbed

jab *noun*
jabs

jabber *verb*
jabbers
jabbering
jabbered

jack *noun*
jacks

jack *verb*
jacks
jacking
jacked

jackal *noun*
jackals

jackass *noun*
jackasses

jackdaw *noun*
jackdaws

jacket *noun*
jackets

jack-in-the-box *noun*
jack-in-the-boxes

jackknife *verb*
jackknifes
jackknifing
jackknifed

jackpot *noun*
jackpots

jacuzzi *noun*
jacuzzis

jade *noun*

jaded

jagged

jaguar *noun*
jaguars

jail *noun*
jails

jail *verb*
jails
jailing
jailed

jailer *noun*
jailers

Jain* *noun*
Jains

jam *noun*
jams

jam *verb*
jams
jamming
jammed

jamboree *noun*
jamborees

jammy *adjective*
jammier
jammiest

jangle *verb*
jangles
jangling
jangled

January *noun*
Januaries

jar *noun*
jars

jar *verb*
jars
jarring
jarred

jaundice

jaunt *noun*
jaunts

jauntiness

jaunty *adjective*
jauntier
jauntiest
jauntily

javelin *noun*
javelins

jaw *noun*
jaws

jay *noun*
jays

jazz

jazzy *adjective*
jazzier
jazziest

jealous *adjective*
jealously

jealousy

jeans

Jeep *noun*
Jeeps

jeer *verb*
jeers
jeering
jeered

jellied

jelly *noun*
jellies

jellyfish *noun*
jellyfish

- -

★ A member of an Indian religion.

a
b
c
d
e
f
g
h
i
j
k
l
m
n
o
p
q
r
s
t
u
v
w
x
y
z

a
b
c
d
e
f
g
h

j

k
l
m
n
o
p
q
r
s
t
u
v
w
x
y
z

jerk verb
jerks
jerking
jerked

jerk noun
jerks

jerky adjective
jerkier
jerkiest
jerkily

jersey noun
jerseys

jest verb
jests
jesting
jested

jest noun
jests

jester noun
jesters

jet noun
jets

jet verb
jets
jetting
jetted

jet-propelled

jetty noun
jetties

Jew noun
Jews

jewel noun
jewels

jewelled

jeweller noun
jewellers

jewellery

Jewish

jib noun
jibs

jiffy noun
jiffies

jig noun
jigs

jig verb
jigs
jigging
jigged

jigsaw noun
jigsaws

jingle verb
jingles
jingling
jingled

jingle noun
jingles

job noun
jobs

jobcentre noun
jobcentres

jockey noun
jockeys

jodhpurs plural noun

jog verb
jogs
jogging
jogged

jogger noun
joggers

jogtrot noun
jogtrots

join verb
joins
joining
joined

join noun
joins

joiner noun
joiners

joinery

joint noun
joints

joint adjective
jointly

joist noun
joists

jojoba

joke verb
jokes
joking
joked

joke noun
jokes

joker noun
jokers

jollity

jolly adjective
jollier
jolliest

jolly adverb

jolly verb
jollies
jollying
jollied

jolt verb
jolts
jolting
jolted

jolt noun
jolts

jostle verb
jostles
jostling
jostled

jot verb
jots
jotting
jotted

jot noun
jots

jotter noun
jotters

joule noun
joules

journal noun
journals

journalism

journalist noun
journalists

journey noun
journeys

journey verb
journeys
journeying
journeyed

joust verb
jousts
jousting
jousted

jovial adjective
jovially

joviality

joy noun
joys

joyful adjective
joyfully

joyous adjective
joyously

joyride noun
joyrides

joystick noun
joysticks

jubilant adjective
jubilantly

jubilation

jubilee noun
jubilees

Judaism

judge verb
judges
judging
judged

judge noun
judges

judgement noun
judgements

judicial adjective
judicially

judicious adjective
judiciously

judo

jug noun
jugs

juggernaut noun
juggernauts

juggle verb
juggles
juggling
juggled

juggler noun
jugglers

juice* noun
juices

juicy adjective
juicier
juiciest

jukebox noun
jukeboxes

July noun
Julys

jumble verb
jumbles
jumbling
jumbled

jumble noun

jumbo jet noun
jumbo jets

jump verb
jumps
jumping
jumped

jump noun
jumps

jumper noun
jumpers

jumpy adjective
jumpier
jumpiest

junction noun
junctions

June noun
Junes

jungle noun
jungles

jungly adjective
junglier
jungliest

junior adjective and noun
juniors

junk noun
junks

junket noun
junkets

juror noun
jurors

jury noun
juries

just adjective
justly

just adverb

justice noun
justices

justifiable adjective
justifiably

justification

justify verb
justifies
justifying
justified

jut verb
juts
jutting
jutted

juvenile

Kk

kaleidoscope noun
kaleidoscopes

kangaroo noun
kangaroos

karaoke

karate

★ **Juice** is the liquid from fruit. **!** deuce.

a

kayak *noun*
kayaks

b

kebab *noun*
kebabs

c

keel *noun*
keels

d

keel *verb*
keels
keeling
keeled

e

f

keen *adjective*
keener
keenest
keenly

g

h

keenness

i

keep *verb*
keeps
keeping
kept

j

k

keep *noun*
keeps

l

keeper *noun*
keepers

m

keg *noun*
kegs

n

o

kennel *noun*
kennels

p

kept see **keep**

q

kerb* *noun*
kerbs

r

kerbstone *noun*
kerbstones

s

kernel☆ *noun*
kerneis

t

kestrel *noun*
kestrels

u

ketchup

v

kettle *noun*
kettles

w

x

kettledrum *noun*
kettledrums

key○ *noun*
keys

keyboard *noun*
keyboards

keyhole *noun*
keyholes

keynote *noun*
keynotes

khaki

kibbutz *noun*
kibbutzim

kick *verb*
kicks
kicking
kicked

kick *noun*
kicks

kick-off *noun*
kick-offs

kid *noun*
kids

kid *verb*
kids
kidding
kidded

kidnap *verb*
kidnaps
kidnapping
kidnapped

kidnapper *noun*
kidnappers

kidney *noun*
kidneys

kill *verb*
kills
killing
killed

killer *noun*
killers

kiln *noun*
kilns

kilo *noun*
kilos

kilogram *noun*
kilograms

kilometre *noun*
kilometres

kilowatt *noun*
kilowatts

kilt *noun*
kilts

kin

kind *adjective*
kinder
kindest
kindly

kind *noun*
kinds

kindergarten *noun*
kindergartens

kind-hearted

kindle *verb*
kindles
kindling
kindled

kindliness

kindling

kindly *adjective*
kindlier
kindliest

kindness

kinetic

king *noun*
kings

kingdom *noun*
kingdoms

kingfisher *noun*
kingfishers

kingly

y

z

★ A **kerb** is the edge of a pavement. **!** curb.
☆ **Kernel** is part of a nut. **!** colonel.
○ A **key** is a device for opening a lock. **!** quay.

134

kink *noun*
kinks

kinky *adjective*
kinkier
kinkiest

kiosk *noun*
kiosks

kipper *noun*
kippers

kiss *verb*
kisses
kissing
kissed

kiss *noun*
kisses

kit *noun*
kits

kitchen *noun*
kitchens

kite *noun*
kites

kitten *noun*
kittens

kitty *noun*
kitties

kiwi *noun*
kiwis

knack

knapsack *noun*
knapsacks

knave *noun*
knaves

knead* *verb*
kneads
kneading
kneaded

knee *noun*
knees

kneecap *noun*
kneecaps

kneel *verb*
kneels
kneeling
knelt

knew☆ see **know**

knickers *plural noun*

knife *noun*
knives

knife *verb*
knifes
knifing
knifed

knight◊ *noun*
knights

knight *verb*
knights
knighting
knighted

knighthood *noun*
knighthoods

knit *verb*
knits
knitting
knitted

knives see **knife**

knob *noun*
knobs

knobbly *adjective*
knobblier
knobbliest

knock *verb*
knocks
knocking
knocked

knock *noun*
knocks

knocker *noun*
knockers

knockout *noun*
knockouts

knot *noun*
knots

knot *verb*
knots
knotting
knotted

knotty *adjective*
knottier
knottiest

know *verb*
knows
knowing
knew
known

know-all *noun*
know-alls

know-how

knowing *adjective*
knowingly

knowledge

knowledgeable
adjective
knowledgeably

knuckle *noun*
knuckles

koala *noun*
koalas

kookaburra *noun*
kookaburras

Koran

kosher

kung fu

Ll

label *noun*
labels

....

★ To **knead** is to work a mixture into a dough. ! **need**.
☆ **Knew** is the past tense of know. ! **new**.
◊ A **knight** is a soldier in old times. ! **night**.

a
b
c
d
e
f
g
h
i
j
k
l
m
n
o
p
q
r
s
t
u
v
w
x
y
z

135

la

label *verb*
labels
labelling
labelled

laboratory *noun*
laboratories

laborious *adjective*
laboriously

labour *noun*
labours

labourer *noun*
labourers

Labrador *noun*
Labradors

laburnum *noun*
laburnums

labyrinth *noun*
labyrinths

lace *noun*
laces

lace *verb*
laces
lacing
laced

lack *verb*
lacks
lacking
lacked

lack *noun*

lacquer

lacrosse

lad *noun*
lads

ladder *noun*
ladders

laden

ladle *noun*
ladles

lady *noun*
ladies

ladybird *noun*
ladybirds

ladylike

ladyship *noun*
ladyships

lag *verb*
lags
lagging
lagged

lager *noun*
lagers

lagoon *noun*
lagoons

laid see **lay**

lain see **lie**

lair *noun*
lairs

lake *noun*
lakes

lama *noun*
lamas

lamb *noun*
lambs

lame *adjective*
lamer
lamest
lamely

lameness

lament *verb*
laments
lamenting
lamented

lament *noun*
laments

lamentation *noun*
lamentations

laminated

lamp *noun*
lamps

lamp-post *noun*
lamp-posts

lampshade *noun*
lampshades

lance *noun*
lances

lance corporal *noun*
lance corporals

land *noun*
lands

land *verb*
lands
landing
landed

landing *noun*
landings

landlady *noun*
landladies

landlord *noun*
landlords

landmark *noun*
landmarks

landowner *noun*
landowners

landscape *noun*
landscapes

landslide *noun*
landslides

lane *noun*
lanes

language *noun*
languages

lankiness

lanky *adjective*
lankier
lankiest

lantern *noun*
lanterns

lap *verb*
laps
lapping
lapped

lap *noun*
laps

lapel *noun*
lapels

lapse *verb*
lapses
lapsing
lapsed

lapse *noun*
lapses

laptop *noun*
laptops

lapwing *noun*
lapwings

larch *noun*
larches

lard

larder *noun*
larders

large *adjective*
larger
largest
largely

largeness

lark *noun*
larks

lark *verb*
larks
larking
larked

larva *noun*
larvae

lasagne *noun*
lasagnes

laser *noun*
lasers

lash *verb*
lashes
lashing
lashed

lash *noun*
lashes

lass *noun*
lasses

lasso *noun*
lassos

lasso *verb*
lassoes
lassoing
lassoed

last *adjective and
adverb*
lastly

last *verb*
lasts
lasting
lasted

last *noun*

latch *noun*
latches

late *adjective and
adverb*
later
latest

lately

lateness

latent

lateral *adjective*
laterally

lathe *noun*
lathes

lather *noun*
lathers

Latin

latitude *noun*
latitudes

latter *adjective*
latterly

lattice *noun*
lattices

laugh *verb*
laughs
laughing
laughed

laugh *noun*
laughs

laughable *adjective*
laughably

laughter

launch *verb*
launches
launching
launched

launch *noun*
launches

launder *verb*
launders
laundering
laundered

launderette *noun*
launderettes

laundry *noun*
laundries

laurel *noun*
laurels

lava

lavatory *noun*
lavatories

lavender

lavish *adjective*
lavishly

law *noun*
laws

lawcourt *noun*
lawcourts

lawful *adjective*
lawfully

lawless *adjective*
lawlessly

lawn *noun*
lawns

lawnmower *noun*
lawnmowers

lawsuit *noun*
lawsuits

lawyer *noun*
lawyers

lax *adjective*
laxly

laxative *noun*
laxatives

lay *verb*
lays
laying
laid

lay see **lie**

layabout *noun*
layabouts

layer *noun*
layers

layman *noun*
laymen

layout *noun*
layouts

laze *verb*
lazes
lazing
lazed

laziness

lazy *adjective*
lazier
laziest
lazily

lead *verb*
leads
leading
led

lead* *noun*
leads

leader *noun*
leaders

leadership

leaf *noun*
leaves

leaflet *noun*
leaflets

leafy *adjective*
leafier
leafiest

league *noun*
leagues

leak *verb*
leaks
leaking
leaked

leak☆ *noun*
leaks

leakage *noun*
leakages

leaky *adjective*
leakier
leakiest

lean *verb*
leans
leaning
leaned *or* leant

lean *adjective*
leaner
leanest

leap *verb*
leaps
leaping
leapt

leap *noun*
leaps

leapfrog

leap year *noun*
leap years

learn *verb*
learns
learning
learnt *or* learned

learned° *adjective*

learner *noun*
learners

lease *noun*
leases

leash *noun*
leashes

least *adjective and noun*

leather *noun*
leathers

leathery

leave *verb*
leaves
leaving
left

leave *noun*

leaves see **leaf**

lectern *noun*
lecterns

lecture *verb*
lectures
lecturing
lectured

lecture *noun*
lectures

lecturer *noun*
lecturers

led see **lead**

ledge *noun*
ledges

lee

leek✛ *noun*
leeks

leer *verb*
leers
leering
leered

leeward

left *adjective and noun*

left see **leave**

left-handed

leftovers *plural noun*

leg *noun*
legs

legacy *noun*
legacies

....

* A **lead** (pronounced *leed*) is a cord for leading a dog. **Lead** (pronounced *led*) is a metal.
☆ A **leak** is a hole or crack that liquid or gas can get through. **!leek**.
° Pronounced *ler-nid*.
✛ A **leek** is a vegetable. **!leak**.

a
b
c
d
e
f
g
h
i
j
k
l
m
n
o
p
q
r
s
t
u
v
w
x
y
z

legal *adjective*
legally

legality

legalize *verb*
legalizes
legalizing
legalized

legend *noun*
legends

legendary

legibility

legible *adjective*
legibly

legion *noun*
legions

legislate *verb*
legislates
legislating
legislated

legislation

legislator *noun*
legislators

legitimacy

legitimate *adjective*
legitimately

leisure

leisurely

lemon *noun*
lemons

lemonade *noun*
lemonades

lend *verb*
lends
lending
lent

length *noun*
lengths

lengthen *verb*
lengthens
lengthening
lengthened

lengthways *adverb*

lengthwise *adverb*

lengthy *adjective*
lengthier
lengthiest
lengthily

lenience

lenient *adjective*
leniently

lens *noun*
lenses

Lent*

lent see **lend**

lentil *noun*
lentils

leopard *noun*
leopards

leotard *noun*
leotards

leper *noun*
lepers

leprosy

less

lessen☆ *verb*
lessens
lessening
lessened

lesser

lesson○ *noun*
lessons

lest *conjunction*

let *verb*
lets
letting
let

-let
-*let* makes nouns meaning 'a small version of', e.g. **booklet**, **piglet**. It also makes words for pieces of jewellery, e.g. **anklet** (worn on the ankle), **bracelet** (from a French word *bras* meaning 'arm')

---

lethal *adjective*
lethally

let's *verb*

letter *noun*
letters

letter box *noun*
letter boxes

lettering

lettuce *noun*
lettuces

leukaemia

level *verb*
levels
levelling
levelled

level *adjective* and *noun*
levels

lever *noun*
levers

leverage

liability *noun*
liabilities

liable

liar *noun*
liars

liberal *adjective*
liberally

★ **Lent** is the Christian time of fasting. **I lent**.
☆ To **lessen** something is to make it less. **I lessen**.
○ A **lesson** is a period of learning. **I lessen**.

a b c d e f g h i j k l m n o p q r s t u v w x y z

li

liberate *verb*
liberates
liberating
liberated

liberation

liberty *noun*
liberties

librarian *noun*
librarians

librarianship

library *noun*
libraries

licence *noun*
licences

license *verb*
licenses
licensing
licensed

lichen *noun*
lichens

lick *verb*
licks
licking
licked

lick *noun*
licks

lid *noun*
lids

lie* *verb*
lies
lying
lay
lain

lie☆ *verb*
lies
lying
lied

lie *noun*
lies

lieutenant *noun*
lieutenants

life *noun*
lives

lifebelt *noun*
lifebelts

lifeboat *noun*
lifeboats

life cycle *noun*
life cycles

lifeguard *noun*
lifeguards

lifeless *adjective*
lifelessly

lifelike

lifelong

lifestyle *noun*
lifestyles

lifetime *noun*
lifetimes

lift *verb*
lifts
lifting
lifted

lift *noun*
lifts

lift-off *noun*
lift-offs

light *adjective*
lighter
lightest
lightly

light *verb*
lights
lighting
lit *or* lighted

light *noun*
lights

lighten *verb*
lightens
lightening
lightened

lighter *noun*
lighters

lighthouse *noun*
lighthouses

lighting

lightning

lightweight

like *verb*
likes
liking
liked

like *preposition*

likeable

likely *adjective*
likelier
likeliest

liken *verb*
likens
likening
likened

likeness *noun*
likenesses

likewise

liking *noun*
likings

lilac *noun*
lilacs

lily *noun*
lilies

limb *noun*
limbs

limber *verb*
limbers
limbering
limbered

lime *noun*
limes

limelight

limerick *noun*
limericks

limestone

★ As in *to lie on the bed.*
☆ Meaning 'to say something untrue'.

limit *noun*
limits

limit *verb*
limits
limiting
limited

limitation *noun*
limitations

limited

limitless

limp *adjective*
limper
limpest
limply

limp *verb*
limps
limping
limped

limp *noun*
limps

limpet *noun*
limpets

line *noun*
lines

line *verb*
lines
lining
lined

linen

liner *noun*
liners

linesman *noun*
linesmen

-ling
-ling makes words for small things, e.g. **duckling**.
-----

linger *verb*
lingers
lingering
lingered

lingerie

linguist *noun*
linguists

linguistic

linguistics

lining *noun*
linings

link *verb*
links
linking
linked

link *noun*
links

lino

linoleum

lint

lion *noun*
lions

lioness *noun*
lionesses

lip *noun*
lips

lip-read *verb*
lip-reads
lip-reading
lip-read

lipstick *noun*
lipsticks

liquid *adjective and noun*
liquids

liquidizer *noun*
liquidizers

liquor *noun*
liquors

liquorice

lisp *noun*
lisps

lisp *verb*
lisps
lisping
lisped

list *noun*
lists

list *verb*
lists
listing
listed

listen *verb*
listens
listening
listened

listener *noun*
listeners

listless *adjective*
listlessly

lit *see* **light**

literacy

literal *adjective*
literally

literary

literate

literature

litmus

litre *noun*
litres

litter *noun*
litters

litter *verb*
litters
littering
littered

little★ *adjective and adverb*
less
least

live *verb*
lives
living
lived

★ You can also use **littler** and **littlest** when you are talking about size.

li - lo

live *adjective*
livelihood *noun*
  livelihoods
liveliness *noun*
lively *adjective*
  livelier
  liveliest
liver *noun*
  livers
livery *noun*
  liveries
lives see **life**
livestock *noun*
livid *adjective*
living *noun*
  livings
lizard *noun*
  lizards
llama *noun*
  llamas
load *verb*
  loads
  loading
  loaded
load *noun*
  loads
loaf *noun*
  loaves
loaf *verb*
  loafs
  loafing
  loafed
loafer *noun*
  loafers
loam *noun*
loamy *adjective*
  loamier
  loamiest

loan* *noun*
  loans
loan *verb*
  loans
  loaning
  loaned
loath☆ *adjective*
loathe○ *verb*
  loathes
  loathing
  loathed
loathsome
loaves see **loaf**
lob *verb*
  lobs
  lobbing
  lobbed
lobby *noun*
  lobbies
lobby *verb*
  lobbies
  lobbying
  lobbied
lobe *noun*
  lobes
lobster *noun*
  lobsters
local *adjective*
  locally
local *noun*
  locals
locality *noun*
  localities
locate *verb*
  locates
  locating
  located
location *noun*
  locations

loch✛ *noun*
  lochs
lock✱ *noun*
  locks
lock *verb*
  locks
  locking
  locked
locker *noun*
  lockers
locket *noun*
  lockets
locomotive *noun*
  locomotives
locust *noun*
  locusts
lodge *noun*
  lodges
lodge *verb*
  lodges
  lodging
  lodged
lodger *noun*
  lodgers
lodgings *plural noun*
loft *noun*
  lofts
lofty *adjective*
  loftier
  loftiest
  loftily
log *noun*
  logs
log *verb*
  logs
  logging
  logged
logarithm *noun*
  logarithms

....

★ A **loan** is a thing that is lent to someone. **!** lone.
☆ **Loath** means 'unwilling'. **!** loathe.
○ To **loathe** is to dislike very much. **!** loath.
✛ A **loch** is a lake in Scotland. **!** lock.
✱ A **lock** is a mechanism for keeping something closed. **!** loch.

logbook *noun*
logbooks

logic

logical *adjective*
logically

logo *noun*
logos

-logy
-*logy* makes words for
subjects of study, e.g.
archaeology (the
study of ancient
remains). Most of
these words end in
-*ology*, but an
important exception is
genealogy. Some
words have plurals,
e.g. **genealogies**.

---

loiter *verb*
loiters
loitering
loitered

loiterer *noun*
loiterers

loll *verb*
lolls
lolling
lolled

lollipop *noun*
lollipops

lolly *noun*
lollies

lone*

loneliness

lonely *adjective*
lonelier
loneliest

long *adjective* and
adverb
longer
longest

long *verb*
longs
longing
longed

longitude *noun*
longitudes

longitudinal *adjective*
longitudinally

loo *noun*
loos

look *verb*
looks
looking
looked

look *noun*
looks

lookout *noun*
lookouts

loom *noun*
looms

loom *verb*
looms
looming
loomed

loop *noun*
loops

loop *verb*
loops
looping
looped

loophole *noun*
loopholes

loose *adjective*
looser
loosest
loosely

loose *verb*
looses
loosing
loosed

loosen *verb*
loosens
loosening
loosened

looseness

loot *verb*
loots
looting
looted

loot *noun*

looter *noun*
looters

lopsided

lord *noun*
lords

lordly

lordship

lorry *noun*
lorries

lose *verb*
loses
losing
lost

loser *noun*
losers

loss *noun*
losses

lot *noun*
lots

lotion *noun*
lotions

lottery *noun*
lotteries

lotto

loud *adjective*
louder
loudest
loudly

loudness

loudspeaker *noun*
loudspeakers

lounge *noun*
lounges

★ **Lone** means 'alone'. **!loan.**

lounge verb
lounges
lounging
lounged

louse noun
lice

lousy adjective
lousier
lousiest
lousily

lout noun
louts

lovable adjective
lovably

love verb
loves
loving
loved

love noun
loves

loveliness

lovely adjective
lovelier
loveliest

lover noun
lovers

loving adjective
lovingly

low adjective
lower
lowest

low verb
lows
lowing
lowed

lower verb
lowers
lowering
lowered

lowland adjective

lowlands plural nouns

lowlander noun
lowlanders

lowliness

lowly adjective
lowlier
lowliest

lowness

loyal adjective
loyally

loyalty noun
loyalties

lozenge noun
lozenges

lubricant noun
lubricants

lubricate verb
lubricates
lubricating
lubricated

lubrication

lucid adjective
lucidly

lucidity

luck

lucky adjective
luckier
luckiest
luckily

ludicrous adjective
ludicrously

ludo

lug verb
lugs
lugging
lugged

luggage

lukewarm

lull verb
lulls
lulling
lulled

lull noun
lulls

lullaby noun
lullabies

lumber verb
lumbers
lumbering
lumbered

lumber noun

lumberjack noun
lumberjacks

luminosity

luminous

lump noun
lumps

lump verb
lumps
lumping
lumped

lumpy adjective
lumpier
lumpiest

lunacy noun
lunacies

lunar

lunatic noun
lunatics

lunch noun
lunches

lung noun
lungs

lunge verb
lunges
lunging
lunging or lunged

lupin noun
lupins

lurch verb
lurches
lurching
lurched

lurch noun
lurches

lure verb
lures
luring
lured

lurk *verb*
  lurks
  lurking
  lurked

luscious *adjective*
  lusciously

lush *adjective*
  lusher
  lushest
  lushly

lushness

lust *noun*
  lusts

lustful *adjective*
  lustfully

lustre *noun*
  lustres

lustrous

lute *noun*
  lutes

luxury *noun*
  luxuries

luxurious *adjective*
  luxuriously

Lycra

-ly
-*ly* makes adverbs
from adjectives, e.g.
slow - slowly. When
the adjective ends in
-*y* following a
consonant, you
change the *y* to *i*, e.g.
happy - happily. -*ly* is
also used to make
some adjectives, e.g.
lovely, and some
words that are
adjectives and
adverbs, e.g. **kindly**,
hourly.

---

lying see **lie**

lynch *verb*
  lynches
  lynching
  lynched

lyre *noun*
  lyres

lyric *noun*
  lyrics

lyrical *adjective*
  lyrically

lyrics *plural noun*

Mm

ma *noun*
  mas

mac *noun*
  macs

macabre

macaroni

machine *noun*
  machines

machinery

mackerel *noun*
  mackerel

mackintosh *noun*
  mackintoshes

mad *adjective*
  madder
  maddest
  madly

madam

madden *verb*
  maddens
  maddening
  maddened

made* see **make**

madman *noun*
  madmen

madness

magazine *noun*
  magazines

maggot *noun*
  maggots

magic *noun* and
adjective

magical *adjective*
  magically

magician *noun*
  magicians

magistrate *noun*
  magistrates

magma

magnesium

magnet *noun*
  magnets

magnetism

magnetic *adjective*
  magnetically

magnetize *verb*
  magnetizes
  magnetizing
  magnetized

magnificent *adjective*
  magnificently

magnificence

magnification

magnifier

magnify *verb*
  magnifies
  magnifying
  magnified

magnitude *noun*
  magnitudes

magnolia *noun*
  magnolias

magpie *noun*
  magpies

mahogany

maid☆ *noun*
  maids

★ You use **made** in e.g. *I made a cake*. **!** **maid**.
☆ A **maid** is a female servant. **!** **made**.

a b c d e f g h i j k l m n o p q r s t u v w x y z

ma

maiden *noun*
maidens

mail* *noun*

mail *verb*
mails
mailing
mailed

maim *verb*
maims
maiming
maimed

main☆ *adjective*
mainly

mainland

mainly

mains *plural noun*

maintain *verb*
maintains
maintaining
maintained

maintenance

maisonette *noun*
maisonettes

maize

majestic *adjective*
majestically

majesty *noun*
majesties

major *adjective*

major *noun*
majors

majority *noun*
majorities

make *verb*
makes
making
made

make *noun*
makes

make-believe

maker *noun*
makers

make-up

maladjusted

malaria

male° *adjective and noun*
males

malevolence

malevolent *adjective*
malevolently

malice

malicious *adjective*
maliciously

mallet *noun*
mallets

malnourished

malnutrition

malt

malted

mammal *noun*
mammals

mammoth *adjective and noun*
mammoths

man *noun*
men

man *verb*
mans
manning
manned

manage *verb*
manages
managing
managed

manageable

management

manager *noun*
managers

manageress *noun*
manageresses

mane✣ *noun*
manes

manger *noun*
mangers

mangle *verb*
mangles
mangling
mangled

mango *noun*
mangoes

manhandle *verb*
manhandles
manhandling
manhandled

manhole *noun*
manholes

mania *noun*
manias

maniac *noun*
maniacs

manic *adjective*
manically

manifesto *noun*
manifestos

manipulate *verb*
manipulates
manipulating
manipulated

manipulation

manipulator

mankind

manliness

manly *adjective*
manlier
manliest

. . . .

★ **Mail** is letters and parcels sent by post. **! male**.

☆ **Main** means 'most important'. **! mane**.

○ A **male** is a man or an animal of the same gender as a man. **! mail**.

✣ A **mane** is the long piece of hair on a horse or lion. **! main**.

146

manner* *noun*
manners

manoeuvrable

manoeuvre *verb*
manoeuvres
manoeuvring
manoeuvred

manoeuvre *noun*
manoeuvres

man-of-war *noun*
men-of-war

manor☆ *noun*
manors

mansion *noun*
mansions

manslaughter

mantelpiece *noun*
mantelpieces

mantle *noun*
mantles

manual *adjective*
manually

manual *noun*
manuals

manufacture *verb*
manufactures
manufacturing
manufactured

manufacture *noun*

manufacturer *noun*
manufacturers

manure

manuscript *noun*
manuscripts

Manx

many *adjective and noun*
more
most

Maori *noun*
Maoris

map *noun*
maps

map *verb*
maps
mapping
mapped

maple *noun*
maples

mar *verb*
mars
marring
marred

marathon *noun*
marathons

marauder *noun*
marauders

marauding

marble *noun*
marbles

March *noun*
Marches

march *verb*
marches
marching
marched

march *noun*
marches

marcher *noun*
marchers

mare⁰ *noun*
mares

margarine

margin *noun*
margins

marginal *adjective*
marginally

marigold *noun*
marigolds

marijuana

marina *noun*
marinas

marine *adjective and noun*
marines

mariner *noun*
mariners

marionette *noun*
marionettes

mark *verb*
marks
marking
marked

mark *noun*
marks

market *noun*
markets

market *verb*
markets
marketing
marketed

marksman *noun*
marksmen

marksmanship

marmalade

maroon *verb*
maroons
marooning
marooned

maroon *adjective and noun*

marquee *noun*
marquees

marriage *noun*
marriages

a
b
c
d
e
f
g
h
i
j
k
l
m
n
o
p
q
r
s
t
u
v
w
x
y
z

· ·

★ You use **manner** in e.g. *a friendly manner*. **!manor**.

☆ A **manor** is a big house in the country. **!manner**.

⊙ A **mare** is a female horse. **!mayor**.

147

ma

a b c d e f g h i j k l m n o p q r s t u v w x y z

marrow *noun*
marrows

marry *verb*
marries
marrying
married

marsh *noun*
marshes

marshal *noun*
marshals

marshmallow *noun*
marshmallows

marshy *adjective*
marshier
marshiest

marsupial *noun*
marsupials

martial

Martian *noun*
Martians

martin *noun*
martins

martyr *noun*
martyrs

martyrdom

marvel *verb*
marvels
marvelling
marvelled

marvel *noun*
marvels

marvellous *adjective*
marvellously

Marxism

Marxist

marzipan

mascot *noun*
mascots

masculine

masculinity

mash *verb*
mashes
mashing
mashed

mash *noun*

mask *noun*
masks

mask *verb*
masks
masking
masked

Mason★ *noun*
Masons

mason☆ *noun*
masons

masonry

Mass○ *noun*
Masses

mass *noun*
masses

mass *verb*
masses
massing
massed

massacre *verb*
massacres
massacring
massacred

massacre *noun*
massacres

massage *verb*
massages
massaging
massaged

massage *noun*

massive *adjective*
massively

mast *noun*
masts

master *noun*
masters

master *verb*
masters
mastering
mastered

masterly

mastermind *noun*
masterminds

masterpiece *noun*
masterpieces

mastery

mat✛ *noun*
mats

matador *noun*
matadors

match *verb*
matches
matching
matched

match *noun*
matches

mate *noun*
mates

mate *verb*
mates
mating
mated

material *noun*
materials

materialistic

maternal *adjective*
maternally

maternity

mathematical
adjective
mathematically

★ You use a capital M when you mean a member of the
  Freemasons.
☆ Use a small m when you mean someone who builds with stone.
○ Use a capital M when you mean the Roman Catholic service.
✛ A **mat** is a covering for a floor. **! matt**.

mathematician noun
mathematicians

mathematics

maths

matinée noun
matinées

matrimonial

matrimony

matrix noun
matrices

matron noun
matrons

matt*

matted

matter verb
matters
mattering
mattered

matter noun
matters

matting

mattress noun
mattresses

mature

maturity

mauve

maximum adjective
and noun
maxima or maximums

May noun
Mays

may verb
might

may

maybe

May Day

mayday☆ noun
maydays

mayonnaise

mayorO noun
mayors

mayoress noun
mayoresses

maypole noun
maypoles

maze noun
mazes

meadow noun
meadows

meagre

meal noun
meals

mean adjective
meaner
meanest
meanly

mean verb
means
meaning
meant

meander verb
meanders
meandering
meandered

meaning noun
meanings

meaningful adjective
meaningfully

meaningless
adjective
meaninglessly

meanness

means plural noun

meantime

meanwhile

measles plural noun

measly adjective
measlier
measliest

measure verb
measures
measuring
measured

measure noun
measures

measurement noun
measurements

meat✦ noun
meats

meaty adjective
meatier
meatiest

mechanic noun
mechanics

mechanical adjective
mechanically

mechanics

mechanism noun
mechanisms

medal noun
medals

medallist noun
medallists

meddle verb
meddles
meddling
meddled

meddler noun
meddlers

meddlesome

media plural noun

median noun
medians

medical adjective
medically

- -

★ **Matt** means 'not shiny'. **!mat.**
☆ An international radio signal.
O You use **mayor** in e.g. *the Mayor of London*. **!mare.**
✦ **Meat** is the flesh of an animal. **!meet.**

a
b
c
d
e
f
g
h
i
j
k
l
m
n
o
p
q
r
s
t
u
v
w
x
y
z

149

me

a **medicine** noun
medicines

medicinal

b **medieval**

c **mediocre**

mediocrity

d **meditate** verb
meditates
e meditating
meditated
f
meditation

g **Mediterranean**

medium adjective

h **medium** noun
media or mediums
i
meek adjective
j meeker
meekest
k meekly

l **meekness**

m **meet*** verb
meets
meeting
n met

o **meeting** noun
meetings

p **megaphone** noun
megaphones

q **melancholy**

mellow adjective
r mellower
mellowest
s
melodious adjective
t melodiously

u **melodrama** noun
melodramas

v **melodramatic**
adjective
melodramatically
w
melody noun
x melodies

y **melodic**

z

melon noun
melons

melt verb
melts
melting
melted

member noun
members

membership

**Member of
Parliament** noun
Members of
Parliament

membrane noun
membranes

memoirs plural noun

memorable adjective
memorably

memorial noun
memorials

memorize verb
memorizes
memorizing
memorized

memory noun
memories

men see **man**

menace verb
menaces
menacing
menaced

menace noun
menaces

menagerie noun
menageries

mend verb
mends
mending
mended

mender noun
menders

menstrual

menstruation

-ment
-ment makes nouns
from adjectives e.g.
contentment. There
is a fixed number of
these, and you cannot
freely add -ment as
you can with -ness.
When the adjective
ends in -y following a
consonant, you
change the y to i, e.g.
merry - **merriment**.

---

mental adjective
mentally

mention verb
mentions
mentioning
mentioned

mention noun
mentions

menu noun
menus

mercenary adjective
and noun
mercenaries

merchandise

merchant noun
merchants

merciful adjective
mercifully

merciless adjective
mercilessly

mercury

mercy noun
mercies

mere adjective

mere noun
meres

merely adverb

....

z ★ People **meet** when they come together. ! **meat**.

150

merge verb
merges
merging
merged

merger noun
mergers

meridian noun
meridians

meringue noun
meringues

merit noun
merits

merit verb
merits
meriting
merited

mermaid noun
mermaids

merriment noun

merry adjective
merrier
merriest
merrily

merry-go-round noun
merry-go-rounds

mesh noun
meshes

mess noun
messes

mess verb
messes
messing
messed

message noun
messages

messenger noun
messengers

Messiah

messiness

messy adjective
messier
messiest
messily

met see **meet**

metal* noun
metals

metallic

metallurgical

metallurgist

metallurgy

metamorphosis
noun
metamorphoses

metaphor noun
metaphors

metaphorical
adjective
metaphorically

meteor noun
meteors

meteoric

meteorite noun
meteorites

meteorological

meteorologist

meteorology

meter☆ noun
meters

methane

method noun
methods

methodical adjective
methodically

Methodist noun
Methodists

meths

methylated spirit

meticulous adjective
meticulously

metre○ noun
metres

metric adjective

metrical adjective
metrically

metronome noun
metronomes

mettle✢

mew verb
mews
mewing
mewed

miaow verb
miaows
miaowing
miaowed

mice see **mouse**

---

micro-
micro- makes words
meaning 'small', e.g.
microwave. When
the word begins with a
vowel you add a
hyphen, e.g.
micro-organism.

---

microbe noun
microbes

microchip noun
microchips

microcomputer noun
microcomputers

microfilm noun
microfilms

★ A **Metal** is a hard substance used to make things. **!mettle**.
☆ A **meter** is a device that shows how much of something has been used. **!metre**.
○ A **metre** is a unit of length. **!meter**.
✢ As in *to be on your mettle*. **!metal**.

mi

microphone *noun*
microphones

microprocessor
noun
microprocessors

microscope *noun*
microscopes

microscopic
adjective
microscopically

microwave *noun*
microwaves

microwave *verb*
microwaves
microwaving
microwaved

mid*

midday

middle *noun*
middles

Middle Ages

Middle East

midge *noun*
midges

midget *noun*
midgets

midland *adjective*

midnight

midst

midsummer

midway

midwife *noun*
midwives

midwifery

might☆ *noun*

might see **may**

mightiness

mighty *adjective*
mightier
mightiest
mightily

migraine *noun*
migraines

migrant *noun*
migrants

migrate *verb*
migrates
migrating
migrated

migration *noun*
migrations

migratory

mike *noun*
mikes

mild *adjective*
milder
mildest
mildly

mildness

mile *noun*
miles

mileage *noun*
mileages

milestone *noun*
milestones

militancy

militant

militarism

militaristic

military

milk *noun*

milk *verb*
milks
milking
milked

milkman *noun*
milkmen

milky *adjective*
milkier
milkiest

Milky Way

mill *noun*
mills

mill *verb*
mills
milling
milled

millennium *noun*
millenniums

miller *noun*
millers

millet

milligram *noun*
milligrams

millilitre *noun*
millilitres

millimetre *noun*
millimetres

million *noun*
millions

millionth

millionaire *noun*
millionaires

millstone *noun*
millstones

milometer *noun*
milometers

mime *verb*
mimes
miming
mimed

mime *noun*
mimes

mimic *verb*
mimics
mimicking
mimicked

mimic *noun*
mimics

. . . .

★ You use a hyphen, e.g. *mid-August*.
☆ **Might** means 'force' or 'strength'. **!** mite.

mimicry

minaret *noun*
minarets

mince *verb*
minces
mincing
minced

mince *noun*

mincemeat

mincer *noun*
mincers

mind *noun*
minds

mind *verb*
minds
minding
minded

mindless *adjective*
mindlessly

mine *adjective*

mine *verb*
mines
mining
mined

mine *noun*
mines

minefield *noun*
minefields

miner *noun*
miners

mineral *noun*
minerals

mingle *verb*
mingles
mingling
mingled

mini-
mini- makes words
meaning 'small', e.g.
miniskirt. You do not
normally need a
hyphen.

mingy *adjective*
mingier
mingiest

miniature *adjective*
and *noun*
miniatures

minibus *noun*
minibuses

minim *noun*
minims

minimal *adjective*
minimally

minimize *verb*
minimizes
minimizing
minimized

minimum *adjective*
and *noun*
minima
minimums

minister *noun*
ministers

ministry *noun*
ministries

mink *noun*
minks

minnow *noun*
minnows

minor *adjective* and
noun
minors

minority *noun*
minorities

minstrel *noun*
minstrels

mint *noun*
mints

mint *verb*
mints
minting
minted

minus *preposition*

minute *adjective*
minutely

minute *noun*
minutes

miracle *noun*
miracles

miraculous *adjective*
miraculously

mirage *noun*
mirages

mirror *noun*
mirrors

mirth

misbehave *verb*
misbehaves
misbehaving
misbehaved

misbehaviour

miscarriage *noun*
miscarriages

miscellaneous

miscellany *noun*
miscellanies

mischief

mischievous
adjective
mischievously

miser *noun*
misers

miserable *adjective*
miserably

miserly

misery *noun*
miseries

misfire *verb*
misfires
misfiring
misfired

misfit *noun*
misfits

misfortune *noun*
misfortunes

mishap *noun*
mishaps

misjudge verb
misjudges
misjudging
misjudged

mislay verb
mislays
mislaying
mislaid

mislead verb
misleads
misleading
misled

misprint noun
misprints

miss verb
misses
missing
missed

miss noun
misses

missile noun
missiles

missing

mission noun
missions

missionary noun
missionaries

misspell verb
misspells
misspelling
misspelt or misspelled

mist* noun
mists

mistake noun
mistakes

mistake verb
mistakes
mistaking
mistook
mistaken

mister

mistiness

mistletoe

mistreat verb
mistreats
mistreating
mistreated

mistreatment

mistress noun
mistresses

mistrust verb
mistrusts
mistrusting
mistrusted

misty adjective
mistier
mistiest
mistily

misunderstand verb
misunderstands
misunderstanding
misunderstood

misunderstanding noun
misunderstandings

misuse verb
misuses
misusing
misused

misuse noun
misuses

mite☆ noun
mites

mitre noun
mitres

mitten noun
mittens

mix verb
mixes
mixing
mixed

mixer noun
mixers

mixture noun
mixtures

mix-up noun
mix-ups

moan verb
moans
moaning
moaned

moan noun
moans

moat noun
moats

mob noun
mobs

mob verb
mobs
mobbing
mobbed

mobile adjective and noun
mobiles

mobility

mobilization

mobilize verb
mobilizes
mobilizing
mobilized

moccasin noun
moccasins

mock adjective

mock verb
mocks
mocking
mocked

mockery noun
mockeries

mock-up noun
mock-ups

mode noun
modes

model noun
models

· ·

★ **Mist** is damp air that is difficult to see through. **! missed**.
☆ A **mite** is a tiny insect. **! might**.

model *verb*
models
modelling
modelled

modem *noun*
modems

moderate *adjective*
moderately

moderate *verb*
moderates
moderating
moderated

moderation

modern

modernity

modernization

modernize *verb*
modernizes
modernizing
modernized

modest *adjective*
modestly

modesty

modification *noun*
modifications

modify *verb*
modifies
modifying
modified

module *noun*
modules

moist *adjective*
moister
moistest

moisture

moisten *verb*
moistens
moistening
moistened

molar *noun*
molars

mole *noun*
moles

molecular

molecule *noun*
molecules

molehill *noun*
molehills

molest *verb*
molests
molesting
molested

mollusc *noun*
molluscs

molten

moment *noun*
moments

momentary *adjective*
momentarily

momentous *adjective*
momentously

momentum

monarch *noun*
monarchs

monarchy *noun*
monarchies

monastery *noun*
monasteries

monastic

Monday *noun*
Mondays

money

mongoose *noun*
mongooses

mongrel *noun*
mongrels

monitor *verb*
monitors
monitoring
monitored

monitor *noun*
monitors

monk *noun*
monks

monkey *noun*
monkeys

monogram *noun*
monograms

monologue *noun*
monologues

monopolize *verb*
monopolizes
monopolizing
monopolized

monopoly *noun*
monopolies

monorail *noun*
monorails

monotonous
adjective
monotonously

monotony

monsoon *noun*
monsoons

monster *noun*
monsters

monstrosity *noun*
monstrosities

monstrous *adjective*
monstrously

month *noun*
months

monthly *adjective and*
adverb

monument *noun*
monuments

monumental
adjective
monumentally

moo *verb*
moos
mooing
mooed

mood *noun*
moods

moodiness

moody *adjective*
moodier
moodiest
moodily

moon *noun*
moons

moonlight

mo

moonlit

moor* *verb*
moors
mooring
moored

moor☆ *noun*
moors

moorhen *noun*
moorhens

mooring *noun*
moorings

moose° *noun*
moose

mop *noun*
mops

mop *verb*
mops
mopping
mopped

mope *verb*
mopes
moping
moped

moped *noun*
mopeds

moraine *noun*
moraines

moral *adjective*
morally

moral *noun*
morals

morale

morality

morals *plural noun*

morbid *adjective*
morbidly

more✛ *adjective, adverb,* and *noun*

moreover

Mormon *noun*
Mormons

morning *noun*
mornings

moron *noun*
morons

moronic *adjective*
moronically

morose *adjective*
morosely

morphine

morris dance *noun*
morris dances

Morse code

morsel *noun*
morsels

mortal *adjective*
mortally

mortality

mortar

mortgage *noun*
mortgages

mortuary *noun*
mortuaries

mosaic *noun*
mosaics

mosque *noun*
mosques

mosquito *noun*
mosquitoes

moss *noun*
mosses

mossy *adjective*
mossier
mossiest

most *adjective, adverb,* and *noun*

mostly *adverb*

motel *noun*
motels

moth *noun*
moths

mother *noun*
mothers

motherhood

mother-in-law *noun*
mothers-in-law

motherly

motion *noun*
motions

motionless

motivate *verb*
motivates
motivating
motivated

motive *noun*
motives

motor *noun*
motors

motorbike *noun*
motorbikes

motor boat *noun*
motor boats

motor car *noun*
motor cars

motorcycle *noun*
motorcycles

motorcyclist *noun*
motorcyclists

motorist *noun*
motorists

motorway *noun*
motorways

mottled

motto *noun*
mottoes

....

★ To **moor** a boat is to tie it up. ❗**more**.
☆ A **moor** is an area of rough land. ❗**more**.
○ A **moose** is an American elk. ❗**mouse**, **mousse**.
✛ You use **more** in e.g. *I'd like more to eat.* ❗**moor**.

156

a b c d e f g h i j k l **m** *n o p q r s t u v w x y z*

mould *verb*
moulds
moulding
moulded

mould *noun*
moulds

mouldy *adjective*
mouldier
mouldiest

moult *verb*
moults
moulting
moulted

mound *noun*
mounds

mount *verb*
mounts
mounting
mounted

mount *noun*
mounts

mountain *noun*
mountains

mountaineer *noun*
mountaineers

mountaineering

mountainous

mourn *verb*
mourns
mourning
mourned

mourner *noun*
mourners

mournful *adjective*
mournfully

mouse* *noun*
mice

mousetrap *noun*
mousetraps

mousse☆ *noun*
mousses

moustache *noun*
moustaches

mousy *adjective*
mousier
mousiest

mouth *noun*
mouths

mouthful *noun*
mouthfuls

mouthpiece *noun*
mouthpieces

movable

move *verb*
moves
moving
moved

move *noun*
moves

movement *noun*
movements

movie *noun*
movies

mow *verb*
mows
mowing
mowed
mown

mower *noun*
mowers

much *adjective,*
adverb, and *noun*

muck *noun*

muck *verb*
mucks
mucking
mucked

mucky *adjective*
muckier
muckiest

mud

muddle *verb*
muddles
muddling
muddled

muddle *noun*
muddles

muddler *noun*
muddlers

muddy *adjective*
muddier
muddiest

mudguard *noun*
mudguards

muesli

muezzin○ *noun*
muezzins

muffle *verb*
muffles
muffling
muffled

mug *noun*
mugs

mug *verb*
mugs
mugging
mugged

mugger *noun*
muggers

muggy *adjective*
muggier
muggiest

mule *noun*
mules

multi-

multi- makes words
with the meaning
'many', e.g.
multicultural. You do
not normally need a
hyphen.

★ A **mouse** is a small animal. **!moose**, **mousse**.
☆ A **mousse** is a creamy pudding. **!moose**, **mouse**.
○ A man who calls Muslims to prayer. Pronounced *moo-ezz-in*.

a
b
c
d
e
f
g
h
i
j
k
l
m
n
o
p
q
r
s
t
u
v
w
x
y
z

mu

multiple *adjective and noun*
multiples

multiplication

multiply *verb*
multiplies
multiplying
multiplied

multiracial

multitude *noun*
multitudes

mumble *verb*
mumbles
mumbling
mumbled

mummify *verb*
mummifies
mummifying
mummified

mummy *noun*
mummies

mumps

munch *verb*
munches
munching
munched

mundane

municipal

mural *noun*
murals

murder *verb*
murders
murdering
murdered

murder *noun*
murders

murderer *noun*
murderers

murderous *adjective*
murderously

murky *adjective*
murkier
murkiest

murmur *verb*
murmurs
murmuring
murmured

murmur *noun*
murmurs

muscle* *noun*
muscles

muscle *verb*
muscles
muscling
muscled

muscular

museum *noun*
museums

mushroom *noun*
mushrooms

mushroom *verb*
mushrooms
mushrooming
mushroomed

music

musical *adjective*
musically

musical *noun*
musicals

musician *noun*
musicians

musket *noun*
muskets

musketeer *noun*
musketeers

Muslim *noun*
Muslims

muslin

mussel☆ *noun*
mussels

must

mustard

muster *verb*
musters
mustering
mustered

mustiness

musty *adjective*
mustier
mustiest

mutation *noun*
mutations

mute *adjective*
mutely

mute *noun*
mutes

muted

mutilate *verb*
mutilates
mutilating
mutilated

mutilation

mutineer *noun*
mutineers

mutiny *noun*
mutinies

mutinous *adjective*
mutinously

mutiny *verb*
mutinies
mutinying
mutinied

mutter *verb*
mutters
muttering
muttered

mutton

mutual *adjective*
mutually

muzzle *verb*
muzzles
muzzling
muzzled

....

★ A **muscle** is a part of the body. ! **mussel**.
☆ A **mussel** is a shellfish. ! **muscle**.

muzzle noun
muzzles

myself

mysterious adjective
mysteriously

mystery noun
mysteries

mystification

mystify verb
mystifies
mystifying
mystified

myth noun
myths

mythical

mythological adjective

mythology

Nn

nab verb
nabs
nabbing
nabbed

nag verb
nags
nagging
nagged

nag noun
nags

nail noun
nails

nail verb
nails
nailing
nailed

naive adjective
naively

naivety

naked

nakedness

name noun
names

name verb
names
naming
named

nameless

namely

nanny noun
nannies

nap noun
naps

napkin noun
napkins

nappy noun
nappies

narcissus noun
narcissi

narcotic noun
narcotics

narrate verb
narrates
narrating
narrated

narration noun
narrations

narrative noun
narratives

narrator noun
narrators

narrow adjective
narrower
narrowest
narrowly

nasal adjective
nasally

nastiness

nasturtium noun
nasturtiums

nasty adjective
nastier
nastiest
nastily

nation noun
nations

national adjective
nationally

nationalism

nationalist

nationality noun
nationalities

nationalization

nationalize verb
nationalizes
nationalizing
nationalized

nationwide adjective

native adjective and noun
natives

Native American noun
Native Americans

nativity noun
nativities

natural adjective
naturally

natural noun
naturals

naturalist noun
naturalists

naturalization

naturalize verb
naturalizes
naturalizing
naturalized

nature noun
natures

naughtiness

naughty adjective
naughtier
naughtiest
naughtily

nausea

nautical

a naval* *adjective*

nave *noun*
naves

navel° *noun*
navels

navigable *adjective*

navigate *verb*
navigates
navigating
navigated

navigation

navigator *noun*
navigators

navy *noun*
navies

Nazi *noun*
Nazis

Nazism

near *adjective* and *adverb*
nearer
nearest

near *preposition*

near *verb*
nears
nearing
neared

nearby

nearly

neat *adjective*
neater
neatest
neatly

neatness

necessarily

necessary

necessity *noun*
necessities

neck *noun*
necks

neckerchief *noun*
neckerchiefs

necklace *noun*
necklaces

nectar

nectarine *noun*
nectarines

need° *verb*
needs
needing
needed

need *noun*
needs

needle *noun*
needles

needless *adjective*
needlessly

needlework

needy *adjective*
needier
neediest

negative *adjective*
negatively

negative *noun*
negatives

neglect *verb*
neglects
neglecting
neglected

neglect *noun*

neglectful *adjective*
neglectfully

negligence

negligent *adjective*
negligently

negligible *adjective*
negligibly

negotiate *verb*
negotiates
negotiating
negotiated

negotiation *noun*
negotiations

negotiator *noun*
negotiators

neigh *verb*
neighs
neighing
neighed

neigh *noun*
neighs

neighbour *noun*
neighbours

neighbouring

neighbourhood *noun*
neighbourhoods

neighbourly

neither *adjective* and *conjunction*

neon

nephew *noun*
nephews

nerve *noun*
nerves

nerve-racking

nervous *adjective*
nervously

nervousness

-ness
-ness makes nouns from adjectives, e.g. **soft - softness**.
When the adjective ends in -y following a consonant, you change the y to i, e.g. **lively - liveliness**.

---

nest *noun*
nests

....

★ **Naval** means 'to do with a navy'. **! navel**.

☆ A **navel** is a small hollow in your stomach. **! naval**.

○ To **need** is to require something. **! knead**.

n

nest *verb*
nests
nesting
nested

nestle *verb*
nestles
nestling
nestled

nestling *noun*
nestlings

net *noun*
nets

net *adjective*

netball

nettle *noun*
nettles

network *noun*
networks

neuter *adjective*

neuter *verb*
neuters
neutering
neutered

neutral *adjective*
neutrally

neutrality

neutralize *verb*
neutralizes
neutralizing
neutralized

neutron *noun*
neutrons

never

nevertheless
conjunction

new* *adjective*
newer
newest
newly

newcomer *noun*
newcomers

newness

news

newsagent *noun*
newsagents

newsletter *noun*
newsletters

newspaper *noun*
newspapers

newt *noun*
newts

New Testament

newton *noun*
newtons

next *adjective* and
adverb

next door

nib *noun*
nibs

nibble *verb*
nibbles
nibbling
nibbled

nice *adjective*
nicer
nicest
nicely

niceness

nicety *noun*
niceties

nick *verb*
nicks
nicking
nicked

nick *noun*
nicks

nickel *noun*
nickels

nickname *noun*
nicknames

nicotine

niece *noun*
nieces

night☆ *noun*
nights

nightclub *noun*
nightclubs

nightdress *noun*
nightdresses

nightfall

nightingale *noun*
nightingales

nightly

nightmare *noun*
nightmares

nightmarish

nil

nimble *adjective*
nimbler
nimblest
nimbly

nine *noun*
nines

nineteen *noun*
nineteens

nineteenth

ninetieth

ninety *noun*
nineties

ninth *adjective*
ninthly

nip *verb*
nips
nipping
nipped

nip *noun*
nips

nipple *noun*
nipples

nippy *adjective*
nippier
nippiest

nit *noun*
nits

a
b
c
d
e
f
g
h
i
j
k
l
m
n
o
p
q
r
s
t
u
v
w
x
y
z

. . . .

* You use **new** in e.g *She has a new bike.* ! **knew**.
☆ **Night** is the opposite of day. ! **knight**.

a

nitrate *noun*
nitrates

nitric acid

nitrogen

b

c

nitty-gritty

d

nitwit *noun*
nitwits

e

nobility

f

noble *adjective*
nobler
noblest
nobly

g

h

noble *noun*
nobles

i

nobleman *noun*
noblemen

j

k

noblewoman *noun*
noblewomen

l

nobody *noun*
nobodies

m

nocturnal *adjective*
nocturnally

n

nod *verb*
nods
nodding
nodded

o

p

noise *noun*
noises

q

noiseless *adjective*
noiselessly

noisiness

r

s

noisy *adjective*
noisier
noisiest
noisily

t

u

nomad *noun*
nomads

v

nomadic

w

no man's land

x

nominate *verb*
nominates
nominating
nominated

nomination *noun*
nominations

-nomy
-nomy makes words
for subjects of study,
e.g. **astronomy** (the
study of the stars).
Most of these words
end in *-onomy*.

---

none*

---

non- makes words
meaning 'not', e.g.
non-existent,
non-smoker. You
use a hyphen to make
these words. When an
un- word has a special
meaning, e.g.
unprofessional, you
can use *non-* to make
a word without the
special meaning, e.g.
non-professional.

---

non-existent

non-fiction

non-flammable

nonsense

nonsensical *adjective*
nonsensically

non-stop

noodle

noon

no one

noose *noun*
nooses

normal *adjective*
normally

normality

north *adjective* and
adverb

north☆ *noun*

north-east *noun* and
adjective

northerly *adjective*
and *noun*
northerlies

northern

northerner *noun*
northerners

northward *adjective*
and *adverb*

northwards *adverb*

north-west

nose *noun*
noses

nose *verb*
noses
nosing
nosed

nosedive *verb*
nosedives
nosediving
nosedived

nosedive *noun*
nosedives

nosiness

nostalgia

nostalgic *adjective*
nostalgically

nostril *noun*
nostrils

....

y

z

★ You use **none** in e.g. *none of us went.* **!nun**.
☆ You use a capital N in **the North**, when you mean a particular
region.

nosy adjective
  nosier
  nosiest
  nosily

notable adjective
  notably

notch noun
  notches

note noun
  notes

note verb
  notes
  noting
  noted

notebook noun
  notebooks

notepaper

nothing

notice verb
  notices
  noticing
  noticed

notice noun
  notices

noticeable adjective
  noticeably

noticeboard noun
  noticeboards

notion noun
  notions

notoriety

notorious adjective
  notoriously

nougat

nought noun
  noughts

noun noun
  nouns

nourish verb
  nourishes
  nourishing
  nourished

nourishment

novel adjective

novel noun
  novels

novelist noun
  novelists

novelty noun
  novelties

November noun
  Novembers

novice noun
  novices

nowadays

nowhere

nozzle noun
  nozzles

nuclear

nucleus noun
  nuclei

nude adjective and
noun
  nudes

nudge verb
  nudges
  nudging
  nudged

nudist noun
  nudists

nudity

nugget noun
  nuggets

nuisance noun
  nuisances

numb adjective
  numbly

number noun
  numbers

number verb
  numbers
  numbering
  numbered

numbness

numeracy

numeral noun
  numerals

numerate

numerator noun
  numerators

numerical adjective
  numerically

numerous

nun* noun
  nuns

nunnery noun
  nunneries

nurse noun
  nurses

nurse verb
  nurses
  nursing
  nursed

nursery noun
  nurseries

nurture verb
  nurtures
  nurturing
  nurtured

nut noun
  nuts

nutcrackers plural
noun

nutmeg noun
  nutmegs

nutrient noun
  nutrients

nutrition

nutritional adjective
  nutritionally

nutritious

nutshell noun
  nutshells

nutty adjective
  nuttier
  nuttiest

....
★ A **nun** is a member of a convent. **I none.**

a
b
c
d
e
f
g
h
i
j
k
l
n
o
p
q
r
s
t
u
v
w
x
y
z

nuzzle *verb*
nuzzles
nuzzling
nuzzled

nylon *adjective and noun*
nylons

nymph *noun*
nymphs

Oo

-o
Most nouns ending in -o, e.g. **hero, potato,** have plurals ending in -oes, e.g. **heroes, potatoes,** but a few end in -os. The most important are **kilos, photos, pianos, radios, ratios, solos, videos, zeros.** Verbs ending in -o usually have the forms -oes and -oed, e.g. **video - videoes - videoed.**

oak *noun*
oaks

oar* *noun*
oars

oarsman *noun*
oarsmen

oarswoman *noun*
oarswomen

oasis *noun*
oases

oath *noun*
oaths

oatmeal

oats *plural noun*

obedience

obedient *adjective*
obediently

obey *verb*
obeys
obeying
obeyed

obituary *noun*
obituaries

object *noun*
objects

object *verb*
objects
objecting
objected

objection *noun*
objections

objectionable

objective *adjective*
objectively

objective *noun*
objectives

objector *noun*
objectors

obligation *noun*
obligations

obligatory

oblige *verb*
obliges
obliging
obliged

oblique *adjective*
obliquely

oblong *adjective and noun*
oblongs

oboe *noun*
oboes

oboist *noun*
oboists

obscene *adjective*
obscenely

obscenity *noun*
obscenities

obscure *adjective*
obscurer
obscurest
obscurely

obscurity

observance *noun*
observances

observant *adjective*
observantly

observation *noun*
observations

observatory *noun*
observatories

observe *verb*
observes
observing
observed

observer *noun*
observers

obsessed

obsession *noun*
obsessions

obsolete

obstacle *noun*
obstacles

obstinacy

obstinate *adjective*
obstinately

obstruct *verb*
obstructs
obstructing
obstructed

obstruction *noun*
obstructions

obstructive *adjective*
obstructively

. . . .

★ An **oar** is used for rowing a boat. **!** or, ore.

obtain *verb*
obtains
obtaining
obtained

obtainable

obtuse *adjective*
obtuser
obtusest
obtusely

obvious *adjective*
obviously

occasion *noun*
occasions

occasional *adjective*
occasionally

occupant *noun*
occupants

occupation *noun*
occupations

occupy *verb*
occupies
occupying
occupied

occur *verb*
occurs
occurring
occurred

occurrence *noun*
occurrences

ocean *noun*
oceans

o'clock

octagon *noun*
octagons

octagonal *adjective*
octagonally

octave *noun*
octaves

October *noun*
Octobers

octopus *noun*
octopuses

odd *adjective*
odder
oddest
oddly

oddity *noun*
oddities

oddments *plural noun*

oddness *noun*

odds *plural noun*

odour *noun*
odours

odorous

oesophagus *noun*
oesophagi *or*
oesophaguses

of★

off☆

offence *noun*
offences

offend *verb*
offends
offending
offended

offender *noun*
offenders

offensive *adjective*
offensively

offer *verb*
offers
offering
offered

offer *noun*
offers

offhand

office *noun*
offices

officer *noun*
officers

official *adjective*
officially

official *noun*
officials

officious *adjective*
officiously

off-licence *noun*
off-licences

offset *verb*
offsets
offsetting
offset

offshore *adjective and adverb*

offside

offspring *noun*
offspring

often

ogre *noun*
ogres

ohm *noun*
ohms

oil *noun*
oils

oil *verb*
oils
oiling
oiled

oilfield *noun*
oilfields

oilskin *noun*
oilskins

oil well *noun*
oil wells

oily *adjective*
oilier
oiliest

ointment *noun*
ointments

old *adjective*
older
oldest

Old Testament

....

★ You use **of** in e.g. *a box of matches.* ! **off**.
☆ You use **off** in e.g. *turn off the light.* ! **of**.

ol - or

olive *noun*	**ooze** *verb*	**opposition**
olives	oozes	
Olympic Games	oozing	**oppress** *verb*
plural noun	oozed	oppresses
Olympics *plural noun*	**opaque**	oppressing
ombudsman *noun*	**open** *adjective*	oppressed
ombudsmen	openly	**oppression**
omelette *noun*	**open** *verb*	**oppressive** *adjective*
omelettes	opens	oppressively
omen *noun*	opening	**oppressor** *noun*
omens	opened	oppressors
ominous *adjective*	**opener** *noun*	**opt** *verb*
ominously	openers	opts
omission* *noun*	**opening** *noun*	opting
omissions	openings	opted
omit *verb*	**opera** *noun*	**optical** *adjective*
omits	operas	optically
omitting	**operate** *verb*	**optician** *noun*
omitted	operates	opticians
omnivorous	operating	**optimism**
once	operated	**optimist** *noun*
one☆ *adjective and*	**operatic**	optimists
noun	**operation** *noun*	**optimistic** *adjective*
ones	operations	optimistically
oneself	**operator** *noun*	**option** *noun*
one-sided	operators	options
one-way	**opinion** *noun*	**optional** *adjective*
ongoing	opinions	optionally
onion *noun*	**opium**	**opulence**
onions	**opponent** *noun*	**opulent** *adjective*
onlooker *noun*	opponents	opulently
onlookers	**opportunity** *noun*	**or**○ *conjunction*
only	opportunities	
onshore *adjective and*	**oppose** *verb*	**oral**✛ *adjective*
adverb	opposes	orally
onto *preposition*	opposing	**orange** *adjective and*
onward *adjective and*	opposed	*noun*
adverb	**opposite** *adjective*	oranges
onwards *adverb*	**opposite** *noun*	**orangeade** *noun*
	opposites	orangeades

. . . .

★ An **omission** is something left out. **!** **emission**.
☆ You use **one** in e.g. *one more time*. **!** **won**.
○ You use **or** in e.g. *Do you want a cake or a biscuit?* **!** **oar**, **ore**.
✛ **Oral** means spoken aloud. **!** **aural**.

166

orang-utan noun
orang-utans

oration noun
orations

orator noun
orators

oratorical

oratorio noun
oratorios

oratory

orbit noun
orbits

orbit verb
orbits
orbiting
orbited

orbital

orchard noun
orchards

orchestra noun
orchestras

orchestral

orchid noun
orchids

ordeal noun
ordeals

order noun
orders

order verb
orders
ordering
ordered

orderliness

orderly

ordinal number noun
ordinal numbers

ordinary adjective
ordinarily

ore* noun
ores

organ noun
organs

organic adjective
organically

organism noun
organisms

organist noun
organists

organization noun
organizations

organize verb
organizes
organizing
organized

organizer noun
organizers

oriental

orienteering

origami

origin noun
origins

original adjective
originally

originality

originate verb
originates
originating
originated

origination

originator noun
originators

ornament noun
ornaments

ornamental adjective
ornamentally

ornamentation

ornithological

ornithologist

ornithology

orphan noun
orphans

orphanage noun
orphanages

orthodox

Orthodox Church

orthodoxy

oscillate verb
oscillates
oscillating
oscillated

oscillation noun
oscillations

ostrich noun
ostriches

other adjective and noun
others

otherwise

otter noun
otters

ought

ounce noun
ounces

ours

ourselves

outback

outboard motor noun
outboard motors

outbreak noun
outbreaks

outburst noun
outbursts

outcast noun
outcasts

outcome noun
outcomes

outcry noun
outcries

outdated

outdo verb
outdoes
outdoing
outdid
outdone

outdoor adjective

outdoors adverb

★ **Ore** is rock with metal in it. **!** oar, or.

a b c d e f g h i j k l m n **o** p q r s t u v w x y z

outer

outfit *noun*
outfits

outgrow *verb*
outgrows
outgrowing
outgrew
outgrown

outhouse *noun*
outhouses

outing *noun*
outings

outlast *verb*
outlasts
outlasting
outlasted

outlaw *noun*
outlaws

outlaw *verb*
outlaws
outlawing
outlawed

outlet *noun*
outlets

outline *noun*
outlines

outline *verb*
outlines
outlining
outlined

outlook *noun*
outlooks

outlying

outnumber *verb*
outnumbers
outnumbering
outnumbered

outpatient *noun*
outpatients

outpost *noun*
outposts

output *verb*
outputs
outputting
output

output *noun*
outputs

outrage *noun*
outrages

outrage *verb*
outrages
outraging
outraged

outrageous *adjective*
outrageously

outright

outset

outside *adverb and preposition*

outside *noun*
outsides

outsider *noun*
outsiders

outskirts *plural noun*

outspoken

outstanding *adjective*
outstandingly

outward *adjective*
outwardly

outwards *adverb*

outweigh *verb*
outweighs
outweighing
outweighed

outwit *verb*
outwits
outwitting
outwitted

oval *adjective and noun*
ovals

ovary *noun*
ovaries

oven *noun*
ovens

over *adverb and preposition*

over *noun*
overs

---

over-

over- makes words meaning 'too' or 'too much', e.g. **overactive** and **overcook**. You do not need a hyphen, except in some words beginning with *e*, e.g. **over-eager**.

---

overall *adjective*

overalls *plural noun*

overarm *adjective*

overboard

overcast

overcoat *noun*
overcoats

overcome *verb*
overcomes
overcoming
overcame
overcome

overdo *verb*
overdoes
overdoing
overdid
overdone

overdose *noun*
overdoses

overdue

overflow *verb*
overflows
overflowing
overflowed

overgrown

overhang *verb*
overhangs
overhanging
overhung

overhaul *verb*
overhauls
overhauling
overhauled

overhead *adjective*

overheads *plural noun*

overhear *verb*
overhears
overhearing
overheard

overland *adjective*

overlap *verb*
overlaps
overlapping
overlapped

overlook *verb*
overlooks
overlooking
overlooked

overnight

overpower *verb*
overpowers
overpowering
overpowered

overrun *verb*
overruns
overrunning
overran
overrun

overseas *adjective and adverb*

oversight *noun*
oversights

oversleep *verb*
oversleeps
oversleeping
overslept

overtake *verb*
overtakes
overtaking
overtook
overtaken

overthrow *verb*
overthrows
overthrowing
overthrew
overthrown

overthrow *noun*
overthrows

overtime

overture *noun*
overtures

overturn *verb*
overturns
overturning
overturned

overwhelm *verb*
overwhelms
overwhelming
overwhelmed

overwork *verb*
overworks
overworking
overworked

overwork *noun*

ovum *noun*
ova

owe *verb*
owes
owing
owed

owl *noun*
owls

own *adjective*

own *verb*
owns
owning
owned

owner *noun*
owners

ownership *noun*

ox *noun*
oxen

oxidation

oxide *noun*
oxides

oxidize *verb*
oxidizes
oxidizing
oxidized

oxygen

oyster *noun*
oysters

ozone

Pp

pa *noun*
pas

pace *noun*
paces

pace *verb*
paces
pacing
paced

pacemaker *noun*
pacemakers

pacification

pacifism

pacifist *noun*
pacifists

pacify *verb*
pacifies
pacifying
pacified

pack *verb*
packs
packing
packed

pack *noun*
packs

package *noun*
packages

packet *noun*
packets

pad *noun*
pads

pad *verb*
pads
padding
padded

padding

paddle *verb*
paddles
paddling
paddled

paddle *noun*
paddles

pa

paddock *noun*
paddocks

paddy *noun*
paddies

padlock *noun*
padlocks

pagan *adjective* and *noun*
pagans

page *noun*
pages

pageant *noun*
pageants

pageantry

pagoda *noun*
pagodas

paid see **pay**

pail* *noun*
pails

pain☆ *noun*
pains

pain *verb*
pains
paining
pained

painful *adjective*
painfully

painkiller *noun*
painkillers

painless *adjective*
painlessly

painstaking

paint *noun*
paints

paint *verb*
paints
painting
painted

paintbox *noun*
paintboxes

paintbrush *noun*
paintbrushes

painter *noun*
painters

painting *noun*
paintings

pair⊙ *noun*
pairs

pair *verb*
pairs
pairing
paired

pal *noun*
pals

palace *noun*
palaces

palate *noun*
palates

pale✛ *adjective*
paler
palest

paleness

palette *noun*
palettes

paling *noun*
palings

palisade *noun*
palisades

pall *verb*
palls
palling
palled

pallid

pallor

palm *noun*
palms

palm *verb*
palms
palming
palmed

palmistry

Palm Sunday

paltry *adjective*
paltrier
paltriest

pampas *plural noun*

pamper *verb*
pampers
pampering
pampered

pamphlet *noun*
pamphlets

pan *noun*
pans

pancake *noun*
pancakes

panda *noun*
pandas

pandemonium

pander *verb*
panders
pandering
pandered

pane* *noun*
panes

panel *noun*
panels

pang *noun*
pangs

....

★ A **pail** is a bucket. **!pale**.
☆ A **pain** is an unpleasant feeling caused by injury or disease.
  !pane.
⊙ A **pair** is a set of two. **!pear**.
✛ **Pale** means 'almost white'. **!pail**.
⊛ A **pane** is a piece of glass in a window. **!pain**.

170

panic

panic *verb*
panics
panicking
panicked

panicky

pannier *noun*
panniers

panorama *noun*
panoramas

panoramic *adjective*
panoramically

pansy *noun*
pansies

pant *verb*
pants
panting
panted

panther *noun*
panthers

panties *plural noun*

pantomime *noun*
pantomimes

pantry *noun*
pantries

pants *plural noun*

paper *noun*
papers

paper *verb*
papers
papering
papered

paperback *noun*
paperbacks

papier mâché

papyrus *noun*
papyri

parable *noun*
parables

parachute *noun*
parachutes

parachutist

parade *noun*
parades

parade *verb*
parades
parading
paraded

paradise

paradox *noun*
paradoxes

paradoxical *adjective*
paradoxically

paraffin

paragraph *noun*
paragraphs

parallel

parallelogram *noun*
parallelograms

paralyse *verb*
paralyses
paralysing
paralysed

paralysis *noun*
paralyses

paralytic *adjective*
paralytically

parapet *noun*
parapets

paraphernalia

paraphrase *verb*
paraphrases
paraphrasing
paraphrased

parasite *noun*
parasites

parasitic *adjective*
parasitically

parasol *noun*
parasols

paratrooper

paratroops *plural noun*

parcel *noun*
parcels

parched

parchment

pardon *verb*
pardons
pardoning
pardoned

pardon *noun*
pardons

pardonable

parent *noun*
parents

parentage

parental

parenthood

parenthesis *noun*
parentheses

parish *noun*
parishes

parishioner *noun*
parishioners

park *noun*
parks

park *verb*
parks
parking
parked

parka *noun*
parkas

parliament *noun*
parliaments

parliamentary

parody *noun*
parodies

parole

parrot *noun*
parrots

parsley

parsnip *noun*
parsnips

parson *noun*
parsons

parsonage *noun*
parsonages

part *noun*
parts

pa

part *verb*
parts
parting
parted

partial *adjective*
partially

partiality

participant *noun*
participants

participate *verb*
participates
participating
participated

participation

participle *noun*
participles

particle *noun*
particles

particular *adjective*
particularly

particulars *plural noun*

parting *noun*
partings

partition *noun*
partitions

partly

partner *noun*
partners

partnership

partridge *noun*
partridges

part-time *adjective*

party *noun*
parties

pass *verb*
passes
passing
passed

pass *noun*
passes

passable

passage *noun*
passages

passageway *noun*
passageways

passed★ see pass

passenger *noun*
passengers

passer-by *noun*
passers-by

passion *noun*
passions

passionate *adjective*
passionately

passive *adjective*
passively

Passover

passport *noun*
passports

password *noun*
passwords

past☆ *noun, adjective,
and preposition*

pasta *noun*
pastas

paste *noun*
pastes

paste *verb*
pastes
pasting
pasted

pastel *noun*
pastels

pasteurization

pasteurize *verb*
pasteurizes
pasteurizing
pasteurized

pastille *noun*
pastilles

pastime *noun*
pastimes

pastoral

pastry *noun*
pastries

pasture *noun*
pastures

pasty *noun*
pasties

pasty *adjective*
pastier
pastiest

pat *verb*
pats
patting
patted

pat *noun*
pats

patch *noun*
patches

patch *verb*
patches
patching
patched

patchwork

patchy *adjective*
patchier
patchiest

patent *adjective*
patently

patent *verb*
patents
patenting
patented

patent *noun*
patents

paternal *adjective*
paternally

path *noun*
paths

pathetic *adjective*
pathetically

★ You use **passed** in e.g. *We passed the house.* **!past**.
☆ You use **past** in e.g. *We went past the house.* **!passed**.

172

patience

patient *adjective*
patiently

patient *noun*
patients

patio *noun*
patios

patriot *noun*
patriots

patriotic *adjective*
patriotically

patriotism

patrol *verb*
patrols
patrolling
patrolled

patrol *noun*
patrols

patron *noun*
patrons

patronage

patronize *verb*
patronizes
patronizing
patronized

patter *verb*
patters
pattering
pattered

patter *noun*
patters

pattern *noun*
patterns

pause *verb*
pauses
pausing
paused

pause *noun*
pauses

pave *verb*
paves
paving
paved

pavement *noun*
pavements

pavilion *noun*
pavilions

paw *noun*
paws

paw *verb*
paws
pawing
pawed

pawn *noun*
pawns

pawn *verb*
pawns
pawning
pawned

pawnbroker *noun*
pawnbrokers

pay *verb*
pays
paying
paid

pay *noun*

payment *noun*
payments

pea *noun*
peas

peace✶

peaceful *adjective*
peacefully

peach *noun*
peaches

peacock *noun*
peacocks

peak✩ *noun*
peaks

peak○ *verb*
peaks
peaking
peaked

peaked

peal✢ *verb*
peals
pealing
pealed

peal✱ *noun*
peals

peanut *noun*
peanuts

pear✻ *noun*
pears

pearl *noun*
pearls

pearly *adjective*
pearlier
pearliest

peasant *noun*
peasants

peasantry

peat

pebble *noun*
pebbles

pebbly *adjective*
pebblier
pebbliest

peck *verb*
pecks
pecking
pecked

a
b
c
d
e
f
g
h
i
j
k
l
m
n
o
p
q
r
s
t
u
v
w
x
y
z

✶ **Peace** is a time when there is no war. **!** **piece.**
✩ A **peak** is the top of something. **!** **peek.**
○ To **peak** is to reach the highest point. **!** **peek.**
✢ To **peal** is to make a ringing sound of bells. **!** **peel.**
✱ A **peal** is a ringing of bells. **!** **peel.**
✻ A **pear** is a fruit. **!** **pair.**

pe

peck *noun*
pecks

peckish

peculiar *adjective*
peculiarly

peculiarity *noun*
peculiarities

pedal *noun*
pedals

pedal *verb*
pedals
pedalling
pedalled

peddle* *verb*
peddles
peddling
peddled

pedestal *noun*
pedestals

pedestrian *noun*
pedestrians

pedestrian *adjective*

pedigree *noun*
pedigrees

pedlar *noun*
pedlars

peek☆ *verb*
peeks
peeking
peeked

peel○ *noun*
peels

peel✣ *verb*
peels
peeling
peeled

peep *verb*
peeps
peeping
peeped

peep *noun*
peeps

peer● *verb*
peers
peering
peered

peer *noun*
peers

peerless

peewit *noun*
peewits

peg *noun*
pegs

peg *verb*
pegs
pegging
pegged

Pekinese *noun*
Pekinese

pelican *noun*
pelicans

pellet *noun*
pellets

pelt *verb*
pelts
pelting
pelted

pelt *noun*
pelts

pen *noun*
pens

penalize *verb*
penalizes
penalizing
penalized

penalty *noun*
penalties

pence see penny

pencil *noun*
pencils

pencil *verb*
pencils
pencilling
pencilled

pendant *noun*
pendants

pendulum *noun*
pendulums

penetrate *verb*
penetrates
penetrating
penetrated

penetration

penfriend *noun*
penfriends

penguin *noun*
penguins

penicillin

peninsula *noun*
peninsulas

peninsular

penis *noun*
penises

penitence

penitent

penknife *noun*
penknives

pennant *noun*
pennants

penniless

penny *noun*
pennies *or* pence

....

★ To **peddle** is to sell things on the street. **!pedal**.
☆ To **peek** is to look secretly at something. **!peak**.
○ **Peel** is the skin of fruit and vegetables. **!peal**.
✣ To **peel** something is to take the skin off it. **!peal**.
● To **peer** is to look closely at something. **!pier**.

174

pension noun
pensions

pensioner noun
pensioners

pentagon noun
pentagons

pentathlon noun
pentathlons

peony noun
peonies

people plural noun

people noun
peoples

pepper noun
peppers

peppermint noun
peppermints

peppery

perceive verb
perceives
perceiving
perceived

per cent

percentage noun
percentages

perceptible adjective
perceptibly

perception noun
perceptions

perceptive adjective
perceptively

perch verb
perches
perching
perched

perch noun
perch

percolator noun
percolators

percussion

percussive

perennial adjective
perennially

perennial noun
perennials

perfect adjective
perfectly

perfect verb
perfects
perfecting
perfected

perfection

perforate verb
perforates
perforating
perforated

perforation noun
perforations

perform verb
performs
performing
performed

performance noun
performances

performer noun
performers

perfume noun
perfumes

perhaps

peril noun
perils

perilous adjective
perilously

perimeter noun
perimeters

period noun
periods

periodic adjective
periodically

periodical noun
periodicals

periscope noun
periscopes

perish verb
perishes
perishing
perished

perishable

perm noun
perms

perm verb
perms
perming
permed

permanence

permanent adjective
permanently

permissible

permission

permissive adjective
permissively

permissiveness

permit verb
permits
permitting
permitted

permit noun
permits

perpendicular

perpetual adjective
perpetually

perpetuate verb
perpetuates
perpetuating
perpetuated

perplex verb
perplexes
perplexing
perplexed

perplexity

persecute verb
persecutes
persecuting
persecuted

persecution noun
persecutions

persecutor noun
persecutors

perseverance

persevere verb
perseveres
persevering
persevered

persist verb
persists
persisting
persisted

persistence

persistent adjective
persistently

person* noun
persons or people

personal adjective
personally

personality noun
personalities

personnel plural noun

perspective noun
perspectives

perspiration

perspire verb
perspires
perspiring
perspired

persuade verb
persuades
persuading
persuaded

persuasion

persuasive adjective
persuasively

perverse adjective
perversely

perversion noun
perversions

perversity

pervert verb
perverts
perverting
perverted

pervert noun
perverts

Pesach☆

pessimism

pessimist noun
pessimists

pessimistic adjective
pessimistically

pest noun
pests

pester verb
pesters
pestering
pestered

pesticide noun
pesticides

pestle noun
pestles

pet noun
pets

petal noun
petals

petition noun
petitions

petrify verb
petrifies
petrifying
petrified

petrochemical noun
petrochemicals

petrol

petroleum

petticoat noun
petticoats

pettiness

petty adjective
pettier
pettiest
pettily

pew noun
pews

pewter

pharmacy noun
pharmacies

phase noun
phases

phase verb
phases
phasing
phased

pheasant noun
pheasants

phenomenal
adjective
phenomenally

phenomenon noun
phenomena

philatelist noun
philatelists

philately

philosopher noun
philosophers

philosophical
adjective
philosophically

philosophy noun
philosophies

phobia noun
phobias

-phobia
-phobia makes words
meaning 'a strong fear
or dislike', e.g.
xenophobia (a
dislike of strangers').
It comes from a Greek
word and is only used
with other Greek or
Latin words.

---

phoenix noun
phoenixes

phone noun
phones

★ The normal plural is **people**: *three people came*. **Persons** is
formal, e.g. in official reports.
☆ The Hebrew name for Passover. Pronounced *pay-sahk*.

phone *verb*
phones
phoning
phoned

-phone
-phone makes words to do with sound, e.g. **telephone**, **saxophone**. You can sometimes make adjectives by using *-phonic*, e.g. **telephonic**, and nouns by using *-phony*, e.g. **telephony**.

phonecard *noun*
phonecards

phone-in *noun*
phone-ins

phosphorescence

phosphorescent

phosphoric

phosphorus

photo *noun*
photos

photo-
photo- makes words to do with light, e.g. **photograph**, **photocopy**. It is also used in more technical words such as **photochemistry** (the chemistry of light) and as a separate word in **photo** (photograph) and **photo finish** (close finish to a race).

photocopier *noun*
photocopiers

photocopy *noun*
photocopies

photocopy *verb*
photocopies
photocopying
photocopied

photoelectric

photograph *noun*
photographs

photograph *verb*
photographs
photographing
photographed

photographer *noun*
photographers

photographic *adjective*
photographically

photography

phrase *noun*
phrases

phrase *verb*
phrases
phrasing
phrased

physical *adjective*
physically

physician *noun*
physicians

physicist *noun*
physicists

physics

physiological *adjective*
physiologically

physiologist *noun*
physiologists

physiology

pi*

pianist *noun*
pianists

piano *noun*
pianos

piccolo *noun*
piccolos

pick *verb*
picks
picking
picked

pick *noun*
picks

pickaxe *noun*
pickaxes

picket *noun*
pickets

picket *verb*
pickets
picketing
picketed

pickle *noun*
pickles

pickle *verb*
pickles
pickling
pickled

pickpocket *noun*
pickpockets

pick-up *noun*
pick-ups

picnic *noun*
picnics

picnic *verb*
picnics
picnicking
picnicked

picnicker *noun*
picnickers

pictogram *noun*
pictograms

pictorial *adjective*
pictorially

a
b
c
d
e
f
g
h
i
j
k
l
m
n
o
p
q
r
s
t
u
v
w
x
y
z

* **Pi** is a Greek letter, used in mathematics. **!** pie.

177

pi

picture noun
pictures

picture verb
pictures
picturing
pictured

picturesque

pie* noun
pies

piece☆ noun
pieces

piece verb
pieces
piecing
pieced

piecemeal

pie chart noun
pie charts

pier° noun
piers

pierce verb
pierces
piercing
pierced

pig noun
pigs

pigeon noun
pigeons

pigeon-hole noun
pigeon-holes

piggy noun
piggies

piggyback noun
piggybacks

piglet noun
piglets

pigment noun
pigments

pigmy noun use
pygmy

pigsty noun
pigsties

pigtail noun
pigtails

pike noun
pikes

pilchard noun
pilchards

pile noun
piles

pile verb
piles
piling
piled

pilfer verb
pilfers
pilfering
pilfered

pilgrim noun
pilgrims

pilgrimage noun
pilgrimages

pill noun
pills

pillage verb
pillages
pillaging
pillaged

pillar noun
pillars

pillion noun
pillions

pillow noun
pillows

pillowcase noun
pillowcases

pilot noun
pilots

pilot verb
pilots
piloting
piloted

pimple noun
pimples

pimply adjective
pimplier
pimpliest

pin noun
pins

pin verb
pins
pinning
pinned

pinafore noun
pinafores

pincer noun
pincers

pinch verb
pinches
pinching
pinched

pinch noun
pinches

pincushion noun
pincushions

pine noun
pines

pine verb
pines
pining
pined

pineapple noun
pineapples

ping-pong

★ A **pie** is a food with pastry. **! pi.**

☆ You use **piece** in e.g. *a piece of cake*. **! peace.**

○ A **pier** is a long building on stilts going into the sea. **! peer.**

178

pink adjective
pinker
pinkest

pink noun
pinks

pint noun
pints

pioneer noun
pioneers

pious adjective
piously

pip noun
pips

pipe noun
pipes

pipe verb
pipes
piping
piped

pipeline noun
pipelines

piper noun
pipers

piracy noun

pirate noun
pirates

pistil* noun
pistils

pistol☆ noun
pistols

piston noun
pistons

pit noun
pits

pit verb
pits
pitting
pitted

pitch noun
pitches

pitch verb
pitches
pitching
pitched

pitch-black

pitcher noun
pitchers

pitchfork noun
pitchforks

pitfall noun
pitfalls

pitiful adjective
pitifully

pitiless adjective
pitilessly

pity verb
pities
pitying
pitied

pity noun

pivot noun
pivots

pivot verb
pivots
pivoting
pivoted

pixie noun
pixies

pizza noun
pizzas

pizzicato

placard noun
placards

place° noun
places

place verb
places
placing
placed

placid adjective
placidly

plague noun
plagues

plague verb
plagues
plaguing
plagued

plaice✦ noun
plaice

plaid noun
plaids

plain* adjective
plainer
plainest
plainly

plain noun
plains

plain clothes

plainness

plaintiff noun
plaintiffs

plaintive

plaintively

plait noun
plaits

plait verb
plaits
plaiting
plaited

plan noun
plans

plan verb
plans
planning
planned

a
b
c
d
e
f
g
h
i
j
k
l
m
n
o
p
q
r
s
t
u
v
w
x
y
z

. . . .

★ A **pistil** is a part of a flower.❗**pistol**.
☆ A **pistol** is a gun.❗**pistil**.
○ You use **place** in e.g. *a place in the country*. ❗**plaice**.
✦ A **plaice** is a fish. ❗**place**.
● **Plain** means 'not pretty or decorated'. ❗**plane**.

179

pl

plane* *noun*
planes

plane☆ *verb*
planes
planing
planed

planet *noun*
planets

planetary

plank *noun*
planks

plankton

planner *noun*
planners

plant *noun*
plants

plant *verb*
plants
planting
planted

plantation *noun*
plantations

planter *noun*
planters

plaque *noun*
plaques

plasma

plaster *noun*
plasters

plaster *verb*
plasters
plastering
plastered

plasterer *noun*
plasterers

plaster of Paris

plastic *adjective and noun*
plastics

Plasticine

plate *noun*
plates

plate *verb*
plates
plating
plated

plateau *noun*
plateaux

plateful *noun*
platefuls

platform *noun*
platforms

platinum

platoon *noun*
platoons

platypus *noun*
platypuses

play *verb*
plays
playing
played

play *noun*
plays

playback *noun*
playbacks

player *noun*
players

playful *adjective*
playfully

playfulness

playground *noun*
playgrounds

playgroup *noun*
playgroups

playmate *noun*
playmates

play-off *noun*
play-offs

playtime *noun*
playtimes

playwright *noun*
playwrights

plea *noun*
pleas

plead *verb*
pleads
pleading
pleaded

pleasant *adjective*
pleasanter
pleasantest
pleasantly

please *verb*
pleases
pleasing
pleased

pleasurable *adjective*
pleasurably

pleasure *noun*
pleasures

pleat *noun*
pleats

pleated

pledge *verb*
pledges
pledging
pledged

pledge *noun*
pledges

plentiful *adjective*
plentifully

plenty

pliable

pliers *plural noun*

plight *noun*
plights

plod *verb*
plods
plodding
plodded

plodder *noun*
plodders

....

★ A **plane** is an aeroplane, a level surface, a tool, or a tree. **! plain**.
☆ To **plane** wood is to make it smooth with a tool. **! plain**.

plop *verb*
plops
plopping
plopped

plop *noun*
plops

plot *noun*
plots

plot *verb*
plots
plotting
plotted

plotter *noun*
plotters

plough *noun*
ploughs

plough *verb*
ploughs
ploughing
ploughed

ploughman *noun*
ploughmen

plover *noun*
plovers

pluck *verb*
plucks
plucking
plucked

pluck *noun*

plucky *adjective*
pluckier
pluckiest
pluckily

plug *noun*
plugs

plug *verb*
plugs
plugging
plugged

plum★ *noun*
plums

plumage

plumb☆ *verb*
plumbs
plumbing
plumbed

plumber *noun*
plumbers

plumbing

plume *noun*
plumes

plumed

plump *adjective*
plumper
plumpest

plump *verb*
plumps
plumping
plumped

plunder *verb*
plunders
plundering
plundered

plunder *noun*

plunderer *noun*
plunderers

plunge *verb*
plunges
plunging
plunged

plunge *noun*
plunges

plural *adjective* and *noun*
plurals

plus *preposition*

plus *noun*
pluses

plutonium

plywood

pneumatic

pneumonia

poach *verb*
poaches
poaching
poached

poacher *noun*
poachers

pocket *noun*
pockets

pocket *verb*
pockets
pocketing
pocketed

pocketful *noun*
pocketfuls

pod *noun*
pods

podgy *adjective*
podgier
podgiest

poem *noun*
poems

poet *noun*
poets

poetic *adjective*
poetically

poetry

point *noun*
points

point *verb*
points
pointing
pointed

point-blank *adjective*

pointed *adjective*
pointedly

pointer *noun*
pointers

pointless *adjective*
pointlessly

★ A **plum** is a fruit. **! plumb.**

☆ To **plumb** water is to see how deep it is. **! plum.**

po

poise *noun*

poise *verb*
poises
poising
poised

poison *noun*
poisons

poison *verb*
poisons
poisoning
poisoned

poisoner *noun*
poisoners

poisonous *adjective*
poisonously

poke *verb*
pokes
poking
poked

poke *noun*
pokes

poker *noun*
pokers

polar

Polaroid

pole* *noun*
poles

police *plural noun*

policeman *noun*
policemen

police officer *noun*
police officers

policewoman *noun*
policewomen

policy *noun*
policies

polio

poliomyelitis

polish *verb*
polishes
polishing
polished

polish *noun*
polishes

polished

polite *adjective*
politer
politest
politely

politeness

political *adjective*
politically

politician *noun*
politicians

politics

polka *noun*
polkas

poll☆ *noun*
polls

pollen

pollute *verb*
pollutes
polluting
polluted

pollution

polo

polo neck *noun*
polo necks

poltergeist *noun*
poltergeists

polygon *noun*
polygons

polystyrene

polythene

pomp

pomposity

pompous *adjective*
pompously

pond *noun*
ponds

ponder *verb*
ponders
pondering
pondered

ponderous *adjective*
ponderously

pony *noun*
ponies

ponytail *noun*
ponytails

pony-trekking

poodle *noun*
poodles

pool *noun*
pools

pool *verb*
pools
pooling
pooled

poor *adjective*
poorer
poorest
poorly

poorly *adjective* and *adverb*

pop *verb*
pops
popping
popped

pop *noun*
pops

popcorn

Pope *noun*
Popes

poplar *noun*
poplars

poppadom *noun*
poppadoms

poppy *noun*
poppies

....

★ A **pole** is a long thin stick. **!poll**.

☆ A **poll** is a vote in an election. **!pole**.

popular *adjective*
popularly
popularity
popularize *verb*
popularizes
popularizing
popularized
populated
population *noun*
populations
populous
porcelain
porch *noun*
porches
porcupine *noun*
porcupines
pore *noun*
pores
pore* *verb*
pores
poring
pored
pork
pornographic
pornography
porosity
porous
porpoise *noun*
porpoises
porridge
port *noun*
ports
portable
portcullis *noun*
portcullises
porter *noun*
porters
porthole *noun*
portholes
portion *noun*
portions

portliness
portly *adjective*
portlier
portliest
portrait *noun*
portraits
portray *verb*
portrays
portraying
portrayed
portrayal *noun*
portrayals
pose *verb*
poses
posing
posed
pose *noun*
poses
poser *noun*
posers
posh *adjective*
posher
poshest
position *noun*
positions
positive *adjective*
positively
positive *noun*
positives
posse *noun*
posses
possess *verb*
possesses
possessing
possessed
possession *noun*
possessions
possessive *adjective*
possessively
possessor *noun*
possessors
possibility *noun*
possibilities

possible *adjective*
possibly
post *verb*
posts
posting
posted
post *noun*
posts
postage
postal
postbox *noun*
postboxes
postcard *noun*
postcards
postcode *noun*
postcodes
poster *noun*
posters
postman *noun*
postmen
postmark *noun*
postmarks
post-mortem *noun*
post-mortems
postpone *verb*
postpones
postponing
postponed
postponement *noun*
postponements
postscript *noun*
postscripts
posture *noun*
postures
posy *noun*
posies
pot *noun*
pots
pot *verb*
pots
potting
potted

★ To **pore** over something is to study it closely. ! **pour**.

a

potassium

potato *noun*
potatoes

b

potency

c

potent *adjective*
potently

d

potential *adjective*
potentially

e

f

potential *noun*
potentials

g

pothole *noun*
potholes

h

potholer *noun*
potholer

i

j

potholing

potion *noun*
potions

k

potter *noun*
potters

l

potter *verb*
potters
pottering
pottered

m

n

pottery *noun*
potteries

p

potty *adjective*
pottier
pottiest
pottily

q

potty *noun*
potties

r

pouch *noun*
pouches

s

t

poultry

u

pounce *verb*
pounces
pouncing
pounced

v

w

pound *noun*
pounds

x

pound *verb*
pounds
pounding
pounded

pour* *verb*
pours
pouring
poured

pout *verb*
pouts
pouting
pouted

poverty

powder *noun*
powders

powder *verb*
powders
powdering
powdered

powdery

power *noun*
powers

powered

powerful *adjective*
powerfully

powerhouse *noun*
powerhouses

powerless

practicable

practical *adjective*
practically

practice *noun*
practices

practise *verb*
practises
practising
practised

prairie *noun*
prairies

praise *verb*
praises
praising
praised

praise *noun*
praises

pram *noun*
prams

prance *verb*
prances
prancing
pranced

prank *noun*
pranks

prawn *noun*
prawns

pray* *verb*
prays
praying
prayed

prayer *noun*
prayers

---

pre-
pre- makes words
meaning 'before', e.g.
pre-date (to exist
before something
else), **prefabricated**
(made in advance).
Many are spelt joined
up, but not all.

---

preach *verb*
preaches
preaching
preached

preacher *noun*
preachers

precarious *adjective*
precariously

precaution *noun*
precautions

★ To **pour** a liquid is to tip it from a jug etc. **I pore**.
☆ To **pray** is to say prayers. **I prey**.

precede *verb*
precedes
preceding
preceded

precedence

precedent *noun*
precedents

precinct *noun*
precincts

precious *adjective*
preciously

precipice *noun*
precipices

précis *noun*
précis

precise *adjective*
precisely

precision

predator *noun*
predators

predatory

predecessor *noun*
predecessors

predict *verb*
predicts
predicting
predicted

predictable *adjective*
predictably

prediction *noun*
predictions

predominance

predominant *adjective*
predominantly

predominate *verb*
predominates
predominating
predominated

preface *noun*
prefaces

prefect *noun*
prefects

prefer *verb*
prefers
preferring
preferred

preferable *adjective*
preferably

preference *noun*
preferences

prefix *noun*
prefixes

pregnancy *noun*
pregnancies

pregnant

prehistoric

prehistory

prejudice *noun*
prejudices

prejudiced

preliminary *adjective
and noun*
preliminaries

prelude *noun*
preludes

premier *noun*
premiers

première *noun*
premières

premises *plural noun*

premium *noun*
premiums

Premium Bond *noun*
Premium Bonds

preoccupation *noun*
preoccupations

preoccupied

prep

preparation *noun*
preparations

preparatory

prepare *verb*
prepares
preparing
prepared

preposition *noun*
prepositions

prescribe *verb*
prescribes
prescribing
prescribed

prescription *noun*
prescriptions

presence

present *adjective*
presently

present *noun*
presents

present *verb*
presents
presenting
presented

presentation *noun*
presentations

presenter *noun*
presenters

preservation

preservative *noun*
preservatives

preserve *verb*
preserves
preserving
preserved

preside *verb*
presides
presiding
presided

presidency *noun*
presidencies

president *noun*
presidents

presidential *adjective*
presidentially

press *verb*
presses
pressing
pressed

press *noun*
presses

pr

press-up *noun*
press-ups

pressure *noun*
pressures

pressurize *verb*
pressurizes
pressurizing
pressurized

prestige *noun*

prestigious *adjective*
prestigiously

presumably

presume *verb*
presumes
presuming
presumed

presumption *noun*
presumptions

presumptuous
adjective
presumptuously

pretence *noun*
pretences

pretend *verb*
pretends
pretending
pretended

pretender *noun*
pretenders

prettiness

pretty *adjective* and
adverb
prettier
prettiest
prettily

prevail *verb*
prevails
prevailing
prevailed

prevalent

prevent *verb*
prevents
preventing
prevented

prevention

preventive

preview *noun*
previews

previous *adjective*
previously

prey* *verb*
preys
preying
preyed

prey *noun*

price *noun*
prices

price *verb*
prices
pricing
priced

priceless

prick *verb*
pricks
pricking
pricked

prick *noun*
pricks

prickle *noun*
prickles

prickly *adjective*
pricklier
prickliest

pride *noun*
prides

priest *noun*
priests

priestess *noun*
priestesses

priesthood

prig *noun*
prigs

priggish *adjective*
priggishly

prim *adjective*
primmer
primmest
primly

primness

primary *adjective*
primarily

primate *noun*
primates

prime *adjective*

prime *verb*
primes
priming
primed

prime *noun*
primes

prime minister *noun*
prime ministers

primer *noun*
primers

primeval

primitive *adjective*
primitively

primrose *noun*
primroses

prince *noun*
princes

princely

princess *noun*
princesses

principal☆ *adjective*
principally

principal○ *noun*
principals

★ To **prey** on animals is to hunt and kill them. **!pray**.
☆ **Principal** means 'chief' or 'main'. **!principle**.
○ A **principal** is a head of a college. **!principle**.

186

principle★ noun
principles

print verb
prints
printing
printed

print noun
prints

printer noun
printers

printout noun
printouts

priority noun
priorities

prise☆ verb
prises
prising
prised

prism noun
prisms

prison noun
prisons

prisoner noun
prisoners

privacy noun

private adjective
privately

private noun
privates

privatization

privatize verb
privatizes
privatizing
privatized

privet

privilege noun
privileges

privileged

prize noun
prizes

prize○ verb
prizes
prizing
prized

pro noun
pros

---

pro-
pro- makes words
meaning 'in favour of',
e.g. **pro-choice**. In
this type of word you
use a hyphen.

---

probability noun
probabilities

probable adjective
probably

probation

probationary

probe verb
probes
probing
probed

probe noun
probes

problem noun
problems

procedure noun
procedures

proceed verb
proceeds
proceeding
proceeded

proceedings plural noun

proceeds plural noun

process noun
processes

process verb
processes
processing
processed

procession noun
processions

proclaim verb
proclaims
proclaiming
proclaimed

proclamation noun
proclamations

prod verb
prods
prodding
prodded

prodigal adjective
prodigally

produce verb
produces
producing
produced

produce noun

producer noun
producers

product noun
products

production noun
productions

productive adjective
productively

productivity

profession noun
professions

professional adjective
professionally

professional noun
professionals

professor noun
professors

- -

★ A **principle** is a rule or belief. **! principal**.
☆ To **prise** something is to open it. **! prize**.
○ To **prize** something is to value it highly. **! prise**.

pr

proficiency
proficient *adjective*
proficiently
profile *noun*
profiles
profit* *noun*
profits
profit *verb*
profits
profiting
profited
profitable *adjective*
profitably
profound *adjective*
profoundly
profundity
profuse *adjective*
profusely
profusion
program☆ *noun*
programs
program *verb*
programs
programming
programmed
programme☆ *noun*
programmes
progress *noun*
progress *verb*
progresses
progressing
progressed
progression
progressive *adjective*
progressively
prohibit *verb*
prohibits
prohibiting
prohibited

prohibition *noun*
prohibitions
project *noun*
projects
project *verb*
projects
projecting
projected
projection *noun*
projections
projectionist *noun*
projectionists
projector *noun*
projectors
prologue *noun*
prologues
prolong *verb*
prolongs
prolonging
prolonged
promenade *noun*
promenades
prominence
prominent *adjective*
prominently
promise *verb*
promises
promising
promised
promise *noun*
promises
promontory *noun*
promontories
promote *verb*
promotes
promoting
promoted
promoter *noun*
promoter
promotion *noun*
promotions

prompt *adjective*
prompter
promptest
promptly
prompt *verb*
prompts
prompting
prompted
prompter *noun*
prompters
promptness
prone
prong *noun*
prongs
pronoun *noun*
pronouns
pronounce *verb*
pronounces
pronouncing
pronounced
pronouncement
noun
pronouncements
pronunciation *noun*
pronunciations
proof *adjective* and
noun
proofs
prop *verb*
props
propping
propped
prop *noun*
props
propaganda
propel *verb*
propels
propelling
propelled
propellant *noun*
propellants

....

★ A **profit** is extra money made by selling something. I **prophet**.
☆ You use **program** when you are talking about computers. In other
   meanings you use **programme**.

188

propeller *noun*
propellers

proper *adjective*
properly

property *noun*
properties

prophecy *noun*
prophecies

prophesy *verb*
prophesies
prophesying
prophesied

prophet* *noun*
prophets

prophetic *adjective*
prophetically

proportion *noun*
proportions

proportional *adjective*
proportionally

proportionate *adjective*
proportionately

propose *verb*
proposes
proposing
proposed

proposal *noun*
proposals

proprietor *noun*
proprietors

propulsion

prose

prosecute *verb*
prosecutes
prosecuting
prosecuted

prosecution *noun*
prosecutions

prosecutor *noun*
prosecutors

prospect *noun*
prospects

prospect *verb*
prospects
prospecting
prospected

prospector *noun*
prospectors

prosper *verb*
prospers
prospering
prospered

prosperity

prosperous *adjective*
prosperously

prostitute *noun*
prostitutes

protect *verb*
protects
protecting
protected

protection

protective *adjective*
protectively

protector *noun*
protectors

protein *noun*
proteins

protest *verb*
protests
protesting
protested

protest *noun*
protests

protester *noun*
protesters

Protestant *noun*
Protestants

proton *noun*
protons

protoplasm

prototype *noun*
prototypes

protractor *noun*
protractors

protrude *verb*
protrudes
protruding
protruded

protrusion *noun*
protrusions

proud *adjective*
prouder
proudest
proudly

prove *verb*
proves
proving
proved

proverb *noun*
proverbs

proverbial *adjective*
proverbially

provide *verb*
provides
providing
provided

province *noun*
provinces

provincial

provision *noun*
provisions

provisional *adjective*
provisionally

provocative *adjective*
provocatively

provoke *verb*
provokes
provoking
provoked

provocation *noun*
provocations

. . . .

★ A **prophet** is someone who makes predictions about the future.
❗ **profit**.

a

prow *noun*
prows

b

prowl *verb*
prowls
prowling
prowled

c

prowler *noun*
prowlers

d

e

prudence

f

prudent *adjective*
prudently

g

prune *noun*
prunes

h

prune *verb*
prunes
pruning
pruned

i

j

pry *verb*
pries
prying
pried

k

l

psalm *noun*
psalms

m

pseudonym *noun*
pseudonyms

n

o

psychiatric

psychiatrist *noun*
psychiatrists

p

psychiatry

psychic

q

psychological
adjective
psychologically

r

psychologist *noun*
psychologists

s

psychology

t

pub *noun*
pubs

u

puberty

v

public *adjective* and
noun
publicly

w

publication *noun*
publications

x

y

z

publicity

publicize *verb*
publicizes
publicizing
publicized

publish *verb*
publishes
publishing
published

publisher *noun*
publishers

puck *noun*
pucks

pucker *verb*
puckers
puckering
puckered

pudding *noun*
puddings

puddle *noun*
puddles

puff *verb*
puffs
puffing
puffed

puff *noun*
puffs

puffin *noun*
puffins

pull *verb*
pulls
pulling
pulled

pull *noun*
pulls

pulley *noun*
pulleys

pullover *noun*
pullovers

pulp *noun*
pulps

pulp *verb*
pulps
pulping
pulped

pulpit *noun*
pulpits

pulse *noun*
pulses

pulverize *verb*
pulverizes
pulverizing
pulverized

puma *noun*
pumas

pumice

pump *verb*
pumps
pumping
pumped

pump *noun*
pumps

pumpkin *noun*
pumpkins

pun *noun*
puns

pun *verb*
puns
punning
punned

punch *verb*
punches
punching
punched

punch *noun*
punches

punch *noun*
punches

punchline *noun*
punchlines

punch-up *noun*
punch-ups

punctual *adjective*
punctually

punctuality

punctuate *verb*
punctuates
punctuating
punctuated

punctuation

puncture *noun*
punctures

punish *verb*
punishes
punishing
punished

punishment *noun*
punishments

punk *noun*
punks

punt *noun*
punts

punt *verb*
punts
punting
punted

puny *adjective*
punier
puniest

pup *noun*
pups

pupa *noun*
pupae

pupil *noun*
pupils

puppet *noun*
puppets

puppy *noun*
puppies

purchase *verb*
purchases
purchasing
purchased

purchase *noun*
purchases

purchaser *noun*
purchasers

purdah

pure *adjective*
purer
purest
purely

purge *verb*
purges
purging
purged

purge *noun*
purges

purification

purifier *noun*
purifiers

purify *verb*
purifies
purifying
purified

Puritan★ *noun*
Puritans

puritan *noun*
puritans

puritanical *adjective*
puritanically

purity

purple *noun*

purpose *noun*
purposes

purposely

purr *verb*
purrs
purring
purred

purse *noun*
purses

pursue *verb*
pursues
pursuing
pursued

pursuer *noun*
pursuers

pursuit *noun*
pursuits

pus☆ *noun*

push *verb*
pushes
pushing
pushed

push *noun*
pushes

pushchair *noun*
pushchairs

puss○ or **pussy** *noun*
pusses *or* pussies

put✢ *verb*
puts
putting
put

putt✱ *verb*
putts
putting
putted

putter *noun*
putters

putty

puzzle *verb*
puzzles
puzzling
puzzled

puzzle *noun*
puzzles

pygmy *noun*
pygmies

pyjamas

pylon *noun*
pylons

★ You use a capital P when you are talking about people in history, and a small p when you mean anyone who is morally strict.

☆ **Pus** is yellow stuff produced in sore places on the body. **! puss**.

○ **Puss** is a word for a cat. **! pus**.

✢ To **put** something somewhere is to place it there. **! putt**.

✱ To **putt** a ball is to tap it gently. **! put**.

a

b

c

d

Qq

e

f

g **quack** verb
quacks
quacking
quacked

h

i **quack** noun
quacks

j

quad noun
quads

k

l **quadrangle** noun
quadrangles

quadrant noun
quadrants

m

quadrilateral noun
quadrilaterals

n

o **quadruple** adjective
and noun

p **quadruple** verb
quadruples
quadrupling
quadrupled

q

quadruplet noun
quadruplets

r

s **quail** verb
quails
quailing
quailed

t

u **quail** noun
quail or quails

v **quaint** adjective
quainter
quaintest
quaintly

w

x

y

z

quaintness noun

quake verb
quakes
quaking
quaked

Quaker noun
Quakers

qualification noun
qualifications

qualify verb
qualifies
qualifying
qualified

quality noun
qualities

quantity noun
quantities

quarantine

quarrel noun
quarrels

quarrel verb
quarrels
quarrelling
quarrelled

quarrelsome

quarry noun
quarries

quart noun
quarts

quarter noun
quarters

quartet noun
quartets

quartz

quaver verb
quavers
quavering
quavered

quaver noun
quavers

quay★ noun
quays

queasy adjective
queasier
queasiest

queen noun
queens

queer adjective
queerer
queerest

quench verb
quenches
quenching
quenched

query verb
queries
querying
queried

query noun
queries

quest noun
quests

question noun
questions

question verb
questions
questioning
questioned

questionable
adjective
questionably

questioner noun
questioner

questionnaire noun
questionnaires

queue☆ noun
queues

queue verb
queues
queueing
queued

....

★ A **quay** is a place where ships tie up. **!key.**
☆ A **queue** is a line of people waiting for something. **!cue.**

quibble verb
quibbles
quibbling
quibbled

quibble noun
quibbles

quiche noun
quiches

quick adjective
quicker
quickest
quickly

quicken verb
quickens
quickening
quickened

quicksand noun
quicksands

quid noun
quid

quiet adjective
quieter
quietest
quietly

quieten verb
quietens
quietening
quietened

quill noun
quills

quilt noun
quilts

quintet noun
quintets

quit verb
quits
quitting
quitted
quit

quitter noun
quitters

quite

quiver verb
quivers
quivering
quivered

quiver noun
quivers

quiz noun
quizzes

quiz verb
quizzes
quizzing
quizzed

quoit noun
quoits

quota noun
quotas

quotation noun
quotations

quote verb
quotes
quoting
quoted

quotient noun
quotients

Rr

rabbi noun
rabbis

rabbit noun
rabbits

rabid

rabies

raccoon noun
raccoons

race noun
races

race verb
races
racing
raced

race noun
races

racecourse noun
racecourses

racer noun
racers

racial adjective
racially

racism

racist noun
racists

rack noun
racks

rack verb
racks
racking
racked

racket noun
rackets

radar

radial adjective
radially

radiance

radiant adjective
radiantly

radiate verb
radiates
radiating
radiated

radiation

radiator noun
radiators

radical adjective
radically

radical noun
radicals

radii see **radius**

a
b
c
d
e
f
g
h
i
j
k
l
m
n
o
p
q
r
s
t
u
v
w
x
y
z

radio noun
radios

radioactive

radioactivity

radish noun
radishes

radium

radius noun
radii

raffle noun
raffles

raffle verb
raffles
raffling
raffled

raft noun
rafts

rafter noun
rafters

rag noun
rags

rage noun
rages

rage verb
rages
raging
raged

ragged

ragtime

raid noun
raids

raid verb
raids
raiding
raided

raider noun
raiders

rail noun
rails

railings plural noun

railway noun
railways

rain verb
rains
raining
rained

rain noun
rains

rainbow noun
rainbows

raincoat noun
raincoats

raindrop noun
raindrops

rainfall

rainforest noun
rainforests

raise verb
raises
raising
raised

raisin noun
raisins

rake verb
rakes
raking
raked

rake noun
rakes

rally verb
rallies
rallying
rallied

rally noun
rallies

ram verb
rams
ramming
rammed

ram noun
rams

Ramadan

ramble noun
rambles

ramble verb
rambles
rambling
rambled

rambler noun
ramblers

ramp noun
ramps

rampage verb
rampages
rampaging
rampaged

rampage noun

ran see **run**

ranch noun
ranches

random

rang see **ring**

range noun
ranges

range verb
ranges
ranging
ranged

ranger* noun
rangers

rank noun
ranks

rank verb
ranks
ranking
ranked

ransack verb
ransacks
ransacking
ransacked

ransom verb
ransoms
ransoming
ransomed

ransom noun
ransoms

· ·

★ You use a capital R when you mean a senior Guide.

194

rap* verb
raps
rapping
rapped

rap noun
raps

rapid adjective
rapidly

rapidity

rapids plural noun

rare adjective
rarer
rarest
rarely

rarity noun
rarities

rascal noun
rascals

rash adjective
rasher
rashest
rashly

rash noun
rashes

rasher noun
rashers

raspberry noun
raspberries

Rastafarian noun
Rastafarians

rat noun
rats

rate noun
rates

rate verb
rates
rating
rated

rather

ratio noun
ratios

ration noun
rations

ration verb
rations
rationing
rationed

rational adjective
rationally

rationalize verb
rationalizes
rationalizing
rationalized

rattle verb
rattles
rattling
rattled

rattle noun
rattles

rattlesnake noun
rattlesnakes

rave verb
raves
raving
raved

rave noun
raves

raven noun
ravens

ravenous adjective
ravenously

ravine noun
ravines

raw adjective
rawer
rawest

ray noun
rays

razor noun
razors

re-
re- makes words
meaning 'again', e.g.
reproduce. These
words are normally
spelt joined up, but a
few need a hyphen so
you don't confuse
them with other
words, e.g. **re-cover** (
to put a new cover
on); **recover** has
another meaning. You
also need a hyphen in
words beginning with
e, e.g. **re-enter**.

reach verb
reaches
reaching
reached

reach noun
reaches

react verb
reacts
reacting
reacted

reaction noun
reactions

reactor noun
reactors

read☆ verb
reads
reading
read

readable

reader noun
readers

readily

readiness

reading noun
readings

★ To **rap** is to knock loudly. **!wrap**.
☆ To **read** is to look at something written or printed. **!reed**.

a
b
c
d
e
f
g
h
i
j
k
l
m
n
o
p
q
r
s
t
u
v
w
x
y
z

a   **ready** *adjective*
     readier
     readiest
b
   real★ *adjective*
c
   realism
d
   realist *noun*
     realists
   realistic *adjective*
e
     realistically
f
   reality *noun*
     realities
g
   realization
h
   realize *verb*
     realizes
i
     realizing
     realized
j
   really
k
   realm *noun*
     realms
l
   reap *verb*
     reaps
m
     reaping
     reaped
n
   reaper *noun*
     reapers
o
   reappear *verb*
     reappears
p
     reappearing
     reappeared
q
   reappearance *noun*
     reappearances
r
   rear *adjective* and
     noun
s
     rears
t
   rear *verb*
     rears
u
     rearing
     reared
v
   rearrange *verb*
     rearranges
w
     rearranging
     rearranged
x
   rearrangement *noun*
y
     rearrangements
z

reason *noun*
   reasons
reason *verb*
   reasons
   reasoning
   reasoned
reasonable *adjective*
   reasonably
reassurance *noun*
   reassurances
reassure *verb*
   reassures
   reassuring
   reassured
rebel *verb*
   rebels
   rebelling
   rebelled
rebel *noun*
   rebels
rebellion *noun*
   rebellions
rebellious *adjective*
   rebelliously
rebound *verb*
   rebounds
   rebounding
   rebounded
rebuild *verb*
   rebuilds
   rebuilding
   rebuilt
recall *verb*
   recalls
   recalling
   recalled
recap *verb*
   recaps
   recapping
   recapped
recapture *verb*
   recaptures
   recapturing
   recaptured

recede *verb*
   recedes
   receding
   receded
receipt *noun*
   receipts
receive *verb*
   receives
   receiving
   received
receiver *noun*
   receivers
recent *adjective*
   recently
receptacle *noun*
   receptacles
reception *noun*
   receptions
receptionist *noun*
   receptionists
recess *noun*
   recesses
recession *noun*
   recessions
recipe *noun*
   recipes
reciprocal *adjective*
   reciprocally
reciprocal *noun*
   reciprocals
recital *noun*
   recitals
recitation *noun*
   recitations
recite *verb*
   recites
   reciting
   recited
reckless *adjective*
   recklessly
recklessness

....

★ **Real** means 'true' or 'existing'. ! **reel**.

reckon verb
reckons
reckoning
reckoned

reclaim verb
reclaims
reclaiming
reclaimed

reclamation noun
reclamations

recline verb
reclines
reclining
reclined

recognition noun

recognizable
adjective
recognizably

recognize verb
recognizes
recognizing
recognized

recoil verb
recoils
recoiling
recoiled

recollect verb
recollects
recollecting
recollected

recollection noun
recollections

recommend verb
recommends
recommending
recommended

recommendation
noun
recommendations

reconcile verb
reconciles
reconciling
reconciled

reconciliation noun
reconciliations

reconstruction noun
reconstructions

record noun
records

record verb
records
recording
recorded

recorder noun
recorders

recover verb
recovers
recovering
recovered

recovery noun
recoveries

recreation noun
recreations

recreational adjective
recreationally

recruit noun
recruits

recruit verb
recruits
recruiting
recruited

rectangle noun
rectangles

rectangular

recur verb
recurs
recurring
recurred

recurrence noun
recurrences

recycle verb
recycles
recycling
recycled

red adjective
redder
reddest

red noun
reds

redden verb
reddens
reddening
reddened

reddish

redeem verb
redeems
redeeming
redeemed

redeemer noun
redeemers

redemption noun
redemptions

redhead noun
redheads

reduce verb
reduces
reducing
reduced

reduction noun
reductions

redundancy noun
redundancies

redundant adjective
redundantly

reed* noun
reeds

reedy

reef noun
reefs

reef knot noun
reef knots

reek verb
reeks
reeking
reeked

a
b
c
d
e
f
g
h
i
j
k
l
m
n
o
p
q
r
s
t
u
v
w
x
y
z

....

★ A **reed** is a plant or a thin strip. **!** read.

a

reel* noun
reels

reflexive adjective
reflexively

refuge noun
refuges

b

reel verb
reels
reeling
reeled

reform verb
reforms
reforming
reformed

refugee noun
refugees

refund verb
refunds
refunding
refunded

c

d

refer verb
refers
referring
referred

reform noun
reforms

refund noun
refunds

e

reformation noun
reformations

f

referee noun
referees

Reformation☆

refusal

reformer noun
reformers

refuse verb
refuses
refusing
refused

g

h

referee verb
referees
refereeing
refereed

refract verb
refracts
refracting
refracted

i

refuse

j

reference noun
references

refraction

regain verb
regains
regaining
regained

k

referendum noun
referendums

refrain verb
refrains
refraining
refrained

l

regard verb
regards
regarding
regarded

refill verb
refills
refilling
refilled

m

refrain noun
refrains

n

regard noun
regards

refill noun
refills

refresh verb
refreshes
refreshing
refreshed

o

regarding preposition

refine verb
refines
refining
refined

p

regardless

refreshment noun
refreshments

q

regatta noun
regattas

refinement noun
refinements

refrigerate verb
refrigerates
refrigerating
refrigerated

r

reggae

refinery noun
refineries

regiment noun
regiments

s

refrigeration

reflect verb
reflects
reflecting
reflected

regimental

t

refrigerator noun
refrigerators

region noun
regions

u

refuel verb
refuels
refuelling
refuelled

reflective adjective
reflectively

regional adjective
regionally

v

w

reflex noun
reflexes

register noun
registers

x

★ A **reel** is a cylinder on which something is wound. **I real**.

y

☆ You use a capital R when you mean the historical religious
movement.

z

198

register verb
registers
registering
registered

registration noun
registrations

regret noun
regrets

regret verb
regrets
regretting
regretted

regretful adjective
regretfully

regrettable adjective
regrettably

regular adjective
regularly

regularity

regulate verb
regulates
regulating
regulated

regulation noun
regulations

regulator noun
regulators

rehearsal noun
rehearsals

rehearse verb
rehearses
rehearsing
rehearsed

reign* verb
reigns
reigning
reigned

reign noun
reigns

rein☆ noun
reins

reindeer noun
reindeer

reinforce verb
reinforces
reinforcing
reinforced

reinforcement noun
reinforcements

reject verb
rejects
rejecting
rejected

reject noun
rejects

rejection noun
rejections

rejoice verb
rejoices
rejoicing
rejoiced

relate verb
relates
relating
related

relation noun
relations

relationship noun
relationships

relative adjective
relatively

relative noun
relatives

relax verb
relaxes
relaxing
relaxed

relaxation

relay verb
relays
relaying
relayed

relay noun
relays

release verb
releases
releasing
released

release noun
releases

relegate verb
relegates
relegating
relegated

relegation

relent verb
relents
relenting
relented

relentless adjective
relentlessly

relevance

relevant adjective
relevantly

reliability

reliable adjective
reliably

reliance

reliant

relic noun
relics

relief noun
reliefs

relieve verb
relieves
relieving
relieved

religion noun
religions

religious adjective
religiously

reluctance

....
★ To **reign** is to rule as a king or queen. **!rein**.
☆ A **rein** is a strap used to guide a horse. **!reign**.

a
b
c
d
e
f
g
h
i
j
k
l
m
n
o
p
q
r
s
t
u
v
w
x
y
z

a
b
c
d
e
f
g
h
i
j
k
l
m
n
o
p
q
r
s
t
u
v
w
x
y
z

reluctant *adjective*
reluctantly

rely *verb*
relies
relying
relied

remain *verb*
remains
remaining
remained

remainder *noun*
remainders

remains

remark *verb*
remarks
remarking
remarked

remark *noun*
remarks

remarkable *adjective*
remarkably

remedial *adjective*
remedially

remedy *noun*
remedies

remember *verb*
remembers
remembering
remembered

remembrance

remind *verb*
reminds
reminding
reminded

reminder *noun*
reminders

reminisce *verb*
reminisces
reminiscing
reminisced

reminiscence *noun*
reminiscences

reminiscent

remnant *noun*
remnants

remorse

remorseful *adjective*
remorsefully

remorseless *adjective*
remorselessly

remote *adjective*
remoter
remotest
remotely

remoteness

removal *noun*
removals

remove *verb*
removes
removing
removed

Renaissance★

render *verb*
renders
rendering
rendered

rendezvous *noun*
rendezvous

renew *verb*
renews
renewing
renewed

renewable

renewal *noun*
renewals

renown

renowned

rent *noun*
rents

rent *verb*
rents
renting
rented

repair *verb*
repairs
repairing
repaired

repair *noun*
repairs

repay *verb*
repays
repaying
repaid

repayment *noun*
repayments

repeat *verb*
repeats
repeating
repeated

repeat *noun*
repeats

repeatedly

repel *verb*
repels
repelling
repelled

repellent

repent *verb*
repents
repenting
repented

repentance

repentant

repetition *noun*
repetitions

repetitive *adjective*
repetitively

replace *verb*
replaces
replacing
replaced

replacement *noun*
replacements

replay *noun*
replays

★ You use a capital R when you mean the historical period.

200

replica noun
replicas

reply verb
replies
replying
replied

reply noun
replies

report verb
reports
reporting
reported

report noun
reports

reporter noun
reporters

repossess verb
repossesses
repossessing
repossessed

represent verb
represents
representing
represented

representation noun
representations

representative
adjective and noun
representatives

repress verb
represses
repressing
repressed

repression noun
repressions

repressive adjective
repressively

reprieve verb
reprieves
reprieving
reprieved

reprieve noun
reprieves

reprimand verb
reprimands
reprimanding
reprimanded

reprisal noun
reprisals

reproach verb
reproaches
reproaching
reproached

reproduce verb
reproduces
reproducing
reproduced

reproduction noun
reproduction

reproductive
adjective
reproductively

reptile noun
reptiles

republic noun
republics

republican adjective
and noun
republicans

Republican*
adjective and noun
Republicans

repulsion

repulsive adjective
repulsively

reputation noun
reputations

request verb
requests
requesting
requested

request noun
requests

require verb
requires
requiring
required

requirement noun
requirements

reread verb
rereads
rereading
reread

rescue verb
rescues
rescuing
rescued

rescue noun
rescues

rescuer noun
rescuers

research noun
researches

researcher noun
researchers

resemblance noun
resemblances

resemble verb
resembles
resembling
resembled

resent verb
resents
resenting
resented

resentful adjective
resentfully

resentment

reservation noun
reservations

reserve verb
reserves
reserving
reserved

reserve noun
reserves

★ You use a capital R when you mean the political party in the USA.

reservoir noun
reservoirs

reshuffle noun
reshuffles

reside verb
resides
residing
resided

residence noun
residences

resident noun
residents

resign verb
resigns
resigning
resigned

resignation noun
resignations

resin noun
resins

resinous

resist verb
resists
resisting
resisted

resistance noun
resistances

resistant

resolute adjective
resolutely

resolution noun
resolutions

resolve verb
resolves
resolving
resolved

resort noun
resorts

resort verb
resorts
resorting
resorted

resound verb
resounds
resounding
resounded

resource noun
resources

respect verb
respects
respecting
respected

respect noun
respects

respectability

respectable adjective
respectably

respectful adjective
respectfully

respective adjective
respectively

respiration

respirator noun
respirators

respiratory

respond verb
responds
responding
responded

response noun
responses

responsibility noun
responsibilities

responsible adjective
responsibly

rest verb
rests
resting
rested

rest noun
rests

restaurant noun
restaurants

restful adjective
restfully

restless adjective
restlessly

restlessness

restoration noun
restorations

restore verb
restores
restoring
restored

restrain verb
restrains
restraining
restrained

restraint noun
restraints

restrict verb
restricts
restricting
restricted

restriction noun
restrictions

restrictive adjective
restrictively

result verb
results
resulting
resulted

result noun
results

resume verb
resumes
resuming
resumed

resumption noun
resumptions

resuscitate verb
resuscitates
resuscitating
resuscitated

retail verb
retails
retailing
retailed

retail noun

retain verb
retains
retaining
retained

retina noun
retinas

retire verb
retires
retiring
retired

retirement

retort verb
retorts
retorting
retorted

retort noun
retorts

retrace verb
retraces
retracing
retraced

retreat verb
retreats
retreating
retreated

retrievable adjective
retrievably

retrieval noun
retrievals

retrieve verb
retrieves
retrieving
retrieved

retriever noun
retrievers

return verb
returns
returning
returned

return noun
returns

reunion noun
reunions

rev verb
revs
revving
revved

rev noun
revs

reveal verb
reveals
revealing
revealed

revelation noun
revelations

revenge

revenue noun
revenues

revere verb
reveres
revering
revered

reverence

Reverend★

reverent★ adjective
reverently

reversal noun
reversals

reverse verb
reverses
reversing
reversed

reverse noun
reverses

reversible adjective
reversibly

review verb
reviews
reviewing
reviewed

review☆ noun
reviews

reviewer noun
reviewers

revise verb
revises
revising
revised

revision noun
revisions

revival noun
revivals

revive verb
revives
reviving
revived

revolt verb
revolts
revolting
revolted

revolt noun
revolts

revolution noun
revolutions

revolutionary
adjective and noun
revolutionaries

revolutionize verb
revolutionizes
revolutionizing
revolutionized

revolve verb
revolves
revolving
revolved

revolver noun
revolvers

revue○ noun
revues

....

★ You use **Reverend** as a title of a member of the clergy, and
reverent as an ordinary word meaning 'showing respect'.

☆ A **review** is a piece of writing about a film, play, etc. **!** revue.

○ A **revue** is an entertainment of short sketches. **!** review.

reward verb
rewards
rewarding
rewarded

reward noun
rewards

rewind verb
rewinds
rewinding
rewound

rewrite verb
rewrites
rewriting
rewrote
rewritten

rheumatic

rheumatism

rhinoceros noun
rhinoceroses
rhinoceros

rhododendron noun
rhododendrons

rhombus noun
rhombuses

rhubarb

rhyme verb
rhymes
rhyming
rhymed

rhyme noun
rhymes

rhythm noun
rhythms

rhythmic or
rhythmical adjective
rhythmically

rib noun
ribs

ribbon noun
ribbons

rice

rich adjective
richer
richest
richly

riches plural noun

richness

rick noun
ricks

rickety

rickshaw noun
rickshaws

ricochet verb
ricochets
ricocheting
ricocheted

rid verb
rids
ridding
rid

riddance

riddle noun
riddles

ride verb
rides
riding
rode
ridden

ride noun
rides

rider noun
riders

ridge noun
ridges

ridicule verb
ridicules
ridiculing
ridiculed

ridiculous adjective
ridiculously

rifle noun
rifles

rift noun
rifts

rig verb
rigs
rigging
rigged

rigging

right adjective
rightly

right* noun
rights

right☆ verb
rights
righting
righted

righteous adjective
righteously

righteousness

rightful adjective
rightfully

right-handed

rightness

rigid adjective
rigidly

rigidity

rim noun
rims

rind noun
rinds

ring noun
rings

ring⊙ verb
rings
ringing
rang
rung

. . . .

★ A **right** is something you are entitled to. **!** rite, **write**.
☆ To **right** something is to make it right. **!** rite, **write**.
⊙ The past tense is **rang** and the past participle is **rung** when you
mean 'to make a sound like a bell'. **!** wring.

ring★ *verb*
rings
ringing
ringed

ring *noun*
rings

ringleader *noun*
ringleaders

ringlet *noun*
ringlets

ringmaster *noun*
ringmasters

rink *noun*
rinks

rinse *verb*
rinses
rinsing
rinsed

rinse *noun*
rinses

riot *verb*
riots
rioting
rioted

riot *noun*
riots

riotous *adjective*
riotously

rip *verb*
rips
ripping
ripped

rip *noun*
rips

ripe *adjective*
riper
ripest

ripen *verb*
ripens
ripening
ripened

ripeness *noun*

rip-off *noun*
rip-offs

ripple *noun*
ripples

ripple *verb*
ripples
rippling
rippled

rise *verb*
rises
rising
rose
risen

rise *noun*
rises

risk *verb*
risks
risking
risked

risk *noun*
risks

risky *adjective*
riskier
riskiest
riskily

risotto *noun*
risottos

rissole *noun*
rissoles

rite☆ *noun*
rites

ritual *noun*
rituals

rival *noun*
rivals

rival *verb*
rivals
rivalling
rivalled

rivalry *noun*
rivalries

river *noun*
rivers

rivet *noun*
rivets

rivet *verb*
rivets
riveting
riveted

road○ *noun*
roads

roadroller *noun*
roadrollers

roadside *noun*
roadsides

roadway *noun*
roadways

roam *verb*
roams
roaming
roamed

roar *verb*
roars
roaring
roared

roar *noun*
roars

roast *verb*
roasts
roasting
roasted

rob *verb*
robs
robbing
robbed

a
b
c
d
e
f
g
h
i
j
k
l
m
n
o
p
q
r
s
t
u
v
w
x
y
z

. . . .
★ The past tense and past participle is **ringed** when you mean 'to put a ring round something'. **!** wring.
☆ A **rite** is a ceremony or ritual. **!** right, write.
○ A **road** is a hard surface for traffic to use. **!** rode.

205

robber noun
robbers

robbery noun
robberies

robe noun
robes

robin noun
robins

robot noun
robots

robust adjective
robustly

rock verb
rocks
rocking
rocked

rock noun
rocks

rocker noun
rockers

rockery noun
rockeries

rocket noun
rockets

rocky adjective
rockier
rockiest
rockily

rod noun
rods

rode★ see **ride**

rodent noun
rodents

rodeo noun
rodeos

rogue noun
rogues

roguish adjective
roguishly

role☆ noun
roles

roll○ verb
rolls
rolling
rolled

roll○ noun
rolls

roller noun
rollers

Roman adjective and noun
Romans

Roman Catholic noun
Roman Catholics

Roman numeral

romantic adjective
romantically

Romany

romp verb
romps
romping
romped

romp noun
romps

rompers plural noun

roof noun
roofs

rook noun
rooks

room noun
rooms

roomful noun
roomfuls

roomy adjective
roomier
roomiest
roomily

roost noun
roosts

root✛ noun
roots

root verb
roots
rooting
rooted

rope noun
ropes

rose noun
roses

rose see **rise**

rosette noun
rosettes

rosy adjective
rosier
rosiest
rosily

rot verb
rots
rotting
rotted

rot noun

rota noun
rotas

rotary

rotate verb
rotates
rotating
rotated

rotation noun
rotations

rotor noun
rotors

rotten

romance noun
romances

- -

★ **Rode** is the past tense of **ride**. ! **road**.
☆ A **role** is a part in a play or film. ! **roll**.
○ A **roll** is a small loaf of bread or an act of rolling. ! **role**.
✛ A **root** is the part of a plant that grows underground. ! **route**.

206

rottenness

rottweiler noun
rottweilers

rough adjective
rougher
roughest
roughly

roughness

roughage

roughen verb
roughens
roughening
roughened

round adjective,
adverb, and
preposition
rounder
roundest
roundly

round noun
rounds

round verb
rounds
rounding
rounded

roundabout adjective
and noun
roundabouts

rounders noun

Roundhead noun
Roundheads

rouse verb
rouses
rousing
roused

rout verb
routs
routing
routed

rout noun
routs

route★ noun
routes

routine noun
routines

routine adjective
routinely

rove verb
roves
roving
roved

rover noun
rovers

row☆ noun
rows

row○ verb
rows
rowing
rowed

rowdiness

rowdy adjective
rowdier
rowdiest
rowdily

rower noun
rowers

rowlock noun
rowlocks

royal adjective
royally

royalty

rub verb
rubs
rubbing
rubbed

rub noun
rubs

rubber noun
rubbers

rubbery

rubbish

rubble

ruby noun
rubies

rucksack noun
rucksacks

rudder noun
rudders

ruddy adjective
ruddier
ruddiest

rude adjective
ruder
rudest
rudely

rudeness

ruffian noun
ruffians

ruffle verb
ruffles
ruffling
ruffled

rug noun
rugs

rugby✦

rugged adjective
ruggedly

rugger

. . . .

★ A **route** is the way you go to get to a place. **I root.**

☆ A **row** is a line of people or things and rhymes with 'go'. A **row** is also a noise or argument and rhymes with 'cow'.

○ To **row** means to use oars to make a boat move and rhymes with 'go'.

✦ You can use a small r when you mean the game.

ruin *verb*
ruins
ruining
ruined

ruin *noun*
ruins

ruinous *adjective*
ruinously

rule *noun*
rules

rule *verb*
rules
ruling
ruled

ruler *noun*
rulers

ruling *noun*
rulings

rum *noun*
rums

rumble *verb*
rumbles
rumbling
rumbled

rumble *noun*
rumbles

rummage *verb*
rummages
rummaging
rummaged

rummy

rumour *noun*
rumours

rump *noun*
rumps

run *verb*
runs
running
ran
run

run *noun*
runs

runaway *noun*
runaways

rung *noun*
rungs

rung see **ring**

runner *noun*
runners

runner-up *noun*
runners-up

runny *adjective*
runnier
runniest
runnily

runway *noun*
runways

rural

rush *verb*
rushes
rushing
rushed

rush *noun*
rushes

rusk *noun*
rusks

rust *noun*

rust *verb*
rusts
rusting
rusted

rustic

rustle *verb*
rustles
rustling
rustled

rustler *noun*
rustlers

rusty *adjective*
rustier
rustiest
rustily

rut *noun*
ruts

ruthless *adjective*
ruthlessly

ruthlessness

rutted

rye* *noun*

Ss

sabbath *noun*
sabbaths

sabotage *noun*

sabotage *verb*
sabotages
sabotaging
sabotaged

saboteur *noun*
saboteurs

sac☆ *noun*
sacs

saccharin

sachet *noun*
sachets

sack◇ *noun*
sacks

sack *verb*
sacks
sacking
sacked

sacred

sacrifice *noun*
sacrifices

sacrificial *adjective*
sacrificially

★ **Rye** is a type of cereal or bread. **!wry.**
☆ A **sac** is a bag-like part of an animal or plant. **!sack.**
◇ A **sack** is a large bag. **!sac.**

sacrifice *verb*
sacrifices
sacrificing
sacrificed

sad *adjective*
sadder
saddest
sadly

sadness

sadden *verb*
saddens
saddening
saddened

saddle *noun*
saddles

saddle *verb*
saddles
saddling
saddled

sadist *noun*
sadists

sadism

sadistic *adjective*
sadistically

safari *noun*
safaris

safe *adjective*
safer
safest
safely

safe *noun*
safes

safeguard *noun*
safeguards

safety

sag *verb*
sags
sagging
sagged

saga *noun*
sagas

sago

said see **say**

sail *verb*
sails
sailing
sailed

sail★ *noun*
sails

sailboard *noun*
sailboards

sailor *noun*
sailors

saint *noun*
saints

saintly *adjective*
saintlier
saintliest

sake

salaam *interjection*

salad *noun*
salads

salami *noun*
salamis

salary *noun*
salaries

sale☆ *noun*
sales

salesman *noun*
salesmen

salesperson *noun*
salespersons

saleswoman *noun*
saleswomen

saline

saliva

sally *verb*
sallies
sallying
sallied

salmon *noun*
salmon

salon *noun*
salons

saloon *noun*
saloons

salt *noun*

salt *verb*
salts
salting
salted

salty *adjective*
saltier
saltiest

salute *verb*
salutes
saluting
saluted

salute *noun*
salutes

salvage *verb*
salvages
salvaging
salvaged

salvation

same

samosa *noun*
samosas

sample *noun*
samples

sample *verb*
samples
sampling
sampled

sanctuary *noun*
sanctuaries

sand *noun*
sands

sand *verb*
sands
sanding
sanded

sander *noun*
sanders

··

★ A **sail** is a sheet that catches the wind to make a boat go. ! **sale**.

☆ You use **sale** in e.g. *The house is for sale.* ! **sail**.

sandal *noun*
sandals

sandbag *noun*
sandbags

sandpaper

sands *plural noun*

sandstone

sandwich *noun*
sandwiches

sandy *adjective*
sandier
sandiest

sane *adjective*
saner
sanest
sanely

sang see **sing**

sanitary

sanitation

sanity

sank see **sink**

Sanskrit

sap *noun*

sap *verb*
saps
sapping
sapped

sapling *noun*
saplings

sapphire *noun*
sapphires

sarcasm

sarcastic *adjective*
sarcastically

sardine *noun*
sardines

sari *noun*
saris

sash *noun*
sashes

sat see **sit**

satchel *noun*
satchels

satellite *noun*
satellites

satin

satire *noun*
satires

satirical *adjective*
satirically

satirist *noun*
satirists

satisfaction

satisfactory *adjective*
satisfactorily

satisfy *verb*
satisfies
satisfying
satisfied

saturate *verb*
saturates
saturating
saturated

saturation

Saturday *noun*
Saturdays

sauce* *noun*
sauces

saucepan *noun*
saucepans

saucer *noun*
saucers

saucy *adjective*
saucier
sauciest
saucily

sauna *noun*
saunas

saunter *verb*
saunters
sauntering
sauntered

sausage *noun*
sausages

savage *adjective*
savagely

savage *noun*
savages

savage *verb*
savages
savaging
savaged

savagery

savannah *noun*
savannahs

save *verb*
saves
saving
saved

saver *noun*
savers

savings *plural noun*

saviour *noun*
saviours

savoury

saw *noun*
saws

saw *verb*
saws
sawing
sawed
sawn

saw see **see**

sawdust

saxophone *noun*
saxophones

say *verb*
says
saying
said

say *noun*

saying *noun*
sayings

scab *noun*
scabs

★ A **sauce** is a liquid you put on food. **!source**.

scabbard *noun*
scabbards

scaffold *noun*
scaffolds

scaffolding *noun*

scald *verb*
scalds
scalding
scalded

scale *noun*
scales

scale *verb*
scales
scaling
scaled

scales *plural noun*

scaly *adjective*
scalier
scaliest

scalp *noun*
scalps

scalp *verb*
scalps
scalping
scalped

scamper *verb*
scampers
scampering
scampered

scampi *plural noun*

scan *verb*
scans
scanning
scanned

scan *noun*
scans

scandal *noun*
scandals

scandalous *adjective*
scandalous

scanner *noun*
scanners

scanty *adjective*
scantier
scantiest
scantily

scapegoat *noun*
scapegoats

scar *noun*
scars

scar *verb*
scars
scarring
scarred

scarce *adjective*
scarcer
scarcest
scarcely

scarcity *noun*
scarcities

scare *verb*
scares
scaring
scared

scare *noun*
scares

scarecrow *noun*
scarecrows

scarf *noun*
scarves

scarlet

scary *adjective*
scarier
scariest
scarily

scatter *verb*
scatters
scattering
scattered

scene* *noun*
scenes

scenery *noun*

scent☆ *noun*
scents

scent *verb*
scents
scenting
scented

sceptic *noun*
sceptics

sceptical *adjective*
sceptically

scepticism

schedule *noun*
schedules

scheme *noun*
schemes

scheme *verb*
schemes
scheming
schemed

schemer *noun*
schemers

scholar *noun*
scholars

scholarly

scholarship *noun*
scholarships

school *noun*
schools

schoolboy *noun*
schoolboys

schoolchild *noun*
schoolchildren

schoolgirl *noun*
schoolgirls

schoolteacher *noun*
schoolteachers

schooner *noun*
schooners

science

scientific *adjective*
scientifically

scientist *noun*
scientists

★ A scene is a place or part of a play. ! seen.
☆ A scent is a smell or perfume. ! cent, sent.

scissors *plural noun*

scoff *verb*
scoffs
scoffing
scoffed

scold *verb*
scolds
scolding
scolded

scone *noun*
scones

scoop *noun*
scoops

scoop *verb*
scoops
scooping
scooped

scooter *noun*
scooters

scope

scorch *verb*
scorches
scorching
scorched

score *noun*
scores

score *verb*
scores
scoring
scored

scorer *noun*
scorers

scorn *noun*

scorn *verb*
scorns
scorning
scorned

scorpion *noun*
scorpions

Scot *noun*
Scots

scoundrel *noun*
scoundrels

scour *verb*
scours
scouring
scoured

Scout* *noun*
Scouts

scout *noun*
scouts

scowl *verb*
scowls
scowling
scowled

scramble *verb*
scrambles
scrambling
scrambled

scramble *noun*
scrambles

scrap *verb*
scraps
scrapping
scrapped

scrap *noun*
scraps

scrape *verb*
scrapes
scraping
scraped

scrape *noun*
scrapes

scraper *noun*
scrapers

scrappy *adjective*
scrappier
scrappiest
scrappily

scratch *verb*
scratches
scratching
scratched

scratch *noun*
scratches

scrawl *verb*
scrawls
scrawling
scrawled

scrawl *noun*
scrawls

scream *verb*
screams
screaming
screamed

scream *noun*
screams

screech *verb*
screeches
screeching
screeched

screech *noun*
screeches

screen *noun*
screens

screen *verb*
screens
screening
screened

screw *noun*
screws

screw *verb*
screws
screwing
screwed

screwdriver *noun*
screwdrivers

scribble *verb*
scribbles
scribbling
scribbled

scribble *noun*
scribbles

scribbler *noun*
scribblers

......

★ You use a capital S when you mean a member of the Scout Association.

script noun
scripts

scripture noun
scriptures

scroll noun
scrolls

scrotum noun
scrotums or scrota

scrounge verb
scrounges
scrounging
scrounged

scrounger noun
scroungers

scrub verb
scrubs
scrubbing
scrubbed

scrub noun
scrubs

scruffy adjective
scruffier
scruffiest
scruffily

scrum noun
scrums

scrummage noun
scrummages

scrutinize verb
scrutinizes
scrutinizing
scrutinized

scrutiny noun
scrutinies

scuba diving

scuffle noun
scuffles

scuffle verb
scuffles
scuffling
scuffled

scullery noun
sculleries

sculptor noun
sculptors

sculpture noun
sculptures

scum noun

scurry verb
scurries
scurrying
scurried

scurvy noun

scuttle verb
scuttles
scuttling
scuttled

scuttle noun
scuttles

scythe noun
scythes

sea* noun
seas

seabed

seafarer noun
seafarers

seafaring

seafood

seagull noun
seagulls

sea horse noun
sea horses

seal verb
seals
sealing
sealed

seal noun
seals

sea lion noun
sea lions

seam☆ noun
seams

seaman noun
seamen

seamanship

seaplane noun
seaplanes

seaport noun
seaports

search verb
searches
searching
searched

search noun
searches

searcher noun
searchers

searchlight noun
searchlights

seashore noun
seashores

seasick

seasickness

seaside

season noun
seasons

season verb
seasons
seasoning
seasoned

seasonal adjective
seasonally

seasoning noun
seasonings

seat noun
seats

seat verb
seats
seating
seated

seat belt noun
seat belts

seaward adjective and adverb

seawards adverb

. . . .

★ A **sea** is an area of salt water. **!** see.
☆ A **seam** is a line of stitching in cloth. **!** seem.

seaweed *noun*
seaweeds

secateurs *plural noun*

secluded

seclusion

second *adjective*
secondly

second *noun*
seconds

second *verb*
seconds
seconding
seconded

secondary

second-hand
adjective

secrecy

secret *adjective*
secretly

secret *noun*
secrets

secretary *noun*
secretaries

secrete *verb*
secretes
secreting
secreted

secretion *noun*
secretions

secretive *adjective*
secretively

secretiveness

sect *noun*
sects

section *noun*
sections

sectional

sector *noun*
sectors

secure *adjective*
securer
securest
securely

secure *verb*
secures
securing
secured

security

sedate *adjective*
sedately

sedation

sedative *noun*
sedatives

sediment

sedimentary

see* *verb*
sees
seeing
saw
seen

seed *noun*
seeds

seedling *noun*
seedlings

seek *verb*
seeks
seeking
sought

seem☆ *verb*
seems
seeming
seemed

seemingly

seen○ see see

seep *verb*
seeps
seeping
seeped

seepage

see-saw *noun*
see-saws

seethe *verb*
seethes
seething
seethed

segment *noun*
segments

segmented

segregate *verb*
segregates
segregating
segregated

segregation

seismograph *noun*
seismographs

seize *verb*
seizes
seizing
seized

seizure *noun*
seizures

seldom

select *verb*
selects
selecting
selected

select *adjective*

self *noun*
selves

self-confidence

self-confident
adjective
self-confidently

self-conscious
adjective
self-consciously

self-contained

selfish *adjective*
selfishly

★ You use **see** in e.g. *I can't see anything.* **! sea**.
☆ You use **seem** in e.g. *they seem tired.* **! seam**.
○ **Seen** is the past participle of **see**. **! scene**.

selfishness

selfless adjective
selflessly

self-service

sell* verb
sells
selling
sold

semaphore

semen

semi-
semi- makes words
meaning 'half', e.g.
semi-automatic,
semi-skimmed. A
few words are spelt
joined up, e.g.
semicircle,
semicolon, but most
of them have
hyphens.

semibreve noun
semibreves

semicircle noun
semicircles

semicircular

semicolon noun
semicolons

semi-detached

semi-final noun
semi-finals

semi-finalist noun
semi-finalists

semitone noun
semitones

semolina

senate noun
senators

senator noun
senators

send verb
sends
sending
sent

senior adjective and
noun
seniors

seniority

sensation noun
sensations

sensational adjective
sensationally

sense noun
senses

sense verb
senses
sensing
sensed

senseless adjective
senselessly

sensible adjective
sensibly

sensitive adjective
sensitively

sensitivity noun
sensitivities

sensitize verb
sensitizes
sensitizing
sensitized

sensor noun
sensors

sent☆ see **send**

sentence noun
sentences

sentence verb
sentences
sentencing
sentenced

sentiment noun
sentiments

sentimental adjective
sentimentally

sentimentality

sentinel noun
sentinels

sentry noun
sentries

separable

separate adjective
separately

separate verb
separates
separating
separated

separation noun
separations

September noun
Septembers

septic

sequel noun
sequels

sequence noun
sequences

sequin noun
sequins

serene adjective
serenely

serenity

sergeant noun
sergeants

sergeant major noun
sergeant majors

serial○ noun
serials

series noun
series

serious adjective
seriously

seriousness

. . . . . .

★ To **sell** something means 'to exchange it for money'. I **cell**.

☆ You use **sent** in e.g. he was sent home. I **cent**, **scent**.

○ A **serial** is a story or programme in separate parts. I **cereal**.

a **sermon** noun
  sermons

b **serpent** noun
  serpents

c **servant** noun
  servants

d **serve** verb
  serves
e serving
  served

f **server** noun
g servers

  serve noun
h serves

i **service** noun
  services

j **service** verb
  services
k servicing
  serviced

l **serviette** noun
m serviettes

  session noun
n sessions

o **set** verb
  sets
  setting
p set

q **set** noun
  sets

r **set square** noun
  set squares

s **sett*** noun
  setts

t **settee** noun
u settees

  setting noun
v settings

  settle verb
w settles
  settling
x settled

settlement noun
  settlements

settler noun
  settlers

set-up noun
  set-ups

seven

seventeen

seventeenth

seventh adjective and
  noun
  seventhly

seventieth

seventy adjective and
  noun
  seventies

sever verb
  severs
  severing
  severed

several adjective
  severally

severe adjective
  severer
  severest
  severely

severity

sew☆ verb
  sews
  sewing
  sewed
  sewn

sewage

sewer noun
  sewers

sex noun
  sexes

sexism

sexist adjective and
  noun
  sexists

sextet noun
  sextets

sexual adjective
  sexually

sexuality

sexy adjective
  sexier
  sexiest
  sexily

shabbiness

shabby adjective
  shabbier
  shabbiest
  shabbily

shack noun
  shacks

shade noun
  shades

shade verb
  shades
  shading
  shaded

shadow noun
  shadows

shadow verb
  shadows
  shadowing
  shadowed

shadowy

shady adjective
  shadier
  shadiest

shaft noun
  shafts

shaggy adjective
  shaggier
  shaggiest
  shaggily

y

z   ★ A **sett** is a badger's burrow.
    ☆ To **sew** is to work with a needle and thread. **! sow**.

shake *verb*
shakes
shaking
shook
shaken

shake* *noun*
shakes

shaky *adjective*
shakier
shakiest
shakily

shall *verb*
should

shallow *adjective*
shallower
shallowest
shallowly

sham *noun*
shams

shamble *verb*
shambles
shambling
shambled

shambles *noun*

shame *verb*
shames
shaming
shamed

shame *noun*

shameful *adjective*
shamefully

shameless *adjective*
shamelessly

shampoo *noun*
shampoos

shampoo *verb*
shampoos
shampooing
shampooed

shamrock

shandy *noun*
shandies

shan't *verb*

shanty *noun*
shanties

shape *noun*
shapes

shape *verb*
shapes
shaping
shaped

shapeless *adjective*
shapelessly

shapely *adjective*
shapelier
shapeliest

share *noun*
shares

share *verb*
shares
sharing
shared

shark *noun*
sharks

sharp *adjective*
sharper
sharpest
sharply

sharp *noun*
sharps

sharpen *verb*
sharpens
sharpening
sharpened

sharpener *noun*
sharpeners

sharpness

shatter *verb*
shatters
shattering
shattered

shave *verb*
shaves
shaving
shaved

shave *noun*
shaves

shaver *noun*
shavers

shavings *plural noun*

shawl *noun*
shawls

she

sheaf *noun*
sheaves

shear☆ *verb*
shears
shearing
sheared
shorn

shearer *noun*
shearers

shears *plural noun*

sheath *noun*
sheaths

sheathe *verb*
sheathes
sheathing
sheathed

shed *noun*
sheds

shed *verb*
sheds
shedding
shed

she'd *verb*

sheen

sheep *noun*
sheep

sheepdog *noun*
sheepdogs

sheepish *adjective*
sheepishly

★ To **shake** is to tremble or quiver. **!sheikh**.
☆ To **shear** is to cut wool from a sheep. **!sheer**.

a
b
c
d
e
f
g
h
i
j
k
l
m
n
o
p
q
r
s
t
u
v
w
x
y
z

sh

sheer* *adjective*
sheerer
sheerest

sheet *noun*
sheets

sheikh *noun*
sheikhs

shelf *noun*
shelves

shell *noun*
shells

shell *verb*
shells
shelling
shelled

she'll *verb*

shellfish *noun*
shellfish

shelter *noun*
shelters

shelter *verb*
shelters
sheltering
sheltered

shelve *verb*
shelves
shelving
shelved

shepherd *noun*
shepherds

sherbet *noun*
sherbets

sheriff *noun*
sheriffs

sherry *noun*
sherries

she's *verb*

shield *noun*
shields

shield *verb*
shields
shielding
shielded

shift *noun*
shifts

shift *verb*
shifts
shifting
shifted

shilling *noun*
shillings

shimmer *verb*
shimmers
shimmering
shimmered

shin *noun*
shins

shine *verb*
shines
shining
shone
shined

shine *noun*

shingle

shiny *adjective*
shinier
shiniest

-ship
-ship makes nouns,
e.g. **friendship**. Other
noun suffixes are
-dom, **-hood**, **-ment**,
and **-ness**.

---

ship *noun*
ships

ship *verb*
ships
shipping
shipped

shipping

shipwreck *noun*
shipwrecks

shipwrecked

shipyard *noun*
shipyards

shire *noun*
shires

shirk *verb*
shirks
shirking
shirked

shirt *noun*
shirts

shiver *verb*
shivers
shivering
shivered

shiver *noun*
shivers

shivery

shoal *noun*
shoals

shock *verb*
shocks
shocking
shocked

shock *noun*
shocks

shoddy *adjective*
shoddier
shoddiest
shoddily

shoe *noun*
shoes

shoelace *noun*
shoelaces

shoestring *noun*
shoestrings

shone see **shine**

shook see **shake**

shoot *verb*
shoots
shooting
shot

. . . .

★ You use **sheer** in e.g. *sheer joy.* **I shear**.

shoot* noun
shoots

shop noun
shops

shop verb
shops
shopping
shopped

shopkeeper noun
shopkeepers

shoplifter noun
shoplifters

shopper noun
shoppers

shopping

shore noun
shores

shorn see **shear**

short adjective
shorter
shortest
shortly

shortness

shortage noun
shortages

shortbread

shortcake noun
shortcakes

shortcoming noun
shortcomings

shorten verb
shortens
shortening
shortened

shorthand

short-handed

shortly

shorts plural noun

short-sighted

shot noun
shots

shot see **shoot**

shotgun noun
shotguns

should

shoulder noun
shoulders

shoulder verb
shoulders
shouldering
shouldered

shout verb
shouts
shouting
shouted

shout noun
shouts

shove verb
shoves
shoving
shoved

shovel noun
shovels

shovel verb
shovels
shovelling
shovelled

show verb
shows
showing
showed
shown

show noun
shows

shower noun
showers

shower verb
showers
showering
showered

showery

showjumper noun
showjumpers

showjumping

showman noun
showmen

showmanship

showroom noun
showrooms

showiness

showy adjective
showier
showiest
showily

shrank see **shrink**

shrapnel

shred noun
shreds

shred verb
shreds
shredding
shredded

shrew noun
shrews

shrewd adjective
shrewder
shrewdest
shrewdly

shrewdness

shriek verb
shrieks
shrieking
shrieked

shriek noun
shrieks

shrill adjective
shriller
shrillest
shrilly

shrillness

shrimp noun
shrimps

shrine noun
shrines

shrink verb
shrinks
shrinking
shrank
shrunk

a
b
c
d
e
f
g
h
i
j
k
l
m
n
o
p
q
r
s
t
u
v
w
x
y
z

. . . .
★ To **shoot** is to fire at someone with a gun. **!chute.**

a
b
c
d
e
f
g
h
i
j
k
l
m
n
o
p
q
r
s
t
u
v
w
x
y
z

shrinkage

shrivel verb
shrivels
shrivelling
shrivelled

shroud noun
shrouds

shroud verb
shrouds
shrouding
shrouded

Shrove Tuesday

shrub noun
shrubs

shrubbery noun
shrubberies

shrug verb
shrugs
shrugging
shrugged

shrug noun
shrugs

shrunk see **shrink**

shrunken adjective

shudder verb
shudders
shuddering
shuddered

shudder noun
shudders

shuffle verb
shuffles
shuffling
shuffled

shuffle noun
shuffles

shunt verb
shunts
shunting
shunted

shunter noun
shunters

shut verb
shuts
shutting
shut

shutter noun
shutters

shuttle noun
shuttles

shuttlecock noun
shuttlecocks

shy adjective
shyer
shyest
shyly

Siamese

sick adjective
sicker
sickest

sicken verb
sickens
sickening
sickened

sickly adjective
sicklier
sickliest

sickness noun
sicknesses

side noun
sides

side verb
sides
siding
sided

sideboard noun
sideboards

sidecar noun
sidecars

sideline noun
sidelines

sideshow noun
sideshows

sideways

siding noun
sidings

siege noun
sieges

sieve noun
sieves

sift verb
sifts
sifting
sifted

sigh verb
sighs
sighing
sighed

sigh noun
sighs

sight* noun
sights

sight verb
sights
sighting
sighted

sightseer noun
sightseers

sightseeing

sign verb
signs
signing
signed

sign noun
signs

signal noun
signals

signal verb
signals
signalling
signalled

signaller noun
signallers

signalman noun
signalmen

signature noun
signatures

. . . .

★ A **sight** is something you see. **!** **site**.

signet* *noun*
signets

significance

significant *adjective*
significantly

signify *verb*
signifies
signifying
signified

signing

signpost *noun*
signposts

Sikh *noun*
Sikhs

silence *noun*
silences

silence *verb*
silences
silencing
silenced

silencer *noun*
silencers

silent *adjective*
silently

silhouette *noun*
silhouettes

silicon

silk

silken

silkworm *noun*
silkworms

silky *adjective*
silkier
silkiest
silkily

sill *noun*
sills

silliness

silly *adjective*
sillier
silliest
sillily

silver

silvery

similar *adjective*
similarly

similarity

simile *noun*
similes

simmer *verb*
simmers
simmering
simmered

simple *adjective*
simpler
simplest

simplicity

simplification

simplify *verb*
simplifies
simplifying
simplified

simply

simulate *verb*
simulates
simulating
simulated

simulation *noun*
simulations

simulator *noun*
simulators

simultaneous
adjective
simultaneously

sin *noun*
sins

sin *verb*
sins
sinning
sinned

since *preposition,*
adverb, and
conjunction

sincere *adjective*
sincerer
sincerest
sincerely

sincerity

sinew *noun*
sinews

sinful *adjective*
sinfully

sinfulness

sing *verb*
sings
singing
sang
sung

singer *noun*
singers

singe *verb*
singes
singeing
singed

single *adjective*
singly

single *noun*
singles

single *verb*
singles
singling
singled

single-handed

singular *adjective*
singularly

singular *noun*
singulars

sinister *adjective*
sinisterly

sink *verb*
sinks
sinking
sank *or* sunk
sunk

sink *noun*
sinks

★ A **signet** is a seal worn in a ring. **!cygnet**.

a
sinner noun
sinners

sinus noun
sinuses

b
c
d
sip verb
sips
sipping
sipped

e
f
siphon noun
siphons

siphon verb
siphons
siphoning
siphoned

g
h
i
sir

siren noun
sirens

j
k
sister noun
sisters

sisterly

l
m
sister-in-law noun
sisters-in-law

n
sit verb
sits
sitting
sat

o
p
sitter noun
sitters

site★ noun
sites

q
r
site verb
sites
siting
sited

s
t
sit-in noun
sit-ins

u
situated

situation noun
situations

v
w
six noun
sixes

x

sixpence noun
sixpences

sixteen noun
sixteens

sixteenth

sixth

sixthly

sixtieth

sixty noun
sixties

size noun
sizes

size verb
sizes
sizing
sized

sizeable

sizzle verb
sizzles
sizzling
sizzled

skate verb
skates
skating
skated

skate☆ noun
skates or skate

skateboard noun
skateboards

skater noun
skaters

skeletal adjective
skeletally

skeleton noun
skeletons

sketch noun
sketches

sketch verb
sketches
sketching
sketched

sketchy adjective
sketchier
sketchiest
sketchily

skewer noun
skewers

ski verb
skis
skiing
skied
ski'd

ski noun
skis

skid verb
skids
skidding
skidded

skid noun
skids

skier noun
skiers

skilful adjective
skilfully

skill noun
skills

skilled

skim verb
skims
skimming
skimmed

skimp verb
skimps
skimping
skimped

skimpy adjective
skimpier
skimpiest
skimpily

skin noun
skins

y
z

★ A **site** is a place where something will be built. **!sight**.
☆ The plural is **skate** when you mean the fish.

skin verb
skins
skinning
skinned

skinny adjective
skinnier
skinniest

skint

skip verb
skips
skipping
skipped

skip noun
skips

skipper noun
skippers

skirt noun
skirts

skirt verb
skirts
skirting
skirted

skirting noun
skirtings

skit noun
skits

skittish adjective
skittishly

skittle noun
skittles

skull noun
skulls

skunk noun
skunks

sky noun
skies

skylark noun
skylarks

skylight noun
skylights

skyscraper noun
skyscrapers

slab noun
slabs

slack adjective
slacker
slackest
slackly

slacken verb
slackens
slackening
slackened

slackness

slacks plural noun

slag heap noun
slag heaps

slain see **slay**

slam verb
slams
slamming
slammed

slang

slant verb
slants
slanting
slanted

slant noun
slants

slap verb
slaps
slapping
slapped

slap noun
slaps

slapstick

slash verb
slashes
slashing
slashed

slash noun
slashes

slat noun
slats

slate noun
slates

slaty adjective
slatier
slatiest

slaughter verb
slaughters
slaughtering
slaughtered

slaughter noun

slaughterhouse
noun
slaughterhouses

slave noun
slaves

slave verb
slaves
slaving
slaved

slavery

slay★ verb
slays
slaying
slew
slain

sled noun
sleds

sledge noun
sledges

sledgehammer noun
sledgehammers

sleek adjective
sleeker
sleekest
sleekly

sleep verb
sleeps
sleeping
slept

sleep noun

sleeper noun
sleepers

sleepiness

sleepless

★ To **slay** people is to kill them. **!sleigh**.

sl

sleepwalker *noun*
sleepwalkers

sleepwalking

sleepy *adjective*
sleepier
sleepiest
sleepily

sleet

sleeve *noun*
sleeves

sleeveless

sleigh* *noun*
sleighs

slender *adjective*
slenderer
slenderest

slept see sleep

slew see slay

slice *noun*
slices

slice *verb*
slices
slicing
sliced

slick *adjective*
slicker
slickest
slickly

slick *noun*
slicks

slide *verb*
slides
sliding
slid

slide *noun*
slides

slight *adjective*
slighter
slightest
slightly

slim *adjective*
slimmer
slimmest
slimly

slim *verb*
slims
slimming
slimmed

slime

slimmer *noun*
slimmers

slimy *adjective*
slimier
slimiest

sling *verb*
slings
slinging
slung

sling *noun*
slings

slink *verb*
slinks
slinking
slunk

slip *verb*
slips
slipping
slipped

slip *noun*
slips

slipper *noun*
slippers

slippery

slipshod

slit *noun*
slits

slit *verb*
slits
slitting
slit

slither *verb*
slithers
slithering
slithered

sliver *noun*
slivers

slog *verb*
slogs
slogging
slogged

slog *noun*
slogs

slogan *noun*
slogans

slop *verb*
slops
slopping
slopped

slope *verb*
slopes
sloping
sloped

slope *noun*
slopes

sloppiness

sloppy *adjective*
sloppier
sloppiest
sloppily

slops *plural noun*

slosh *verb*
sloshes
sloshing
sloshed

slot *noun*
slots

sloth *noun*
sloths

slouch *verb*
slouches
slouching
slouched

slovenly

★ A **sleigh** is a vehicle for sliding on snow. **!** slay.

224

slow *adjective*
slower
slowest
slowly

slow *verb*
slows
slowing
slowed

slowcoach *noun*
slowcoaches

slowness

sludge

slug *noun*
slugs

slum *noun*
slums

slumber

slumber *verb*
slumbers
slumbering
slumbered

slump *verb*
slumps
slumping
slumped

slump *noun*
slumps

slung see **sling**

slunk see **slink**

slur *noun*
slurs

slush

slushy *adjective*
slushier
slushiest
slushily

sly *adjective*
slyer
slyest
slyly

slyness

smack *verb*
smacks
smacking
smacked

smack *noun*
smacks

small *adjective*
smaller
smallest

smallpox

smart *adjective*
smarter
smartest
smartly

smart *verb*
smarts
smarting
smarted

smarten *verb*
smartens
smartening
smartened

smartness

smash *verb*
smashes
smashing
smashed

smash *noun*
smashes

smashing

smear *verb*
smears
smearing
smeared

smear *noun*
smears

smell *verb*
smells
smelling
smelt *or* smelled

smell *noun*
smells

smelly *adjective*
smellier
smelliest

smelt *verb*
smelts
smelting
smelted

smile *noun*
smiles

smile *verb*
smiles
smiling
smiled

smith *noun*
smiths

smithereens *plural noun*

smock *noun*
smocks

smog

smoke *noun*

smoke *verb*
smokes
smoking
smoked

smokeless

smoker *noun*
smokers

smoky *adjective*
smokier
smokiest

smooth *adjective*
smoother
smoothest
smoothly

smooth *verb*
smooths
smoothing
smoothed

smoothness

smother *verb*
smothers
smothering
smothered

smoulder *verb*
smoulders
smouldering
smouldered

smudge *verb*
smudges
smudging
smudged

smudge *noun*
smudges

smuggle *verb*
smuggles
smuggling
smuggled

smuggler *noun*
smugglers

smut *noun*
smuts

smutty *adjective*
smuttier
smuttiest
smuttily

snack *noun*
snacks

snag *noun*
snags

snail *noun*
snails

snake *noun*
snakes

snaky *adjective*
snakier
snakiest

snap *verb*
snaps
snapping
snapped

snap *noun*
snaps

snappy *adjective*
snappier
snappiest
snappily

snapshot *noun*
snapshots

snare *noun*
snares

snare *verb*
snares
snaring
snared

snarl *verb*
snarls
snarling
snarled

snarl *noun*
snarls

snatch *verb*
snatches
snatching
snatched

snatch *noun*
snatches

sneak *verb*
sneaks
sneaking
sneaked

sneak *noun*
sneaks

sneaky *adjective*
sneakier
sneakiest
sneakily

sneer *verb*
sneers
sneering
sneered

sneeze *verb*
sneezes
sneezing
sneezed

sneeze *noun*
sneezes

sniff *verb*
sniffs
sniffing
sniffed

sniff *noun*
sniffs

snigger *verb*
sniggers
sniggering
sniggered

snigger *noun*
sniggers

snip *verb*
snips
snipping
snipped

snip *noun*
snips

snipe *verb*
snipes
sniping
sniped

sniper *noun*
snipers

snippet *noun*
snippets

snivel *verb*
snivels
snivelling
snivelled

snob *noun*
snobs

snobbery *noun*

snobbish *adjective*
snobbishly

snooker *noun*

snoop *verb*
snoops
snooping
snooped

snooper *noun*
snoopers

snore *verb*
snores
snoring
snored

snorkel *noun*
snorkels

snort *verb*
snorts
snorting
snorted

snort *noun*
snorts

snout *noun*
snouts

snow *noun*

a b c d e f g h i j k l m n o p q r s t u v w x y z

snow verb
snows
snowing
snowed

snowball noun
snowballs

snowdrop noun
snowdrops

snowflake noun
snowflakes

snowman noun
snowmen

snowplough noun
snowploughs

snowshoe noun
snowshoes

snowstorm noun
snowstorms

snowy adjective
snowier
snowiest

snub verb
snubs
snubbing
snubbed

snuff

snug adjective
snugger
snuggest
snugly

snuggle verb
snuggles
snuggling
snuggled

soak verb
soaks
soaking
soaked

so-and-so noun
so-and-so´s

soap noun
soaps

soapiness noun

soapy adjective
soapier
soapiest
soapily

soar★ verb
soars
soaring
soared

sob verb
sobs
sobbing
sobbed

sob noun
sobs

sober adjective
soberly

sobriety

so-called

soccer

sociability

sociable adjective
sociably

social adjective
socially

socialism

socialist noun
socialists

society noun
societies

sociological adjective
sociologically

sociologist noun
sociologists

sociology

sock noun
socks

sock verb
socks
socking
socked

socket noun
sockets

soda

sodium

sofa noun
sofas

soft adjective
softer
softest
softly

soften verb
softens
softening
softened

softness

software

soggy adjective
soggier
soggiest
soggily

soil noun

soil verb
soils
soiling
soiled

solar

sold see **sell**

solder noun

solder verb
solders
soldering
soldered

soldier noun
soldiers

sole☆ noun
soles

sole adjective
solely

solemn adjective
solemnly

solemnity

· ·

★ To **soar** is to rise or fly high. **!sore**.
☆ A **sole** is a sh or a part of a shoe. **!soul**.

a
b
c
d
e
f
g
h
i
j
k
l
m
n
o
p
q
r
t
u
v
w
x
y
z

solicitor *noun*
solicitors

solid *adjective*
solidly

solid *noun*
solids

solidify *verb*
solidifies
solidifying
solidified

solidity

soliloquy *noun*
soliloquies

solitary

solitude

solo *noun*
solos

soloist *noun*
soloists

solstice *noun*
solstices

solubility

soluble *adjective*
solubly

solution *noun*
solutions

solve *verb*
solves
solving
solved

solvent *adjective and noun*
solvents

sombre *adjective*
sombrely

some★ *adjective and pronoun*

somebody

somehow

someone

somersault *noun*
somersaults

something

sometime

sometimes

somewhat

somewhere

son☆ *noun*
sons

sonar *noun*
sonars

song *noun*
songs

songbird *noun*
songbirds

sonic *adjective*
sonically

sonnet *noun*
sonnets

soon *adverb*
sooner
soonest

soot

soothe *verb*
soothes
soothing
soothed

sooty *adjective*
sootier
sootiest

sophisticated

sophistication

sopping

soppy *adjective*
soppier
soppiest
soppily

soprano *noun*
sopranos

sorcerer *noun*
sorcerers

sorceress *noun*
sorceresses

sorcery

sore○ *adjective*
sorer
sorest
sorely

sore *noun*
sores

soreness

sorrow *noun*
sorrows

sorrowful *adjective*
sorrowfully

sorry *adjective*
sorrier
sorriest

sort *noun*
sorts

sort *verb*
sorts
sorting
sorted

sought see **seek**

soul✚ *noun*
souls

sound *noun*
sounds

sound *verb*
sounds
sounding
sounded

sound *adjective*
sounder
soundest
soundly

★ You use **some** in e.g. *Have some cake.* **!** **sum**.
☆ A **son** is a male child. **!** **sun**.
○ You use **sore** in e.g. *I've got a sore tooth.* **!** **soar**.
✚ A **soul** is a person's spirit. **!** **sole**.

228

soundness

soundtrack *noun*
soundtracks

soup *noun*
soups

sour *adjective*
sourer
sourest
sourly

source* *noun*
sources

sourness

south *adjective* and *adverb*

south☆ *noun*

south-east *noun* and *adjective*

southerly *adjective* and *noun*
southerlies

southern *adjective*

southerner *noun*
southerners

southward *adjective* and *adverb*

southwards *adverb*

south-west *noun* and *adjective*

souvenir *noun*
souvenirs

sovereign *noun*
sovereigns

sow◦ *verb*
sows
sowing
sowed
sown

sow *noun*
sows

sower *noun*
sowers

soya bean *noun*
soya beans

space *noun*
spaces

space *verb*
spaces
spacing
spaced

spacecraft *noun*
spacecraft

spaceman *noun*
spacemen

spaceship *noun*
spaceships

spacewoman *noun*
spacewomen

spacious *adjective*
spaciously

spaciousness

spade *noun*
spades

spaghetti

span *verb*
spans
spanning
spanned

span *noun*
spans

spaniel *noun*
spaniels

spank *verb*
spanks
spanking
spanked

spanner *noun*
spanners

spar *noun*
spars

spar *verb*
spars
sparring
sparred

spare *verb*
spares
sparing
spared

spare *adjective* and *noun*
spares

sparing *adjective*
sparingly

spark *noun*
sparks

spark *verb*
sparks
sparking
sparked

sparkle *verb*
sparkles
sparkling
sparkled

sparkler *noun*
sparklers

sparrow *noun*
sparrows

sparse *adjective*
sparser
sparsest
sparsely

sparseness

spastic *noun*
spastics

spat see **spit**

spatter *verb*
spatters
spattering
spattered

spawn *noun*

a
b
c
d
e
f
g
h
i
j
k
l
m
n
o
p
q
r
s
t
u
v
w
x
y
z

······································

★ The **source** is where something comes from. !**sauce**.

☆ You use a capital S in **the South**, when you mean a particular region.

◦ To **sow** is to put seed in the ground. !**sew**.

229

sp

spawn verb
spawns
spawning
spawned

speak verb
speaks
speaking
spoke
spoken

speaker noun
speakers

spear noun
spears

spear verb
spears
spearing
speared

special adjective
specially

specialist noun
specialists

speciality noun
specialities

specialization

specialize verb
specializes
specializing
specialized

species noun
species

specific adjective
specifically

specification noun
specifications

specify verb
specifies
specifying
specified

specimen noun
specimens

speck noun
specks

speckled

spectacle noun
spectacles

spectacular adjective
spectacularly

spectator noun
spectators

spectre noun
spectres

spectrum noun
spectra

speech noun
speeches

speechless

speed noun
speeds

speed* verb
speeds
speeding
sped or speeded

speedboat noun
speedboats

speedometer noun
speedometers

speedway noun
speedways

speedy adjective
speedier
speediest
speedily

spell verb
spells
spelling
spelt
spelled

spell noun
spells

spelling noun
spellings

spend verb
spends
spending
spent

sperm noun
sperms or sperm

sphere noun
spheres

spherical adjective
spherically

spice noun
spices

spicy adjective
spicier
spiciest

spider noun
spiders

spied see **spy**

spike noun
spikes

spiky adjective
spikier
spikiest

spill☆ verb
spills
spilling
spilt or spilled

spill noun
spills

spin verb
spins
spinning
spun

....

★ You use **sped** in e.g. *Cars sped past* and **speeded** in e.g. *They speeded up the process.*

☆ You use **spilled** in e.g. *I spilled the milk.* You use **spilt** in e.g. *I can see spilt milk.* You use **spilled** or **spilt** in e.g. *I have spilled/spilt the milk.*

230

spin noun
spins

spinach

spindle noun
spindles

spin-drier noun
spin-driers

spine noun
spines

spinal

spin-off noun
spin-offs

spinster noun
spinsters

spiny adjective
spiniest
spiniest

spiral adjective
spirally

spire noun
spires

spirit noun
spirits

spiritual adjective
spiritually

spiritual noun
spirituals

spiritualism noun

spiritualist noun
spiritualists

spit verb
spits
spitting
spat

spit noun
spits

spite

spiteful adjective
spitefully

spittle

splash verb
splashes
splashing
splashed

splash noun
splashes

splashdown noun
splashdowns

splendid adjective
splendidly

splendour

splint noun
splints

splinter noun
splinters

splinter verb
splinters
splintering
splintered

split verb
splits
splitting
split

split noun
splits

splutter verb
splutters
spluttering
spluttered

spoil* verb
spoils
spoiling
spoilt or spoiled

spoils plural noun

spoilsport noun
spoilsports

spoke noun
spokes

spoke see **speak**

spoken see **speak**

spokesperson noun
spokespersons

sponge noun
sponges

sponge verb
sponges
sponging
sponged

sponger noun
spongers

sponginess noun

spongy adjective
spongier
spongiest
spongily

sponsor noun
sponsors

sponsorship noun
sponsorships

spontaneity

spontaneous
adjective
spontaneously

spooky adjective
spookier
spookiest
spookily

spool noun
spools

spoon noun
spoons

spoon verb
spoons
spooning
spooned

spoonful noun
spoonfuls

sport noun
sports

sporting

★ You use **spoiled** in e.g. *They spoiled the party*. You use **spoilt** in e.g. *a spoilt child*. You use **spoiled** or **spoilt** in e.g. *They have spoiled/spoilt the party*.

sportsman noun
sportsmen

sportsmanship

sportswoman noun
sportswomen

spot noun
spots

spot verb
spots
spotting
spotted

spotless adjective
spotlessly

spotlight noun
spotlights

spotter noun
spotters

spotty adjective
spottier
spottiest
spottily

spout noun
spouts

spout verb
spouts
spouting
spouted

sprain verb
sprains
spraining
sprained

sprain noun
sprains

sprang see **spring**

sprawl verb
sprawls
sprawling
sprawled

spray verb
sprays
spraying
sprayed

spray noun
sprays

spread verb
spreads
spreading
spread

spread noun
spreads

spreadsheet noun
spreadsheets

sprightliness

sprightly adjective
sprightlier
sprightliest

spring verb
springs
springing
sprang
sprung

spring noun
springs

springboard noun
springboards

spring-clean verb
spring-cleans
spring-cleaning
spring-cleaned

springtime

springy adjective
springier
springiest

sprinkle verb
sprinkles
sprinkling
sprinkled

sprinkler noun
sprinklers

sprint verb
sprints
sprinting
sprinted

sprinter noun
sprinters

sprout verb
sprouts
sprouting
sprouted

sprout noun
sprouts

spruce noun
spruces

spruce adjective
sprucer
sprucest

sprung see **spring**

spud noun
spuds

spun see **spin**

spur noun
spurs

spur verb
spurs
spurring
spurred

spurt verb
spurts
spurting
spurted

spurt noun
spurts

spy noun
spies

spy verb
spies
spying
spied

squabble verb
squabbles
squabbling
squabbled

squabble noun
squabbles

squad noun
squads

squadron noun
squadrons

squalid adjective
squalidly

squall noun
squalls

squally *adjective*
squallier
squalliest

squalor

squander *verb*
squanders
squandering
squandered

square *adjective*
squarely

square *noun*
squares

square *verb*
squares
squaring
squared

squareness

squash *verb*
squashes
squashing
squashed

squash *noun*
squashes

squat *verb*
squats
squatting
squatted

squat *adjective*
squatter
squattest
squatly

squatter *noun*
squatters

squaw *noun*
squaws

squawk *verb*
squawks
squawking
squawked

squawk *noun*
squawks

squeak *verb*
squeaks
squeaking
squeaked

squeak *noun*
squeaks

squeaky *adjective*
squeakier
squeakiest
squeakily

squeal *verb*
squeals
squealing
squealed

squeal *noun*
squeals

squeeze *verb*
squeezes
squeezing
squeezed

squeeze *noun*
squeezes

squeezer *noun*
squeezers

squelch *verb*
squelches
squelching
squelched

squelch *noun*
squelches

squid *noun*
squid
squids

squint *verb*
squints
squinting
squinted

squint *noun*
squints

squire *noun*
squires

squirm *verb*
squirms
squirming
squirmed

squirrel *noun*
squirrels

squirt *verb*
squirts
squirting
squirted

stab *verb*
stabs
stabbing
stabbed

stab *noun*
stabs

stability

stabilize *verb*
stabilizes
stabilizing
stabilized

stabilizer *noun*
stabilizers

stable *adjective*
stabler
stablest
stably

stable *noun*
stables

stack *verb*
stacks
stacking
stacked

stack *noun*
stacks

stadium *noun*
stadiums *or* stadia

staff *noun*
staffs

stag *noun*
stags

stage *noun*
stages

stage *verb*
stages
staging
staged

stagecoach *noun*
stagecoaches

st

stagger verb
staggers
staggering
staggered

stagnant adjective
stagnantly

stain noun
stains

stain verb
stains
staining
stained

stainless

stair★ noun
stairs

staircase noun
staircases

stake☆ noun
stakes

stake verb
stakes
staking
staked

stalactite noun
stalactites

stalagmite noun
stalagmites

stale adjective
staler
stalest

stalk noun
stalks

stalk verb
stalks
stalking
stalked

stall noun
stalls

stall verb
stalls
stalling
stalled

stallion noun
stallions

stalls plural noun

stamen noun
stamens

stamina

stammer verb
stammers
stammering
stammered

stammer noun
stammers

stamp noun
stamps

stamp verb
stamps
stamping
stamped

stampede noun
stampedes

stand verb
stands
standing
stood

stand noun
stands

standard adjective
and noun
standards

standardize verb
standardizes
standardizing
standardized

standby noun
standbys

standstill noun
standstills

stank see **stink**

stanza noun
stanzas

staple noun
staples

staple adjective

stapler noun
staplers

star noun
stars

starry adjective
starrier
starriest
starrily

star verb
stars
starring
starred

starboard

starch noun
starches

starchy adjective
starchier
starchiest

stare◎ verb
stares
staring
stared

starfish noun
starfish or starfishes

starling noun
starlings

start verb
starts
starting
started

start noun
starts

starter noun
starters

· ·

★ A **stair** is one of a set of steps. **!** stare.

☆ A **stake** is a pointed stick or post. **!** steak.

◎ To **stare** is to look at something without moving your eyes. **!** stair.

startle *verb*
startles
startling
startled

starvation

starve *verb*
starves
starving
starved

state *noun*
states

state *verb*
states
stating
stated

stateliness

stately *adjective*
statelier
stateliest

statement *noun*
statements

statesman *noun*
statesmen

statesmanship

stateswoman *noun*
stateswomen

static *adjective*
statically

station *noun*
stations

station *verb*
stations
stationing
stationed

stationary* *adjective*

stationery☆ *noun*

stationmaster *noun*
stationmasters

statistic *noun*
statistics

statistical *adjective*
statistically

statistician *noun*
statisticians

statistics

statue *noun*
statues

status *noun*
statuses

staunch *adjective*
stauncher
staunchest
staunchly

stave *noun*
staves

stave *verb*
staves
staving
staved
stove

stay *verb*
stays
staying
stayed

stay *noun*
stays

steadiness

steady *adjective*
steadier
steadiest
steadily

steady *verb*
steadies
steadying
steadied

steak○ *noun*
steaks

steal✢ *verb*
steals
stealing
stole
stolen

stealth

stealthy *adjective*
stealthier
stealthiest
stealthily

steam *noun*

steam *verb*
steams
steaming
steamed

steamy *adjective*
steamier
steamiest
steamily

steamer *noun*
steamers

steamroller *noun*
steamrollers

steamship *noun*
steamships

steed *noun*
steeds

steel *noun*

steel● *verb*
steels
steeling
steeled

steely *adjective*
steelier
steeliest

steep *adjective*
steeper
steepest
steeply

★ **Stationary** means 'not moving'. **!stationery**.
☆ **Stationery** means 'paper and envelopes'. **!stationary**.
○ A **steak** is a thick slice of meat. **!stake**.
✢ To **steal** is to take something that is not yours. **!steel**.
● To **steel** yourself is to find courage to do something hard. **!steal**.

st

steepness

steeple *noun*
steeples

steeplechase *noun*
steeplechases

steeplejack *noun*
steeplejacks

steer *verb*
steers
steering
steered

steer *noun*
steers

stem *noun*
stems

stem *verb*
stems
stemming
stemmed

stench *noun*
stenches

stencil *noun*
stencils

step* *noun*
steps

step *verb*
steps
stepping
stepped

stepchild *noun*
stepchildren

stepfather *noun*
stepfathers

stepladder *noun*
stepladders

stepmother *noun*
stepmothers

steppe☆ *noun*
steppes

stereo *adjective and
noun*
stereos

stereophonic
adjective
stereophonically

sterile

sterility

sterilization

sterilize *verb*
sterilizes
sterilizing
sterilized

sterling

stern *noun*
sterns

stern *adjective*
sterner
sternest
sternly

sternness

stethoscope *noun*
stethoscopes

stew *verb*
stews
stewing
stewed

stew *noun*
stews

steward *noun*
stewards

stewardess *noun*
stewardesses

stick *verb*
sticks
sticking
stuck

stick *noun*
sticks

sticker *noun*
stickers

stickiness

stickleback *noun*
sticklebacks

sticky *adjective*
stickier
stickiest
stickily

stiff *adjective*
stiffer
stiffest
stiffly

stiffen *verb*
stiffens
stiffening
stiffened

stiffness

stifle *verb*
stifles
stifling
stifled

stile *noun*
stiles

still *adjective*
stiller
stillest

still *adverb*

still *verb*
stills
stilling
stilled

stillness

stilts

stimulant *noun*
stimulants

stimulate *verb*
stimulates
stimulating
stimulated

stimulation

stimulus *noun*
stimuli

sting *noun*
stings

a
b
c
d
e
f
g
h
i
j
k
l
m
n
o
p
q
r
s
t
u
v
w
x
y
z

★ A **step** is a movement of the feet or part of a stair. **! steppe**.

☆ A **steppe** is a grassy plain. **! step**.

236

sting *verb*
stings
stinging
stung

stingy *adjective*
stingier
stingiest
stingily

stink *noun*
stinks

stink *verb*
stinks
stinking
stank
stunk

stir *verb*
stirs
stirring
stirred

stir *noun*
stirs

stirrup *noun*
stirrups

stitch *noun*
stitches

stoat *noun*
stoats

stock *noun*
stocks

stock *verb*
stocks
stocking
stocked

stockade *noun*
stockades

stockbroker *noun*
stockbrokers

stocking *noun*
stockings

stockpile *noun*
stockpiles

stocks *plural noun*

stocky *adjective*
stockier
stockiest
stockily

stodgy *adjective*
stodgier
stodgiest
stodgily

stoke *verb*
stokes
stoking
stoked

stole *noun*
stoles

stole see **steal**

stolen see **steal**

stomach *noun*
stomachs

stomach *verb*
stomachs
stomaching
stomached

stone *noun*
stones *or* stone

stone *verb*
stones
stoning
stoned

stony *adjective*
stonier
stoniest

stood see **stand**

stool *noun*
stools

stoop *verb*
stoops
stooping
stooped

stop *verb*
stops
stopping
stopped

stop *noun*
stops

stoppage *noun*
stoppages

stopper *noun*
stoppers

stopwatch *noun*
stopwatches

storage

store *verb*
stores
storing
stored

store *noun*
stores

storey* *noun*
storeys

stork *noun*
storks

storm *noun*
storms

storm *verb*
storms
storming
stormed

stormy *adjective*
stormier
stormiest
stormily

story☆ *noun*
stories

stout *adjective*
stouter
stoutest
stoutly

stoutness

stove *noun*
stoves

. . . .
★ A **storey** is a floor of a building. **!story**.
☆ You use **story** in e.g. *read me a story*. **!storey**.

st

stove see **stave**

stow verb
stows
stowing
stowed

stowaway noun
stowaways

straddle verb
straddles
straddling
straddled

straggle verb
straggles
straggling
straggled

straggler noun
stragglers

straggly adjective
stragglier
straggliest

straight* adjective
straighter
straightest

straighten verb
straightens
straightening
straightened

straightforward
adjective
straightforwardly

strain verb
strains
straining
strained

strain noun
strains

strainer noun
strainers

strait☆ noun
straits

straits○ plural noun

strand noun
strands

stranded

strange adjective
stranger
strangest
strangely

strangeness

stranger noun
strangers

strangle verb
strangles
strangling
strangled

strangler noun
stranglers

strangulation

strap noun
straps

strap verb
straps
strapping
strapped

strategic adjective
strategically

strategist noun
strategists

strategy noun
strategies

stratum noun
strata

straw noun
straws

strawberry noun
strawberries

stray verb
strays
straying
strayed

stray adjective

streak noun
streaks

streak verb
streaks
streaking
streaked

streaky adjective
streakier
streakiest
streakily

stream noun
streams

stream verb
streams
streaming
streamed

streamer noun
streamers

streamline verb
streamlines
streamlining
streamlined

street noun
streets

strength noun
strengths

strengthen verb
strengthens
strengthening
strengthened

strenuous adjective
strenuously

stress noun
stresses

stress verb
stresses
stressing
stressed

stretch verb
stretches
stretching
stretched

....

★ **Straight** means 'not curving or bending'. ! strait.
☆ A **strait** is a narrow stretch of water. ! straight.
○ You use **straits** in the phrase *in dire straits*.

a b c d e f g h i j k l m n o p q r **s** t u v w x y z

238

stretch *noun*
stretches

stretcher *noun*
stretchers

strew *verb*
strews
strewing
strewed
strewn

stricken

strict *adjective*
stricter
strictest
strictly

strictness

stride *verb*
strides
striding
strode
stridden

stride *noun*
strides

strife

strike *verb*
strikes
striking
struck

strike *noun*
strikes

striker *noun*
strikers

striking *adjective*
strikingly

string *noun*
strings

string *verb*
strings
stringing
strung

stringiness

stringy *adjective*
stringier
stringiest
stringily

strip *verb*
strips
stripping
stripped

strip *noun*
strips

stripe *noun*
stripes

striped

stripy *adjective*
stripier
stripiest

strive *verb*
strives
striving
strove
striven

strobe *noun*
strobes

strode see **stride**

stroke *noun*
strokes

stroke *verb*
strokes
stroking
stroked

stroll *verb*
strolls
strolling
strolled

stroll *noun*
strolls

strong *adjective*
stronger
strongest
strongly

stronghold *noun*
strongholds

strove see **strive**

struck see **strike**

structural *adjective*
structurally

structure *noun*
structures

struggle *verb*
struggles
struggling
struggled

struggle *noun*
struggles

strum *verb*
strums
strumming
strummed

strung see **string**

strut *verb*
struts
strutting
strutted

strut *noun*
struts

stub *verb*
stubs
stubbing
stubbed

stub *noun*
stubs

stubble

stubborn *adjective*
stubbornly

stubbornness

stuck see **stick**

stuck-up

stud *noun*
studs

student *noun*
students

studio *noun*
studios

studious *adjective*
studiously

study *verb*
studies
studying
studied

study *noun*
studies

stuff *noun*

stuff verb
stuffs
stuffing
stuffed

stuffiness noun

stuffing noun
stuffings

stuffy adjective
stuffier
stuffiest
stuffily

stumble verb
stumbles
stumbling
stumbled

stump noun
stumps

stump verb
stumps
stumping
stumped

stun verb
stuns
stunning
stunned

stung see sting

stunk see stink

stunt noun
stunts

stupendous adjective
stupendously

stupid adjective
stupider
stupidest
stupidly

stupidity

sturdiness

sturdy adjective
sturdier
sturdiest
sturdily

stutter verb
stutters
stuttering
stuttered

stutter noun
stutters

sty* noun
sties

style noun
styles

style verb
styles
styling
styled

stylish adjective
stylishly

stylus noun
styluses

subcontinent noun
subcontinents

subdivide verb
subdivides
subdividing
subdivided

subdivision noun
subdivisions

subdue verb
subdues
subduing
subdued

subject adjective and
noun
subjects

subject verb
subjects
subjecting
subjected

subjective adjective
subjectively

submarine noun
submarines

submerge verb
submerges
submerging
submerged

submersion

submission noun
submissions

submissive adjective
submissively

submit verb
submits
submitting
submitted

subordinate adjective
and noun
subordinates

subordinate verb
subordinates
subordinating
subordinated

subordination

subscribe verb
subscribes
subscribing
subscribed

subscriber noun
subscribers

subscription noun
subscriptions

subsequent adjective
subsequently

subside verb
subsides
subsiding
subsided

subsidence

subsidize verb
subsidizes
subsidizing
subsidized

subsidy noun
subsidies

★ A **sty** is a place for pigs or a swelling on the eye. In the second
meaning you can also use *stye*, plural *styes*.

substance noun
substances

substantial adjective
substantially

substitute verb
substitutes
substituting
substituted

substitute noun
substitutes

substitution noun
substitutions

subtle adjective
subtler
subtlest
subtly

subtlety noun
subtleties

subtract verb
subtracts
subtracting
subtracted

subtraction noun
subtractions

suburb noun
suburbs

suburban adjective

suburbia noun

subway noun
subways

succeed verb
succeeds
succeeding
succeeded

success noun
successes

successful adjective
successfully

succession noun
successions

successive adjective
successively

successor noun
successors

such

suck verb
sucks
sucking
sucked

suck noun
sucks

suction noun

sudden adjective
suddenly

suddenness noun

suds plural noun

sue verb
sues
suing
sued

suede noun

suet noun

suffer verb
suffers
suffering
suffered

sufficiency noun

sufficient adjective
sufficiently

suffix noun
suffixes

suffocate verb
suffocates
suffocating
suffocated

suffocation noun

sugar noun

sugary adjective

suggest verb
suggests
suggesting
suggested

suggestion noun
suggestions

suicidal adjective
suicidally

suicide noun
suicides

suit* noun
suits

suit verb
suits
suiting
suited

suitability noun

suitable adjective
suitably

suitcase noun
suitcases

suite☆ noun
suites

suitor noun
suitors

sulk verb
sulks
sulking
sulked

sulkiness noun

sulky adjective
sulkier
sulkiest
sulkily

sullen adjective
sullenly

sullenness noun

sulphur noun

sulphuric acid noun

sultan noun
sultans

sultana noun
sultanas

· ·
★ A **suit** is a set of matching clothes. **!suite**.
☆ A **suite** is a set of furniture or a group of rooms. **!suit**.

sum* noun
sums

sum verb
sums
summing
summed

summarize verb
summarizes
summarizing
summarized

summary noun
summaries

summer noun
summers

summertime

summit noun
summits

summon verb
summons
summoning
summoned

summons noun
summonses

sun☆ noun
suns

sun verb
suns
sunning
sunned

sunbathe verb
sunbathes
sunbathing
sunbathed

sunburn

sunburned or
sunburnt

sundae○ noun
sundaes

Sunday✢ noun
Sundays

sundial noun
sundials

sunflower noun
sunflowers

sung see **sing**

sunglasses

sunk see **sink**

sunlight

sunlit

sunny adjective
sunnier
sunniest
sunnily

sunrise noun
sunrises

sunset noun
sunsets

sunshade noun
sunshades

sunshine

sunspot noun
sunspots

sunstroke

suntan noun
suntans

suntanned

super

---

super- makes words
meaning 'very good'
or 'extra', e.g.
supermarket,
supermodel. They
are normally spelt
joined up.

---

superb adjective
superbly

superficial adjective
superficially

superfluous adjective
superfluously

superintend verb
superintends
superintending
superintended

superintendent noun
superintendents

superior adjective and
noun
superiors

superiority

superlative adjective
superlatively

superlative noun
superlatives

supermarket noun
supermarkets

supernatural
adjective
supernaturally

supersonic adjective
supersonically

superstition noun
superstitions

superstitious
adjective
superstitiously

supervise verb
supervises
supervising
supervised

supervision

supervisor

supper noun
suppers

. . . .

★ A **sum** is an amount or total. **I some**.
☆ A **sun** is a large star. **I son**.
○ A **sundae** is a cocktail of fruit and ice cream. **I Sunday**.
✢ **Sunday** is a day of the week. **I sundae**.

supple *adjective*
suppler
supplest
supplely

supplement *noun*
supplements

supplementary

suppleness

supply *verb*
supplies
supplying
supplied

supplier *noun*
suppliers

supply *noun*
supplies

support *verb*
supports
supporting
supported

support *noun*
supports

supporter *noun*
supporters

suppose *verb*
supposes
supposing
supposed

supposedly

supposition *noun*
suppositions

suppress *verb*
suppresses
suppressing
suppressed

suppression

supremacy

supreme *adjective*
supremely

sure *adjective*
surer
surest
surely

surf *noun*

surf *verb*
surfs
surfing
surfed

surface *noun*
surfaces

surface *verb*
surfaces
surfacing
surfaced

surfboard *noun*
surfboards

surfer *noun*
surfers

surge *verb*
surges
surging
surged

surge *noun*
surges

surgeon *noun*
surgeons

surgery *noun*
surgeries

surgical *adjective*
surgically

surname *noun*
surnames

surpass *verb*
surpasses
surpassing
surpassed

surplus *noun*
surpluses

surprise *verb*
surprises
surprising
surprised

surprise *noun*
surprises

surrender *verb*
surrenders
surrendering
surrendered

surrender *noun*
surrenders

surround *verb*
surrounds
surrounding
surrounded

surroundings *plural noun*

survey *noun*
surveys

survey *verb*
surveys
surveying
surveyed

surveyor *noun*
surveyors

survival

survive *verb*
survives
surviving
survived

survivor *noun*
survivors

suspect *verb*
suspects
suspecting
suspected

suspect *noun*
suspects

suspend *verb*
suspends
suspending
suspended

suspense

suspension *noun*
suspensions

suspicion *noun*
suspicions

suspicious *adjective*
suspiciously

sustain *verb*
sustains
sustaining
sustained

SW

swagger *verb*
swaggers
swaggering
swaggered

swallow *verb*
swallows
swallowing
swallowed

swallow *noun*
swallows

swam see **swim**

swamp *verb*
swamps
swamping
swamped

swamp *noun*
swamps

swampy *adjective*
swampier
swampiest

swan *noun*
swans

swank *verb*
swanks
swanking
swanked

swap *verb*
swaps
swapping
swapped

swap *noun*
swaps

swarm *noun*
swarms

swarm *verb*
swarms
swarming
swarmed

swastika *noun*
swastikas

swat* *verb*
swats
swatting
swatted

swatter *noun*
swatters

sway *verb*
sways
swaying
swayed

swear *verb*
swears
swearing
swore
sworn

sweat *verb*
sweats
sweating
sweated

sweat *noun*

sweater *noun*
sweaters

sweatshirt *noun*
sweatshirts

sweaty *adjective*
sweatier
sweatiest
sweatily

swede *noun*
swedes

sweep *verb*
sweeps
sweeping
swept

sweep *noun*
sweeps

sweeper *noun*
sweepers

sweet *adjective*
sweeter
sweetest
sweetly

sweet *noun*
sweets

sweetcorn

sweeten *verb*
sweetens
sweetening
sweetened

sweetener *noun*
sweeteners

sweetheart *noun*
sweethearts

sweetness

swell *verb*
swells
swelling
swelled
swollen

swell *noun*
swells

swelling *noun*
swellings

swelter *verb*
swelters
sweltering
sweltered

swept see **sweep**

swerve *verb*
swerves
swerving
swerved

swerve *noun*
swerves

swift *adjective*
swifter
swiftest
swiftly

swift *noun*
swifts

swiftness

swill *verb*
swills
swilling
swilled

swill *noun*

★ To **swat** an insect is to hit it. ! **swot**.

244

swim verb
swims
swimming
swam
swum

swim noun
swims

swimmer noun
swimmers

swimsuit noun
swimsuits

swindle verb
swindles
swindling
swindled

swindler noun
swindlers

swindle noun
swindles

swine noun
swine or swines

swing verb
swings
swinging
swung

swing noun
swings

swipe verb
swipes
swiping
swiped

swipe noun
swipes

swirl verb
swirls
swirling
swirled

swirl noun
swirls

swish verb
swishes
swishing
swished

swish noun
swishes

Swiss roll noun
Swiss rolls

switch verb
switches
switching
switched

switch noun
switches

switchboard noun
switchboards

swivel verb
swivels
swivelling
swivelled

swollen see **swell**

swoon verb
swoons
swooning
swooned

swoop verb
swoops
swooping
swooped

swoop noun
swoops

swop verb
swops
swopping
swopped

sword noun
swords

swore see **swear**

sworn see **swear**

swot* verb
swots
swotting
swotted

swot noun
swots

swum see **swim**

swung see **swing**

sycamore noun
sycamores

syllabic adjective
syllabically

syllable noun
syllables

syllabus noun
syllabuses

symbol noun
symbols

symbolic adjective
symbolically

symbolism noun

symbolize verb
symbolizes
symbolizing
symbolized

symmetrical
adjective
symmetrically

symmetry noun

sympathetic adjective
sympathetically

sympathize verb
sympathizes
sympathizing
sympathized

sympathy noun
sympathies

symphonic adjective
symphonically

symphony noun
symphonies

symptom noun
symptoms

symptomatic
adjective
symptomatically

synagogue noun
synagogues

synchronization
noun

a
b
c
d
e
f
g
h
i
j
k
l
m
n
o
p
q
r
s
t
u
v
w
x
y
z

....

★ To **swot** is to study hard. **!swat**.

245

synchronize *verb*
synchronizes
synchronizing
synchronized

syncopated

synonym *noun*
synonyms

synonymous *adjective*
synonymously

synthesis *noun*
syntheses

synthesize *verb*
synthesizes
synthesizing
synthesized

synthesizer *noun*
synthesizers

synthetic *adjective*
synthetically

syringe *noun*
syringes

syrup *noun*
syrups

syrupy

system *noun*
systems

systematic *adjective*
systematically

Tt

-t
See the note at **-ed.**

tab *noun*
tabs

tabby *noun*
tabbies

table *noun*
tables

tablecloth *noun*
tablecloths

tablespoon *noun*
tablespoons

tablespoonful *noun*
tablespoonfuls

tablet *noun*
tablets

tack *noun*
tacks

tack *verb*
tacks
tacking
tacked

tackle *verb*
tackles
tackling
tackled

tackle *noun*
tackles

tacky *adjective*
tackier
tackiest
tackily

tact

tactful *adjective*
tactfully

tactical *adjective*
tactically

tactics *plural noun*

tactless *adjective*
tactlessly

tadpole *noun*
tadpoles

tag *noun*
tags

tag *verb*
tags
tagging
tagged

tail★ *noun*
tails

tail *verb*
tails
tailing
tailed

tailback *noun*
tailbacks

tailless

tailor *noun*
tailors

take *verb*
takes
taking
took
taken

takeaway *noun*
takeaways

takings *plural noun*

talc

talcum powder

tale☆ *noun*
tales

talent *noun*
talents

talented

talk *verb*
talks
talking
talked

talk *noun*
talks

talkative *adjective*
talkatively

talker *noun*
talkers

tall *adjective*
taller
tallest

★ A **tail** is a part at the back of an animal. ! **tale**.
☆ A **tale** is a story. ! **tail**.

tally verb
tallies
tallying
tallied

Talmud

talon noun
talons

tambourine noun
tambourines

tame adjective
tamer
tamest
tamely

tame verb
tames
taming
tamed

tameness

tamer noun
tamers

tamper verb
tampers
tampering
tampered

tampon noun
tampons

tan noun
tans

tan verb
tans
tanning
tanned

tandem noun
tandems

tang noun
tangs

tangent noun
tangents

tangerine noun
tangerines

tangle verb
tangles
tangling
tangled

tangle noun
tangles

tank noun
tanks

tankard noun
tankards

tanker noun
tankers

tanner noun
tanners

tantalize verb
tantalizes
tantalizing
tantalized

tantrum noun
tantrums

tap noun
taps

tap verb
taps
tapping
tapped

tap dance noun
tap dances

tap dancer noun
tap dancers

tap dancing

tape noun
tapes

tape verb
tapes
taping
taped

tape-measure noun
tape-measures

taper verb
tapers
tapering
tapered

taper noun
tapers

tape recorder noun
tape recorders

tapestry noun
tapestries

tapeworm noun
tapeworms

tapioca

tar noun

tar verb
tars
tarring
tarred

tarantula noun
tarantulas

target noun
targets

target verb
targets
targeting
targeted

tarmac

tarmacadam

tarnish verb
tarnishes
tarnishing
tarnished

tarpaulin noun
tarpaulins

tarry adjective
tarrier
tarriest

tart noun
tarts

tart adjective
tarter
tartest
tartly

tartan noun
tartans

task noun
tasks

tassel noun
tassels

taste verb
tastes
tasting
tasted

taste noun
tastes

tasteful *adjective*
tastefully

tasteless *adjective*
tastelessly

tasty *adjective*
tastier
tastiest
tastily

tattered

tatters *plural noun*

tattoo *noun*
tattoos

tattoo *verb*
tattoos
tattooing
tattooed

tatty *adjective*
tattier
tattiest
tattily

taught see **teach**

taunt *verb*
taunts
taunting
taunted

taunt *noun*
taunts

taut *adjective*
tauter
tautest
tautly

tautness

tavern *noun*
taverns

tawny *adjective*
tawnier
tawniest

tax *noun*
taxes

tax *verb*
taxes
taxing
taxed

taxable

taxation

taxi *noun*
taxis

taxi *verb*
taxis
taxiing
taxied

taxpayer *noun*
taxpayers

tea★ *noun*
teas

teabag *noun*
teabags

teacake *noun*
teacakes

teach *verb*
teaches
teaching
taught

teacher *noun*
teachers

tea cloth or **tea
towel** *noun*
tea cloths *or* tea
towels

teacup *noun*
teacups

teak

team☆ *noun*
teams

teapot *noun*
teapots

tear *verb*
tears
tearing
tore
torn

tear○ *noun*
tears

tearful *adjective*
tearfully

tear gas

tease *verb*
teases
teasing
teased

teaspoon *noun*
teaspoons

teaspoonful *noun*
teaspoonfuls

teat *noun*
teats

tech *noun*
techs

technical *adjective*
technically

technicality *noun*
technicalities

technician *noun*
technicians

technique *noun*
techniques

technological
adjective
technologically

technology *noun*
technologies

teddy bear *noun*
teddy bears

tedious *adjective*
tediously

tediousness

....

★ **Tea** is a hot drink. ! **tee**.

☆ You use **team** in e.g. *a football team*. ! **teem**.

○ A **tear** is a drop of water from an eye and rhymes with 'here', or a
split in something and rhymes with 'hair'.

tedium

tee* *noun*
tees

teem☆ *verb*
teems
teeming
teemed

teenage

teenager *noun*
teenagers

teens

teeth see **tooth**

teetotal

teetotaller *noun*
teetotallers

telecommunications
plural noun

telegram *noun*
telegrams

telegraph *noun*
telegraphs

telegraphic *adjective*
telegraphically

telegraphy

telepathic *adjective*
telepathically

telepathy

telephone *noun*
telephones

telephone *verb*
telephones
telephoning
telephoned

telephonist *noun*
telephonists

telescope *noun*
telescopes

telescopic *adjective*
telescopically

teletext

televise *verb*
televises
televising
televised

television *noun*
televisions

tell *verb*
tells
telling
told

tell-tale *adjective* and
noun
tell-tales

telly *noun*
tellies

temper *noun*
tempers

temperate

temperature *noun*
temperatures

tempest *noun*
tempests

tempestuous
adjective
tempestuously

temple *noun*
temples

tempo *noun*
tempos

temporary *adjective*
temporarily

tempt *verb*
tempts
tempting
tempted

temptation *noun*
temptations

tempter *noun*
tempters

temptress *noun*
temptresses

ten *noun*
tens

tenancy *noun*
tenancies

tenant *noun*
tenants

tend *verb*
tends
tending
tended

tendency *noun*
tendencies

tender *adjective*
tenderer
tenderest
tenderly

tender *noun*
tenders

tender *verb*
tenders
tendering
tendered

tenderness

tendon *noun*
tendons

tendril *noun*
tendrils

tennis

tenor *noun*
tenors

tenpin bowling

tense *adjective*
tenser
tensest
tensely

tense *noun*
tenses

tension *noun*
tensions

tent *noun*
tents

. . . .

★ A **tee** is part of a golf course. ! **tea**.

☆ You use **teem** in e.g. *a place teeming with people*. ! **team**.

a
b
c
d
e
f
g
h
i
j
k
l
m
n
o
p
q
r
s
t
u
v
w
x
y
z

tentacle *noun*
tentacles

tenth

tenthly

tepid

term *noun*
terms

term *verb*
terms
terming
termed

terminal *noun*
terminals

terminate *verb*
terminates
terminating
terminated

termination *noun*
terminations

terminus *noun*
termini

terrace *noun*
terraces

terrapin *noun*
terrapins

terrible *adjective*
terribly

terrier *noun*
terriers

terrific *adjective*
terrifically

terrify *verb*
terrifies
terrifying
terrified

territorial *adjective*
territorially

territory *noun*
territories

terror *noun*
terrors

terrorism

terrorist *adjective and noun*
terrorists

terrorize *verb*
terrorizes
terrorizing
terrorized

tessellation *noun*
tessellations

test *noun*
tests

test *verb*
tests
testing
tested

testament *noun*
testaments

testicle *noun*
testicles

testify *verb*
testifies
testifying
testified

testimonial *noun*
testimonials

testimony *noun*
testimonies

testy *adjective*
testier
testiest

tether *verb*
tethers
tethering
tethered

tether *noun*
tethers

text *noun*
texts

textbook *noun*
textbooks

textile *noun*
textiles

texture *noun*
textures

than

thank *verb*
thanks
thanking
thanked

thankful *adjective*
thankfully

thankless *adjective*
thanklessly

thanks *plural noun*

that *adjective, pronoun, and conjunction*

thatch *noun*

thatch *verb*
thatches
thatching
thatched

thatcher *noun*
thatchers

thaw *verb*
thaws
thawing
thawed

theatre *noun*
theatres

theatrical *adjective*
theatrically

thee

theft *noun*
thefts

their*

theirs☆

them

★ You use **their** in e.g. *this is their house*. ! *there*, *they're*.
☆ You use **theirs** in e.g. *the house is theirs*. Note that there is no apostrophe in this word.

theme *noun*
themes

theme park *noun*
theme parks

themselves

then

theologian *noun*
theologians

theological *adjective*
theologically

theology

theorem *noun*
theorems

theoretical *adjective*
theoretically

theory *noun*
theories

therapist *noun*
therapists

therapy *noun*
therapies

there* *adverb*

thereabouts

therefore

thermal *adjective*
thermally

thermometer *noun*
thermometers

Thermos *noun*
Thermoses

thermostat *noun*
thermostats

thermostatic *adjective*
thermostatically

thesaurus *noun*
thesauri *or*
thesauruses

these

they

they'd *verb*

they'll *verb*

they're☆ *verb*

they've *verb*

thick *adjective*
thicker
thickest
thickly

thicken *verb*
thickens
thickening
thickened

thicket *noun*
thickets

thickness *noun*
thicknesses

thief *noun*
thieves

thigh *noun*
thighs

thimble *noun*
thimbles

thin *adjective*
thinner
thinnest
thinly

thin *verb*
thins
thinning
thinned

thine

thing *noun*
things

think *verb*
thinks
thinking
thought

thinker *noun*
thinkers

thinness

third

thirdly

Third World

thirst

thirsty *adjective*
thirstier
thirstiest
thirstily

thirteen

thirteenth

thirtieth

thirty *noun*
thirties

this

thistle *noun*
thistles

thorn *noun*
thorns

thorny *adjective*
thornier
thorniest

thorough *adjective*
thoroughly

thoroughness

those

thou

though

thought *noun*
thoughts

thought see think

thoughtful *adjective*
thoughtfully

thoughtfulness

thoughtless *adjective*
thoughtlessly

thoughtlessness

thousand *noun*
thousands

thousandth

. . . .
★ You use **there** in e.g. *Look over there.* **!** their, they're.
☆ **They're** is short for *they are.* **!** their, there.

a

thrash* verb
thrashes
thrashing
thrashed

thread noun
threads

thread verb
threads
threading
threaded

threadbare

threat noun
threats

threaten verb
threatens
threatening
threatened

three noun
threes

three-dimensional adjective
three-dimensionally

thresh☆ verb
threshes
threshing
threshed

threshold noun
thresholds

threw see **throw**

thrift

thrifty adjective
thriftier
thriftiest
thriftily

thrill noun
thrills

thrill verb
thrills
thrilling
thrilled

thriller noun
thrillers

thrive verb
thrives
thriving
thrived or throve or
thriven

throat noun
throats

throb verb
throbs
throbbing
throbbed

throb noun
throbs

throne noun
thrones

throng noun
throngs

throttle verb
throttles
throttling
throttled

throttle noun
throttles

through

throughout

throve see **thrive**

throw verb
throws
throwing
threw
thrown

throw noun
throws

thrush noun
thrushes

thrust verb
thrusts
thrusting
thrust

thud noun
thuds

thud verb
thuds
thudding
thudded

thumb noun
thumbs

thump verb
thumps
thumping
thumped

thump noun
thumps

thunder noun

thunder verb
thunders
thundering
thundered

thunderous adjective
thunderously

thunderstorm noun
thunderstorms

Thursday noun
Thursdays

thus

thy

tick verb
ticks
ticking
ticked

tick noun
ticks

ticket noun
tickets

tickle verb
tickles
tickling
tickled

ticklish adjective
ticklishly

tidal

tiddler noun
tiddlers

b
c
d
e
f
g
h
i
j
k
l
m
n
o
p
q
r
s
t
u
v
w
x
y
z

....

★ To **thrash** someone is to beat them. **! thresh**.
☆ To **thresh** corn is to beat it to separate the grain. **! thrash**.

tiddlywink *noun*
tiddlywinks

tide *noun*
tides

tide *verb*
tides
tiding
tided

tidiness

tidy *adjective*
tidier
tidiest
tidily

tie *verb*
ties
tying
tied

tie *noun*
ties

tie-break *noun*
tie-breaks

tiger *noun*
tigers

tight *adjective*
tighter
tightest
tightly

tighten *verb*
tightens
tightening
tightened

tightness

tightrope *noun*
tightropes

tights *plural noun*

tigress *noun*
tigresses

tile *noun*
tiles

tiled

till *preposition and conjunction*

till *noun*
tills

till *verb*
tills
tilling
tilled

tiller *noun*
tillers

tilt *verb*
tilts
tilting
tilted

tilt *noun*
tilts

timber *noun*
timbers

time *noun*
times

time *verb*
times
timing
timed

timer *noun*
timers

times

timetable *noun*
timetables

timid *adjective*
timidly

timidity

timing

timpani *plural noun*

tin *noun*
tins

tin *verb*
tins
tinning
tinned

tingle *verb*
tingles
tingling
tingled

tingle *noun*
tingles

tinker *verb*
tinkers
tinkering
tinkered

tinker *noun*
tinkers

tinkle *verb*
tinkles
tinkling
tinkled

tinkle *noun*
tinkles

tinny *adjective*
tinnier
tinniest
tinnily

tinsel

tint *noun*
tints

tint *verb*
tints
tinting
tinted

tiny *adjective*
tinier
tiniest

tip *verb*
tips
tipping
tipped

tip *noun*
tips

tiptoe *verb*
tiptoes
tiptoeing
tiptoed

tiptoe *noun*
tiptoes

tire★ *verb*
tires
tiring
tired

★ To **tire** is to become tired. **! tyre.**

a
b
c
d
e
f
g
h
i
j
k
l
m
n
o
p
q
r
s
t
u
v
w
x
y
z

tired

tireless *adjective*
tirelessly

tiresome *adjective*
tiresomely

tissue *noun*
tissues

tit *noun*
tits

titbit *noun*
titbits

title *noun*
titles

titter *verb*
titters
tittering
tittered

to* *preposition*

toad *noun*
toads

toadstool *noun*
toadstools

toast *verb*
toasts
toasting
toasted

toast *noun*
toasts

toaster *noun*
toasters

tobacco *noun*
tobaccos

tobacconist *noun*
tobacconists

toboggan *noun*
toboggans
tobogganing

today

toddler *noun*
toddlers

toe☆ *noun*
toes

toffee *noun*
toffees

toga *noun*
togas

together

toil *verb*
toils
toiling
toiled

toilet *noun*
toilets

token *noun*
tokens

told see **tell**

tolerable *adjective*
tolerably

tolerance

tolerant *adjective*
tolerantly

tolerate *verb*
tolerates
tolerating
tolerated

toll *noun*
tolls

toll *verb*
tolls
tolling
tolled

tomahawk *noun*
tomahawks

tomato *noun*
tomatoes

tomb *noun*
tombs

tomboy *noun*
tomboys

tombstone *noun*
tombstones

tomcat *noun*
tomcats

tommy-gun *noun*
tommy-guns

tomorrow

tom-tom *noun*
tom-toms

ton○ *noun*
tons

tonal *adjective*
tonally

tone *noun*
tones

tone *verb*
tones
toning
toned

tone-deaf

tongs *plural noun*

tongue *noun*
tongues

tonic *noun*
tonics

tonight

tonne✢ *noun*
tonnes

tonsillitis

tonsils *plural noun*

too* *adverb*

took see **take**

tool *noun*
tools

tooth *noun*
teeth

....

★ You use **to** in e.g. *go to bed* or *I want to stay*. **! too, two.**
☆ A **toe** is a part of a foot. **! tow.**
○ A **ton** is a non-metric unit of weight. **! tonne.**
✢ A **tonne** is a metric unit of weight. **! ton.**
● You use **too** in e.g. *it's too late* or *I want to come too*. **! to, two.**

toothache

toothbrush *noun*
toothbrushes

toothed

toothpaste *noun*
toothpastes

top *noun*
tops

top *verb*
tops
topping
topped

topic *noun*
topics

topical *adjective*
topically

topicality

topless

topmost

topping *noun*
toppings

topple *verb*
topples
toppling
toppled

topsy-turvy

torch *noun*
torches

tore see **tear**

toreador *noun*
toreadors

torment *verb*
torments
tormenting
tormented

torment *noun*
torments

tormentor *noun*
tormentors

torn see **tear**

tornado *noun*
tornadoes

torpedo *noun*
torpedoes

torpedo *verb*
torpedoes
torpedoing
torpedoed

torrent *noun*
torrents

torrential *adjective*
torrentially

torso *noun*
torsos

tortoise *noun*
tortoises

torture *verb*
tortures
torturing
tortured

torture *noun*
tortures

torturer *noun*
torturers

Tory *noun*
Tories

toss *verb*
tosses
tossing
tossed

toss *noun*
tosses

total *noun*
totals

total *adjective*
totally

total *verb*
totals
totalling
totalled

totalitarian

totem pole *noun*
totem poles

totter *verb*
totters
tottering
tottered

touch *verb*
touches
touching
touched

touch *noun*
touches

touchy *adjective*
touchier
touchiest
touchily

tough *adjective*
tougher
toughest
toughly

toughen *verb*
toughens
toughening
toughened

toughness

tour *noun*
tours

tourism

tourist *noun*
tourists

tournament *noun*
tournaments

tow★ *verb*
tows
towing
towed

tow *noun*

toward or **towards**

towel *noun*
towels

towelling

tower *noun*
towers

a
b
c
d
e
f
g
h
i
j
k
l
m
n
o
p
q
r
t
u
v
w
x
y
z

★ To **tow** something is to pull it along. **!** **toe**.

tower *verb*
towers
towering
towered

town *noun*
towns

towpath *noun*
towpaths

toxic *adjective*
toxically

toy *noun*
toys

toy *verb*
toys
toying
toyed

toyshop *noun*
toyshops

trace *noun*
traces

trace *verb*
traces
tracing
traced

traceable

track *noun*
tracks

track *verb*
tracks
tracking
tracked

tracker *noun*
trackers

tracksuit *noun*
tracksuits

tract *noun*
tracts

traction

tractor *noun*
tractors

trade *noun*
trades

trade *verb*
trades
trading
traded

trademark *noun*
trademarks

trader *noun*
traders

tradesman *noun*
tradesmen

trade union *noun*
trade unions

tradition *noun*
traditions

traditional *adjective*
traditionally

traffic *noun*
traffics

traffic *verb*
traffics
trafficking
trafficked

tragedy *noun*
tragedies

tragic *adjective*
tragically

trail *noun*
trails

trail *verb*
trails
trailing
trailed

trailer *noun*
trailers

train *noun*
trains

train *verb*
trains
training
trained

trainer *noun*
trainers

traitor *noun*
traitors

tram *noun*
trams

tramp *noun*
tramps

tramp *verb*
tramps
tramping
tramped

trample *verb*
tramples
trampling
trampled

trampoline *noun*
trampolines

trance *noun*
trances

tranquil *adjective*
tranquilly

tranquillity*

tranquillizer *noun*
tranquillizers

transact *verb*
transacts
transacting
transacted

transaction *noun*
transactions

transatlantic

transfer *verb*
transfers
transferring
transferred

transfer *noun*
transfers

transferable

transference

transform *verb*
transforms
transforming
transformed

transformation *noun*
transformations

....

★ Note that there are two ls in this word.

256

transformer *noun*
transformers

transfusion *noun*
transfusions

transistor *noun*
transistors

transition *noun*
transitions

transitional *adjective*
transitionally

transitive *adjective*
transitively

translate *verb*
translates
translating
translated

translation *noun*
translations

translator *noun*
translators

translucent

transmission *noun*
transmissions

transmit *verb*
transmits
transmitting
transmitted

transmitter *noun*
transmitters

transparency *noun*
transparencies

transparent *adjective*
transparently

transpire *verb*
transpires
transpiring
transpired

transplant *verb*
transplants
transplanting
transplanted

transplant *noun*
transplants

transplantation *noun*
transplantations

transport *verb*
transports
transporting
transported

transportation

transport *noun*

transporter *noun*
transporters

trap *verb*
traps
trapping
trapped

trap *noun*
traps

trapdoor *noun*
trapdoors

trapeze *noun*
trapezes

trapezium *noun*
trapeziums

trapezoid *noun*
trapezoids

trapper *noun*
trappers

trash

trashy *adjective*
trashier
trashiest
trashily

travel *verb*
travels
travelling
travelled

travel *noun*

traveller *noun*
travellers

traveller's cheque
noun
traveller's cheques

trawler *noun*
trawlers

tray *noun*
trays

treacherous *adjective*
treacherously

treachery

treacle

tread *verb*
treads
treading
trod
trodden

tread *noun*
treads

treason

treasure *noun*
treasures

treasure *verb*
treasures
treasuring
treasured

treasurer *noun*
treasurers

treasury *noun*
treasuries

treat *verb*
treats
treating
treated

treat *noun*
treats

treatment *noun*
treatments

treaty *noun*
treaties

treble *adjective and
noun*
trebles

treble *verb*
trebles
trebling
trebled

tree *noun*
trees

trek *verb*
treks
trekking
trekked

trek *noun*
treks

tr

trellis noun
trellises

tremble verb
trembles
trembling
trembled

tremble noun
trembles

tremendous adjective
tremendously

tremor noun
tremors

trench noun
trenches

trend noun
trends

trendiness

trendy adjective
trendier
trendiest
trendily

trespass verb
trespasses
trespassing
trespassed

trespasser noun
trespassers

trestle noun
trestles

trial noun
trials

triangle noun
triangles

triangular

tribal adjective
tribally

tribe noun
tribes

tribesman noun
tribesmen

tributary noun
tributaries

tribute noun
tributes

trick noun
tricks

trick verb
tricks
tricking
tricked

trickery

trickster noun
tricksters

trickle verb
trickles
trickling
trickled

trickle noun
trickles

tricky adjective
trickier
trickiest
trickily

tricycle noun
tricycles

tried see **try**

trifle noun
trifles

trifle verb
trifles
trifling
trifled

trifling

trigger noun
triggers

trigger verb
triggers
triggering
triggered

trillion noun
trillions

trim adjective
trimmer
trimmest
trimly

trim verb
trims
trimming
trimmed

trim noun
trims

Trinity★

trio noun
trios

trip verb
trips
tripping
tripped

trip noun
trips

tripe

triple adjective
triply

triple noun
triples

triple verb
triples
tripling
tripled

triplet noun
triplets

tripod noun
tripods

triumph noun
triumphs

triumphant adjective
triumphantly

trivial adjective
trivially

triviality noun
trivialities

trod see **tread**

trodden see **tread**

★ You use a capital T when you mean the three persons of God in Christianity.

258

troll noun
trolls

trolley noun
trolleys

trombone noun
trombones

troop noun
troops

troop verb
troops
trooping
trooped

troops plural noun

trophy noun
trophies

tropic noun
tropics

tropical adjective

trot verb
trots
trotting
trotted

trot noun
trots

trouble noun
troubles

trouble verb
troubles
troubling
troubled

troublesome

trough noun
troughs

trousers plural noun

trout noun
trout

trowel noun
trowels

truancy noun
truancies

truant noun
truants

truce noun
truces

truck noun
trucks

trudge verb
trudges
trudging
trudged

true adjective
truer
truest
truly

trump noun
trumps

trump verb
trumps
trumping
trumped

trumpet noun
trumpets

trumpet verb
trumpets
trumpeting
trumpeted

trumpeter noun
trumpeters

truncheon noun
truncheons

trundle verb
trundles
trundling
trundled

trunk noun
trunks

trunks plural noun

trust verb
trusts
trusting
trusted

trust

trustful adjective
trustfully

trustworthy adjective
trustworthily

trusty adjective
trustier
trustiest
trustily

truth noun
truths

truthful adjective
truthfully

truthfulness

try verb
tries
trying
tried

try noun
tries

T-shirt noun
T-shirts

tub noun
tubs

tuba noun
tubas

tube noun
tubes

tuber noun
tubers

tubing

tubular

tuck verb
tucks
tucking
tucked

tuck noun
tucks

Tuesday noun
Tuesdays

tuft noun
tufts

tug noun
tugs

tug verb
tugs
tugging
tugged

tulip noun
tulips

a
b
c
d
e
f
g
h
i
j
k
l
m
n
o
p
q
r
s
t
u
v
w
x
y
z

tumble *verb*
tumbles
tumbling
tumbled

tumble *noun*
tumbles

tumble-drier *noun*
tumble-driers

tumbler *noun*
tumblers

tummy *noun*
tummies

tumour *noun*
tumours

tumult

tumultuous *adjective*
tumultuously

tuna *noun*
tuna *or* tunas

tundra

tune *noun*
tunes

tune *verb*
tunes
tuning
tuned

tuneful *adjective*
tunefully

tunic *noun*
tunics

tunnel *noun*
tunnels

tunnel *verb*
tunnels
tunnelling
tunnelled

turban *noun*
turbans

turbine *noun*
turbines

turbulence

turbulent *adjective*
turbulently

turf *noun*
turfs *or* turves

turkey *noun*
turkeys

Turkish bath *noun*
Turkish baths

Turkish delight

turmoil

turn *verb*
turns
turning
turned

turn *noun*
turns

turncoat *noun*
turncoats

turnip *noun*
turnips

turnover *noun*
turnovers

turnstile *noun*
turnstiles

turntable *noun*
turntables

turpentine

turquoise

turret *noun*
turrets

turtle *noun*
turtles

tusk *noun*
tusks

tussle *verb*
tussles
tussling
tussled

tussle *noun*
tussles

tutor *noun*
tutors

tweak *verb*
tweaks
tweaking
tweaked

tweak *noun*
tweaks

tweed

tweezers *plural noun*

twelve *noun*
twelves

twelfth

twentieth

twenty *noun*
twenties

twice

twiddle *verb*
twiddles
twiddling
twiddled

twiddle *noun*
twiddles

twig *noun*
twigs

twig *verb*
twigs
twigging
twigged

twilight

twin *noun*
twins

twin *verb*
twins
twinning
twinned

twine

twinkle *verb*
twinkles
twinkling
twinkled

twinkle *noun*
twinkles

twirl *verb*
twirls
twirling
twirled

twirl *noun*
twirls

twist *verb*
twists
twisting
twisted

twist *noun*
twists

twister *noun*
twisters

twitch *verb*
twitches
twitching
twitched

twitch *noun*
twitches

twitter *verb*
twitters
twittering
twittered

two* *adjective and*
noun
twos

tying see **tie**

type *noun*
types

type *verb*
types
typing
typed

typewriter *noun*
typewriters

typewritten

typhoon *noun*
typhoons

typical *adjective*
typically

typist *noun*
typists

tyranny *noun*
tyrannies

tyrannical *adjective*
tyrannically

tyrant *noun*
tyrants

tyre☆ *noun*
tyres

Uu

udder *noun*
udders

ugliness

ugly *adjective*
uglier
ugliest

ulcer *noun*
ulcers

ultimate *adjective*
ultimately

ultraviolet

umbilical cord *noun*
umbilical cords

umbrella *noun*
umbrellas

umpire *noun*
umpires

> **un-**
> *un-* makes words
> meaning 'not', e.g.
> **unable,**
> **unhappiness.** Some
> of these words have
> special meanings,
> e.g. **unprofessional.**
> See the note at **non-**.

unable

unaided

unanimous *adjective*
unanimously

unavoidable
adjective
unavoidably

unaware

unawares

unbearable *adjective*
unbearably

unbelievable
adjective
unbelievably

unblock *verb*
unblocks
unblocking
unblocked

unborn

uncalled for

uncanny *adjective*
uncannier
uncanniest

uncertain *adjective*
uncertainly

uncertainty

uncle *noun*
uncles

uncomfortable
adjective
uncomfortably

uncommon *adjective*
uncommonly

unconscious
adjective
unconsciously

unconsciousness

uncontrollable
adjective
uncontrollably

uncountable

uncouth

★ You use **two** in e.g. *two people* or *there are two of them.* **!** to, too.
☆ A **tyre** is a rubber cover for a wheel. **!** tire.

un

uncover *verb*
uncovers
uncovering
uncovered

undecided

undeniable *adjective*
undeniably

under

underarm *adjective*

underclothes *plural noun*

underdeveloped

underdone

underfoot

undergo *verb*
undergoes
undergoing
underwent
undergone

undergraduate *noun*
undergraduates

underground *adjective* and *noun*
undergrounds

undergrowth

underhand

underlie *verb*
underlies
underlying
underlay
underlain

underline *verb*
underlines
underlining
underlined

undermine *verb*
undermines
undermining
undermined

underneath *preposition*

underpants *plural noun*

underpass *noun*
underpasses

underprivileged

understand *verb*
understands
understanding
understood

understandable *adjective*
understandably

understanding

undertake *verb*
undertakes
undertaking
undertook
undertaken

undertaker *noun*
undertakers

undertaking *noun*
undertakings

underwater

underwear

underworld

undesirable *adjective*
undesirably

undeveloped

undo *verb*
undoes
undoing
undid
undone

undoubted *adjective*
undoubtedly

undress *verb*
undresses
undressing
undressed

unearth *verb*
unearths
unearthing
unearthed

unearthly

unease

uneasiness

uneasy *adjective*
uneasier
uneasiest
uneasily

uneatable

unemployed

unemployment

uneven *adjective*
unevenly

unevenness

unexpected *adjective*
unexpectedly

unfair *adjective*
unfairly

unfairness

unfaithful *adjective*
unfaithfully

unfamiliar

unfamiliarity

unfasten *verb*
unfastens
unfastening
unfastened

unfavourable *adjective*
unfavourably

unfinished

unfit

unfold *verb*
unfolds
unfolding
unfolded

unforgettable *adjective*
unforgettably

unforgivable *adjective*
unforgivably

unfortunate *adjective*
unfortunately

unfreeze *verb*
unfreezes
unfreezing
unfroze
unfrozen

unfriendliness

unfriendly

ungrateful *adjective*
ungratefully

unhappiness

unhappy *adjective*
unhappier
unhappiest
unhappily

unhealthy *adjective*
unhealthier
unhealthiest
unhealthily

unheard-of

unicorn *noun*
unicorns

unification

uniform *noun*
uniforms

uniform *adjective*
uniformly

uniformed

uniformity

unify *verb*
unifies
unifying
unified

unimportance

unimportant

uninhabited

unintentional
adjective
unintentionally

uninterested

uninteresting

union *noun*
unions

unique *adjective*
uniquely

uniqueness

unisex

unison

unit *noun*
units

---

unite *verb*
unites
uniting
united

unity *noun*
unities

universal *adjective*
universally

universe

university *noun*
universities

unjust *adjective*
unjustly

unkind *adjective*
unkinder
unkindest
unkindly

unkindness

unknown

unleaded

unless

unlike

unlikely *adjective*
unlikelier
unlikeliest

unload *verb*
unloads
unloading
unloaded

unlock *verb*
unlocks
unlocking
unlocked

unlucky *adjective*
unluckier
unluckiest
unluckily

unmistakable
adjective
unmistakably

unnatural *adjective*
unnaturally

unnecessary
adjective
unnecessarily

---

unoccupied

unpack *verb*
unpacks
unpacking
unpacked

unpleasant *adjective*
unpleasantly

unpleasantness

unplug *verb*
unplugs
unplugging
unplugged

unpopular *adjective*
unpopularly

unpopularity

unravel *verb*
unravels
unravelling
unravelled

unreal

unreasonable
adjective
unreasonably

unrest

unroll *verb*
unrolls
unrolling
unrolled

unruliness

unruly *adjective*
unrulier
unruliest

unscrew *verb*
unscrews
unscrewing
unscrewed

unseemly

unseen

unselfish *adjective*
unselfishly

unselfishness

unsightly

unskilled

a b c d e f g h i j k l m n o p q r s t **u** v w x y z

unsound *adjective*
unsoundly

unsteadiness

unsteady *adjective*
unsteadier
unsteadiest
unsteadily

unsuccessful
adjective
unsuccessfully

unsuitable *adjective*
unsuitably

unthinkable *adjective*
unthinkably

untidiness

untidy *adjective*
untidier
untidiest
untidily

untie *verb*
unties
untying
untied

until

untimely

unto

untold

untoward

untrue *adjective*
untruly

untruthful *adjective*
untruthfully

unused

unusual *adjective*
unusually

unwanted

unwell

unwilling *adjective*
unwillingly

unwillingness

unwind *verb*
unwinds
unwinding
unwound

unwrap *verb*
unwraps
unwrapping
unwrapped

unzip *verb*
unzips
unzipping
unzipped

update *verb*
updates
updating
updated

upgrade *verb*
upgrades
upgrading
upgraded

upheaval *noun*
upheavals

uphill

uphold *verb*
upholds
upholding
upheld

upholstery

upkeep

uplands *plural noun*

upon

upper

upright *adjective*
uprightly

upright *noun*
uprights

uprising *noun*
uprisings

uproar *noun*
uproars

upset *verb*
upsets
upsetting
upset

upset *noun*
upsets

upshot

upside down

upstairs

upstart *noun*
upstarts

upstream *adjective*

uptake

uptight

upward *adjective* and
adverb

upwards *adverb*

uranium

urban

urbanization

urbanize *verb*
urbanizes
urbanizing
urbanized

urchin *noun*
urchins

Urdu

urge *verb*
urges
urging
urged

urge *noun*
urges

urgency

urgent *adjective*
urgently

urinary

urinate *verb*
urinates
urinating
urinated

urination

urine

urn *noun*
urns

-us
Most nouns ending in -us come from Latin words, e.g. **bonus** and **terminus**. They normally have plurals ending in -uses, e.g. **bonuses** and **terminuses**. Some more technical words have plurals ending in -i, e.g. **nucleus** - **nuclei**.

usable

usage noun
usages

use verb
uses
using
used

use noun
uses

useful adjective
usefully

usefulness

useless adjective
uselessly

uselessness

user noun
users

user-friendly
adjective
user-friendlier
user-friendliest

usher noun
ushers

usher verb
ushers
ushering
ushered

usherette noun
usherettes

usual adjective
usually

usurp verb
usurps
usurping
usurped

usurper noun
usurpers

utensil noun
utensils

uterus noun
uteri

utilization

utilize verb
utilizes
utilizing
utilized

utmost

utter adjective

utter verb
utters
uttering
uttered

utterance noun
utterances

utterly adverb

U-turn noun
U-turns

Vv

vacancy noun
vacancies

vacant adjective
vacantly

vacate verb
vacates
vacating
vacated

vacation noun
vacations

vaccinate verb
vaccinates
vaccinating
vaccinated

vaccination noun
vaccinations

vaccine noun
vaccines

vacuum noun
vacuums

vagina noun
vaginas

vague adjective
vaguer
vaguest
vaguely

vagueness

vain* adjective
vainer
vainest
vainly

vale☆ noun
vales

valentine noun
valentines

valiant adjective
valiantly

valid adjective
validly

validity

valley noun
valleys

valour

valuable adjective
valuably

valuables plural noun

★ **Vain** means 'conceited' or 'proud'. **!** vane, vein.
☆ A **vale** is a valley. **!** veil.

valuation noun
valuations

value noun
values

value verb
values
valuing
valued

valueless

valuer noun
valuers

valve noun
valves

vampire noun
vampires

van noun
vans

vandal noun
vandals

vandalism

vane* noun
vanes

vanilla

vanish verb
vanishes
vanishing
vanished

vanity

vanquish verb
vanquishes
vanquishing
vanquished

vaporize verb
vaporizes
vaporizing
vaporized

vapour noun
vapours

variable adjective
variably

variable noun
variables

variation noun
variations

varied

variety noun
varieties

various adjective
variously

varnish noun
varnishes

varnish verb
varnishes
varnishing
varnished

vary verb
varies
varying
varied

vase noun
vases

vast adjective
vastly

vastness

vat noun
vats

vault verb
vaults
vaulting
vaulted

vault noun
vaults

veal

vector noun
vectors

Veda

veer verb
veers
veering
veered

vegan noun
vegans

vegetable noun
vegetables

vegetarian noun
vegetarians

vegetate verb
vegetates
vegetating
vegetated

vegetation

vehicle noun
vehicles

veil☆ noun
veils

veil verb
veils
veiling
veiled

vein⊙ noun
veins

velocity noun
velocities

velvet

velvety

vendetta noun
vendettas

vendor noun
vendors

venerable adjective
venerably

venereal disease noun
venereal diseases

venetian blind noun
venetian blinds

vengeance

venison

....

★ A **vane** is a pointer that shows which way the wind is blowing.
  I vain, vein.

☆ A **veil** is a covering for the face. **I vale.**

⊙ A **vein** carries blood to the heart. **I vain, vane.**

266

Venn diagram *noun*
Venn diagrams

venom

venomous *adjective*
venomously

vent *noun*
vents

ventilate *verb*
ventilates
ventilating
ventilated

ventilation

ventilator *noun*
ventilators

ventriloquism

ventriloquist *noun*
ventriloquists

venture *verb*
ventures
venturing
ventured

venture *noun*
ventures

veranda *noun*
verandas

verb *noun*
verbs

verdict *noun*
verdicts

verge *verb*
verges
verging
verged

verge *noun*
verges

verification

verify *verb*
verifies
verifying
verified

vermin

verruca *noun*
verrucas

versatile

versatility

verse *noun*
verses

version *noun*
versions

versus

vertebra *noun*
vertebrae

vertebrate *noun*
vertebrates

vertex *noun*
vertices

vertical *adjective*
vertically

very

Vesak

vessel *noun*
vessels

vest *noun*
vests

vested *adjective*
vested

vestment *noun*
vestments

vestry *noun*
vestries

vet *noun*
vets

veteran *noun*
veterans

veterinary

veto *verb*
vetoes
vetoing
vetoed

veto *noun*
vetoes

vex *verb*
vexes
vexing
vexed

vexation

via

viaduct *noun*
viaducts

vibrate *verb*
vibrates
vibrating
vibrated

vibration *noun*
vibrations

vicar *noun*
vicars

vicarage *noun*
vicarages

vice *noun*
vices

vice-president *noun*
vice-presidents

vice versa

vicinity *noun*
vicinities

vicious *adjective*
viciously

viciousness

victim *noun*
victims

victimize *verb*
victimizes
victimizing
victimized

victor *noun*
victors

Victorian *adjective*
and *noun*
Victorians

victorious *adjective*
victoriously

victory *noun*
victories

video *noun*
videos

video *verb*
videoes
videoing
videoed

videotape *noun*
videotapes

view *noun*
views

view *verb*
views
viewing
viewed

viewer *noun*
viewers

vigilance

vigilant *adjective*
vigilantly

vigorous *adjective*
vigorously

vigour

Viking *noun*
Vikings

vile *adjective*
viler
vilest
vilely

villa *noun*
villas

village *noun*
villages

villager *noun*
villagers

villain *noun*
villains

villainous *adjective*
villainously

villainy

vine *noun*
vines

vinegar

vineyard *noun*
vineyards

vintage *noun*
vintages

vinyl

viola *noun*
violas

violate *verb*
violates
violating
violated

violation *noun*
violations

violator *noun*
violators

violence

violent *adjective*
violently

violet *noun*
violets

violin *noun*
violins

violinist *noun*
violinists

viper *noun*
vipers

virgin *noun*
virgins

virginity

virtual *adjective*
virtually

virtue *noun*
virtues

virtuous *adjective*
virtuously

virus *noun*
viruses

visa *noun*
visas

visibility

visible *adjective*
visibly

vision *noun*
visions

visit *verb*
visits
visiting
visited

visit *noun*
visits

visitor *noun*
visitors

visor *noun*
visors

visual *adjective*
visually

visualize *verb*
visualizes
visualizing
visualized

vital *adjective*
vitally

vitality

vitamin *noun*
vitamins

vivid *adjective*
vividly

vividness

vivisection *noun*
vivisections

vixen *noun*
vixens

vocabulary *noun*
vocabularies

vocal *adjective*
vocally

vocalist *noun*
vocalists

vocation *noun*
vocations

vocational *adjective*
vocationally

vodka *noun*
vodkas

voice *noun*
voices

voice *verb*
voices
voicing
voiced

volcanic

volcano *noun*
volcanoes

a
b
c
d
e
f
g
h
i
j
k
l
m
n
o
p
q
r
s
t
u
v
w
x
y
z

vole noun
voles

volley noun
volleys

volleyball

volt noun
volts

voltage noun
voltages

volume noun
volumes

voluntary adjective
voluntarily

volunteer verb
volunteers
volunteering
volunteered

volunteer noun
volunteers

vomit verb
vomits
vomiting
vomited

vote verb
votes
voting
voted

vote noun
votes

voter noun
voters

vouch verb
vouches
vouching
vouched

voucher noun
vouchers

vow noun
vows

vow verb
vows
vowing
vowed

vowel noun
vowels

voyage noun
voyages

voyager noun
voyagers

vulgar adjective
vulgarly

vulnerable adjective
vulnerably

vulture noun
vultures

vulva noun
vulvas

Ww

wad noun
wads

waddle verb
waddles
waddling
waddled

waddle noun
waddles

wade verb
wades
wading
waded

wafer noun
wafers

wag verb
wags
wagging
wagged

wag noun
wags

wage noun
wages

wage verb
wages
waging
waged

wager noun
wagers

wager verb
wagers
wagering
wagered

waggle verb
waggles
waggling
waggled

wagon noun
wagons

wagtail noun
wagtails

wail verb
wails
wailing
wailed

wail* noun
wails

waist☆ noun
waists

waistcoat noun
waistcoats

wait○ verb
waits
waiting
waited

wait noun
waits

waiter noun
waiters

a
b
c
d
e
f
g
h
i
j
k
l
m
n
o
p
q
r
s
t
u
v
w
x
y
z

269

★ A **wail** is a loud sad cry. **whale**.

☆ A person's **waist** is the narrow part around their middle. **waste**.

○ To **wait** is to delay, pause, or rest. **weight**.

a **waitress** noun
waitresses

b **waive*** verb
waives
c waiving
waived

d **wake** verb
wakes
e waking
woke
f woken

g **wake** noun
wakes
h
waken verb
i wakens
wakening
j wakened

k **walk** verb
walks
l walking
walked
m
walk noun
n walks

o **walkabout** noun
walkabouts

p **walker** noun
walkers
q
walkie-talkie noun
r walkie-talkies

Walkman noun
s Walkmans

t **wall** noun
walls
u
wall verb
v walls
walling
walled

x **wallaby** noun
wallabies

wallet noun
wallets

wallflower noun
wallflowers

wallop verb
wallops
walloping
walloped

wallow verb
wallows
wallowing
wallowed

wallpaper noun
wallpapers

walnut noun
walnuts

walrus noun
walruses

waltz noun
waltzes

waltz verb
waltzes
waltzing
waltzed

wand noun
wands

wander verb
wanders
wandering
wandered

wanderer noun
wanderers

wane verb
wanes
waning
waned

wangle verb
wangles
wangling
wangled

want verb
wants
wanting
wanted

want noun
wants

war noun
wars

warble verb
warbles
warbling
warbled

warble noun
warbles

warbler noun
warblers

ward noun
wards

ward verb
wards
warding
warded

warden noun
wardens

warder noun
warders

wardrobe noun
wardrobes

ware☆ noun
wares

warehouse noun
warehouses

warfare

warhead noun
warheads

wariness

warlike

warm adjective
warmer
warmest
warmly

★ To **waive** a right is to say you do not need it. **!** wave.
☆ **Wares** are manufactured goods. **!** wear, where.

warm verb
warms
warming
warmed

warmth

warn verb
warns
warning
warned

warning noun
warnings

warp verb
warps
warping
warped

warp noun
warps

warrant noun
warrants

warrant verb
warrants
warranting
warranted

warren noun
warrens

warrior noun
warriors

warship noun
warships

wart noun
warts

wary adjective
warier
wariest
warily

was

wash verb
washes
washing
washed

wash noun
washes

washable

washbasin noun
washbasins

washer noun
washers

washing

washing-up

wash-out noun
wash-outs

wasn't verb

wasp noun
wasps

wastage

waste* verb
wastes
wasting
wasted

waste adjective and
noun
wastes

wasteful adjective
wastefully

watch verb
watches
watching
watched

watch noun
watches

watchdog noun
watchdogs

watcher noun
watchers

watchful adjective
watchfully

watchfulness

watchman noun
watchmen

water noun
waters

water verb
waters
watering
watered

watercolour noun
watercolours

watercress

waterfall noun
waterfalls

waterlogged

watermark noun
watermarks

waterproof

water-skiing

watertight

waterway noun
waterways

waterworks noun
waterworks

watery

watt☆ noun
watts

wave○ verb
waves
waving
waved

wave noun
waves

waveband noun
wavebands

wavelength noun
wavelengths

waver verb
wavers
wavering
wavered

a
b
c
d
e
f
g
h
i
j
k
l
m
n
o
p
q
r
s
t
u
v
w
x
y
z

★ To **waste** something is to use more of it than is needed. **!waist**.

☆ A **watt** is a unit of electricity. **!what**.

○ To **wave** is to move your arm in greeting. **!waive**.

wavy *adjective*
wavier
waviest
wavily

wax *noun*
waxes

wax *verb*
waxes
waxing
waxed

waxwork *noun*
waxworks

waxy *adjective*
waxier
waxiest

way* *noun*
ways

weak° *adjective*
weaker
weakest
weakly

weakness

weaken *verb*
weakens
weakening
weakened

weakling *noun*
weaklings

wealth

wealthy *adjective*
wealthier
wealthiest
wealthily

weapon *noun*
weapons

wear° *verb*
wears
wearing
wore
worn

wear *noun*

wearer *noun*
wearers

weariness

weary *adjective*
wearier
weariest
wearily

weasel *noun*
weasels

weather *noun*

weather *verb*
weathers
weathering
weathered

weathercock *noun*
weathercocks

weave✛ *verb*
weaves
weaving
weaved *or* wove
woven

weaver *noun*
weavers

web *noun*
webs

webbed

website *noun*
websites

wed *verb*
weds
wedding
wedded
wed

we'd *verb*

wedding *noun*
weddings

wedge *noun*
wedges

wedge *verb*
wedges
wedging
wedged

Wednesday *noun*
Wednesdays

weed *noun*
weeds

weed *verb*
weeds
weeding
weeded

weedy *adjective*
weedier
weediest
weedily

week* *noun*
weeks

weekday *noun*
weekdays

weekend *noun*
weekends

weekly *adjective* and *adverb*

weep *verb*
weeps
weeping
wept

. . . .

★ You use **way** in e.g. *can you tell me the way?* ! **weigh**, **whey**.
☆ **Weak** means 'not strong'. ! **week**.
◦ To **wear** clothes is to be dressed in them. ! **ware**, **where**.
✛ The past tense is **weaved** in e.g. *she weaved her way through the crowd* and **wove** in e.g. *she wove a shawl.*
● A **week** is a period of seven days. ! **weak**.

weft

weigh* *verb*
weighs
weighing
weighed

weight☆ *noun*
weights

weightless

weightlifting

weighty *adjective*
weightier
weightiest
weightily

weir *noun*
weirs

weird *adjective*
weirder
weirdest
weirdly

weirdness

welcome *noun*
welcomes

welcome *verb*
welcomes
welcoming
welcomed

weld *verb*
welds
welding
welded

welder *noun*
welders

welfare

well *noun*
wells

well *adjective and adverb*
better
best

we'll *verb*

well-being

wellington boots
plural noun

well-known

went see **go**

wept see **weep**

were see **are**

we're *verb*

werewolf *noun*
werewolves

west *adjective and adverb*

west○ *noun*

westerly *adjective and noun*
westerlies

western *adjective*

western *noun*
westerns

westward *adjective and adverb*

westwards *adverb*

wet *adjective*
wetter
wettest

wet *verb*
wets
wetting
wetted

wetness

we've *abbreviation*

whack *verb*
whacks
whacking
whacked

whack *noun*
whacks

whale✣ *noun*
whales

whaler *noun*
whalers

whaling

wharf *noun*
wharves *or* wharfs

what✱

whatever

wheat

wheel *noun*
wheels

wheel *verb*
wheels
wheeling
wheeled

wheelbarrow *noun*
wheelbarrows

wheelchair *noun*
wheelchairs

wheeze *verb*
wheezes
wheezing
wheezed

whelk *noun*
whelks

when

whenever *conjunction*

· ·

★ You use **weigh** in e.g. *how much do you weigh?* **!** way, whey.

☆ **Weight** is how heavy something is. **! wait**.

○ You use a capital W in **the West**, when you mean a particular region.

✣ A **whale** is a large sea mammal. **! wail**.

✱ You use **what** in e.g. *what are they doing?* or *I don't know what you mean.* **! watt**.

a
b
c
d
e
f
g
h
i
j
k
l
m
n
o
p
q
r
s
t
u
v
w
x
y
z

273

wh

where*	whip *verb*	whistle *verb*
whereabouts	whips	whistles
whereas	whipping	whistling
whereupon	whipped	whistled
wherever	whirl *verb*	whistle *noun*
whether *conjunction*	whirls	whistles
whey☆	whirling	whistler *noun*
which○	whirled	whistlers
whichever	whirl *noun*	white *adjective*
whiff *noun*	whirls	whiter
whiffs	whirlpool *noun*	whitest
while *adjective* and *noun*	whirlpools	whiteness
	whirlwind *noun*	whitish
while *verb*	whirlwinds	white *noun*
whiles	whirr *verb*	whites
whiling	whirrs	whiten *verb*
whiled	whirring	whitens
	whirred	whitening
whilst *conjunction*	whirr *noun*	whitened
	whirrs	whitewash *noun*
whimper *verb*	whisk *verb*	whitewash *verb*
whimpers	whisks	whitewashes
whimpering	whisking	whitewashing
whimpered	whisked	whitewashed
whimper *noun*	whisk *noun*	Whitsun
whimpers	whisks	Whit Sunday
whine *verb*	whisker *noun*	whiz *verb*
whines	whiskers	whizzes
whining		whizzing
whined	whisky *noun*	whizzed
whine✛ *noun*	whiskies	who
whines	whisper *verb*	whoever
whinny *verb*	whispers	whole* *adjective*
whinnies	whispering	wholly
whinnying	whispered	whole *noun*
whinnied	whisper *noun*	wholes
whip *noun*	whispers	wholefood *noun*
whips	whist	wholefoods

★ You use **where** in e.g. *where are you?* **!ware, wear.**
☆ **Whey** is a watery liquid from milk. **! way, weigh.**
○ You use **which** in e.g. *which one is that?* **! witch.**
✛ A **whine** is a high piercing sound. **! wine.**
● You use **whole** in e.g. *I saw the whole lm.* **! hole.**

274

wholemeal

wholesale *adjective*

wholesome *adjective*

wholly *adverb*

whom

whoop *noun*
whoops

whoopee *interjection*

whooping cough

who's* *verb*

whose☆ *adjective*

why

wick *noun*
wicks

wicked *adjective*
wickeder
wickedest
wickedly

wickedness

wicker

wickerwork

wicket *noun*
wickets

wicketkeeper *noun*
wicketkeepers

wide *adjective*
adverb
wider
widest
widely

widen *verb*
widens
widening
widened

widespread

widow *noun*
widows

widower *noun*
widowers

width *noun*
widths

wield *verb*
wields
wielding
wielded

wife *noun*
wives

wig *noun*
wigs

wiggle *verb*
wiggles
wiggling
wiggled

wiggle *noun*
wiggles

wigwam *noun*
wigwams

wild *adjective*
wilder
wildest
wildly

wilderness *noun*
wildernesses

wildness

wildlife

wilful *adjective*
wilfully

wilfulness

wiliness

will *verb*
would

will *noun*
wills

willing *adjective*
willingly

willingness

willow *noun*
willows

wilt *verb*
wilts
wilting
wilted

wily *adjective*
wilier
wiliest

wimp *noun*
wimps

win *verb*
wins
winning
won

win *noun*
wins

wince *verb*
winces
wincing
winced

winch *noun*
winches

winch *verb*
winches
winching
winched

wind *noun*
winds

wind *verb*
winds
winding
wound

windfall *noun*
windfalls

windmill *noun*
windmills

window *noun*
windows

windpipe *noun*
windpipes

- -

★ You use **who's** in *who's* (who is) *that?* and *I don't know who's* (who has) *done it.* **! whose**.

☆ You use **whose** in *whose is this?* and *I don't know whose it is.* **! who's**.

a b c d e f g h i j k l m n o p q r s t u v **w** x y z

a **windscreen** noun
windscreens

windsurfer

b **windsurfing**

c **windward**

windy adjective
windier
windiest
windily

d **wine*** noun
wines

g **wing** noun
wings

h **wing** verb
wings
winging
winged

winged

l **wingless**

m **wingspan** noun
wingspans

n **wink** verb
winks
winking
winked

o **wink** noun
winks

p **winkle** noun
winkles

q **winkle** verb
winkles
winkling
winkled

u **winner** noun
winners

winnings plural noun

w **winter** noun
winters

wintertime

wintry adjective
wintrier
wintriest

wipe verb
wipes
wiping
wiped

wipe noun
wipes

wiper noun
wipers

wire noun
wires

wire verb
wires
wiring
wired

wireless noun
wirelesses

wiring

wiry adjective
wirier
wiriest
wirily

wisdom

wise adjective
wiser
wisest
wisely

wish verb
wishes
wishing
wished

wish noun
wishes

wishbone noun
wishbones

wisp noun
wisps

wispy adjective
wispier
wispiest
wispily

wistful adjective
wistfully

wistfulness

wit noun
wits

witch☆ noun
witches

witchcraft

with

withdraw verb
withdraws
withdrawing
withdrew
withdrawn

withdrawal noun
withdrawals

wither verb
withers
withering
withered

withhold verb
withholds
withholding
withheld

within

without

withstand verb
withstands
withstanding
withstood

witness noun
witnesses

wittiness

★ **Wine** is a drink. **!** whine.
☆ A **witch** is someone who uses witchcraft. **!** which.

witty *adjective*
wittier
wittiest
wittily

wizard *noun*
wizards

wizardry

wobble *verb*
wobbles
wobbling
wobbled

wobble *noun*
wobbles

wobbly *adjective*
wobblier
wobbliest

woe *noun*
woes

woeful *adjective*
woefully

wok *noun*
woks

woke see **wake**

woken see **wake**

wolf *noun*
wolves

woman *noun*
women

womb *noun*
wombs

won* see **win**

wonder *noun*
wonders

wonder *verb*
wonders
wondering
wondered

wonderful *adjective*
wonderfully

won't *verb*

wood☆ *noun*
woods

wooded

wooden

woodland *noun*
woodlands

woodlouse *noun*
woodlice

woodpecker *noun*
woodpeckers

woodwind

woodwork

woodworm *noun*
woodworm *or*
woodworms

woody *adjective*
woodier
woodiest

wool

woollen

woollens *plural noun*

woolliness

woolly *adjective*
woollier
woolliest

word *noun*
words

word *verb*
words
wording
worded

wording

wordy *adjective*
wordier
wordiest

wore see **wear**

work *noun*
works

work *verb*
works
working
worked

workable

worker *noun*
workers

workforce *noun*
workforces

workman *noun*
workmen

workmanship

workout *noun*
workouts

works *plural noun*

worksheet *noun*
worksheets

workshop *noun*
workshops

world *noun*
worlds

worldliness

worldly *adjective*
worldlier
worldliest

worldwide *adjective*

worm *noun*
worms

worm *verb*
worms
worming
wormed

worn see **wear**

worry *verb*
worries
worrying
worried

worrier *noun*
worriers

a
b
c
d
e
f
g
h
i
j
k
l
m
n
o
p
q
r
s
t
u
v
w
x
y
z

★ You use **won** in e.g. *I won a prize*. **! one**.
☆ **Wood** is material from trees or a lot of trees growing together.
! would.

277

worry noun
worries

worse adjective and adverb

worsen verb
worsens
worsening
worsened

worship verb
worships
worshipping
worshipped

worship noun

worshipper noun
worshippers

worst adjective and adverb

worth

worthiness

worthless adjective
worthlessly

worthwhile

worthy adjective
worthier
worthiest
worthily

would★ see will

wouldn't verb

wound noun
wounds

wound verb
wounds
wounding
wounded

wound see wind

wove see weave

woven see weave

wrap☆ verb
wraps
wrapping
wrapped

wrap noun
wraps

wrapper noun
wrappers

wrapping noun
wrappings

wrath

wrathful adjective
wrathfully

wreath noun
wreaths

wreathe verb
wreathes
wreathing
wreathed

wreck verb
wrecks
wrecking
wrecked

wreck noun
wrecks

wreckage noun
wreckages

wrecker noun
wreckers

wren noun
wrens

wrench verb
wrenches
wrenching
wrenched

wrench noun
wrenches

wrestle verb
wrestles
wrestling
wrestled

wrestler noun
wrestlers

wretch noun
wretches

wretched adjective
wretchedly

wriggle verb
wriggles
wriggling
wriggled

wriggle noun
wriggles

wriggly adjective
wrigglier
wriggliest

wring○ verb
wrings
wringing
wrung

wrinkle noun
wrinkles

wrinkle verb
wrinkles
wrinkling
wrinkled

wrist noun
wrists

wristwatch noun
wristwatches

write✛ verb
writes
writing
wrote
written

writer noun
writers

a
b
c
d
e
f
g
h
i
j
k
l
m
n
o
p
q
r
s
t
u
v
w
x
y
z

....

★ You use **would** in e.g. *would you like to come to tea?* **!** wood.

☆ To **wrap** something is to cover it in paper etc. **!** rap.

○ To **wring** something is to squeeze it hard. **!** ring.

✛ You use **write** in e.g. *to write a letter.* **!** right, rite.

writhe verb
writhes
writhing
writhed

writing noun
writings

written see **write**

wrong adjective and adverb
wrongly

wrong noun
wrongs

wrong verb
wrongs
wronging
wronged

wrote see **write**

wrung see **wring**

wry★ adjective
wryer
wryest

Xx

xenophobia

Xmas noun
Xmases

X-ray noun
X-rays

X-ray verb
X-rays
X-raying
X-rayed

xylophone noun
xylophones

Yy

-y and **-ey**
Nouns ending in **-y** following a consonant, e.g. **story**, make plurals ending in **-ies**, e.g. **stories**, and verbs, e.g. **try**, make forms in **-ies** and **-ied**, e.g. **tries, tried**.
Nouns ending in **-ey**, e.g. **journey**, make plurals ending in **-eys**, e.g. **journeys**.

yacht noun
yachts

yachtsman noun
yachtsmen

yachtswoman noun
yachtswomen

yam noun
yams

yank verb
yanks
yanking
yanked

yap verb
yaps
yapping
yapped

yap noun
yaps

yard noun
yards

yard noun
yards

yarn noun
yarns

yawn verb
yawns
yawning
yawned

yawn noun
yawns

year noun
years

yearly adjective and adverb

yearn verb
yearns
yearning
yearned

yeast

yell noun
yells

yell verb
yells
yelling
yelled

yellow adjective and noun
yellower
yellowest

yelp verb
yelps
yelping
yelped

yelp noun
yelps

yen☆ noun
yens or yen

yeoman noun
yeomen

★ You use **wry** in e.g. *a wry smile*. **!** rye.

☆ The plural is **yens** when you mean 'a longing' and **yen** for Japanese money.

a
b
c
d
e
f
g
h
i
j
k
l
m
n
o
p
q
r
s
t
u
v

w
x
y

z

yesterday *adjective*
and *noun*
yesterdays

yet

yeti *noun*
yetis

yew* *noun*
yews

yield *verb*
yields
yielding
yielded

yield *noun*
yields

yippee

yodel *verb*
yodels
yodelling
yodelled

yodeller *noun*
yodellers

yoga

yoghurt *noun*
yoghurts

yoke☆ *noun*
yokes

yoke *verb*
yokes
yoking
yoked

yolk○ *noun*
yolks

Yom Kippur

yonder

you✢

you'd *verb*

you'll *verb*

young *adjective*
younger
youngest

young *plural noun*

youngster *noun*
youngsters

your

you're *abbreviation*

yours

yourself *pronoun*
yourselves

youth *noun*
youths

youthful *adjective*
youthfully

you've *abbreviation*

yo-yo *noun*
yo-yos

yuppie *noun*
yuppies

Zz

zany *adjective*
zanier
zaniest
zanily

zap *verb*
zaps
zapping
zapped

zeal

zealous *adjective*
zealously

zebra *noun*
zebras

zenith *noun*
zeniths

zero *noun*
zeros

zest

zigzag *noun*
zigzags

zigzag *verb*
zigzags
zigzagging
zigzagged

zinc

zip *noun*
zips

zip *verb*
zips
zipping
zipped

zodiac

zombie *noun*
zombies

zone *noun*
zones

zoo *noun*
zoos

zoological *adjective*
zoologically

zoologist *noun*
zoologists

zoology

zoom *verb*
zooms
zooming
zoomed

★ A **yew** is a tree. **!ewe, yew.**
☆ A **yoke** is a piece of wood put across animals pulling a cart. **!yolk.**
○ A **yolk** is the yellow part of an egg. **!yoke.**
✢ You use **you** in e.g. *I love you.* **!ewe, yew.**